LET WIVES BE SUBMISSIVE

SOCIETY OF BIBLICAL LITERATURE
MONOGRAPH SERIES

editor
James Crenshaw

associate editor
Robert Tannehill

NUMBER 26
LET WIVES BE SUBMISSIVE
The Domestic Code in I Peter

David L. Balch

DAVID L. BALCH

LET WIVES BE SUBMISSIVE
The Domestic Code in I Peter

SCHOLARS PRESS

Distributed by
Scholars Press
101 Salem Street
P.O. Box 2268
Chico, CA 95927

LET WIVES BE SUBMISSIVE
The Domestic Code in I Peter

David L. Balch

Library of Congress Cataloging in Publication Data

Balch, David L
  Let wives be submissive.

  (Monograph series — The Society of Biblical Literature ;
no. 26)
  Includes bibliographical references and index.
  1. Bible. N.T. 1 Peter — Criticism, interpretation, etc.
2. Family — Biblical teaching. 3. Domestic relations —
Biblical teaching. 4. Philosophy, Ancient. 5. Stoics. I.
Title. II. Series: Society of Biblical Literature.
Monograph series ; no. 26.
BS2795.2.B34   241'.63   80-21203
ISBN 0-89130-428-2
ISBN 0-89130-429-0 (pbk.)

Printed in the United States of America
1   2   3   4   5
Edwards Brothers, Inc.
Ann Arbor, Michigan 48106

CONTENTS

List of Abbreviations*

Aristotle, *Pol.*	Aristotle, *Politics*
_____ , *NE*	Aristotle, *Nicomachean Ethics*
_____ , *MM*	Pseudo-Aristotle, *Magna Moralia* (*Great Ethics*)
Dio Chrysostom, *Dis.*	Dio Chrysostom, *Discourses*
Diog. Laert.	Diogenes Laertius, *Lives and Opinions of Eminent Philosphers*
Dionysius Hal., *Rom. Ant.*	Dionysius of Halicarnassus, *Roman Antiquities*
Epictetus, *Dis.*	Epictetus, *Discourses*
Hense	Stobaeus, *Anthologium*, vols. 3–5, ed. O. Hense
Lutz	*Musonius Rufus. The Roman Socrates*, ed. C. Lutz
Or.	*Orations*
ps.	pseudo
Rep.	*Republic*
RhM	*Rheinisches Museum für Philologie*
Seneca, *Ep.*	Seneca, *Epistles*
Stob.	Stobaeus, *Anthologium*, 5 vols., ed. C. Wachsmuth and O. Hense
Thesleff	*The Pythagorean Texts of the Hellenistic Period*, ed. H. Thesleff
Wachsmuth	Stobaeus, *Anthologium*, vols. 1–2, ed. C. Wachsmuth

*Other abbreviations are given in the *Journal of Biblical Literature* 95 (1976) 331–346. Editions and/or translations are cited in the text by the editor's or translator's last name; full bibliographical data are given in the bibliography.

Preface

This study began as a research project suggested to me by Professor Abraham J. Malherbe for his seminar on "Hellenistic Moralists and the New Testament." His suggestions and criticisms shaped and corrected my work. I am grateful for his willingness to share his knowledge of Hellenistic literature and philosophy. His recent book on *Social Aspects of Early Christianity* contains the kind of insight from which I benefited over several years of study.

Both Professors Nils A. Dahl and Wayne A. Meeks of Yale University have made contributions to the interpretation of texts important for this study. The concern for religion and society evident in the following pages is a product of the stimulating years I spent at Union Theological Seminary in New York. The debt to German scholarship also evident in these pages is the fruit of a Fulbright Grant to study in Tübingen from 1968 to early 1970 with the provocative Professor Ernst Käsemann. He excited my interest in the interpretation of canonical texts for contemporary hearers of the Word. I plan to publish a separate article discussing the meaning of the domestic code in 1 Peter for Christian ethics. A grant from the Ecumenical Institute for Advanced Theological Studies in Jerusalem provided both the time and the context for research in 1972–1973, as well as the occasion for critical suggestions from Professors Oscar Cullman, James A. Sanders, and Charles Carlston.

Franklin and Marshall College and Linfield College made funds available which supported my research. I am grateful to the typists, Sylvia Balch, Esther Moshos, and Cheryl (Finlayson) LaRocca. Students who helped with the indices are Margaret JoAnn Berger, Paul Carberry, Niccolo Lorimer and Mary Sherman. Librarians at the institutions named above, along with those at Lancaster Theological Seminary and Hebrew University, have been very helpful. I appreciate the considerable efforts both of Professor (now Dean) Leander Keck and Professor Robert C. Tannehill, associate editor of the Society of Biblical Literature Monograph Series, toward publishing the book.

I dedicate this work to the teacher who introduced me to historical research, Dr. Everett Ferguson, and to my wife, Sylvia. For the past fifteen years Dr. Ferguson has been a model for me of a great teacher who is concerned both about responsible scholarship and about the church. During my graduate studies and teaching career, Sylvia has continued to insist that marriage takes time and effort despite the potentially destructive demands of the individualistic, professional competition highly valued by our culture.

Chapter I

Contemporary Interpretations of 1 Peter and of Household Ethics in the New Testament

The Form of the New Testament Codes of Household Ethics

This study seeks to trace the origin and function of the code of household ethics found in 1 Peter, where slaves are exhorted to be submissive to their masters, wives to be submissive to their husbands, and husbands to live considerately with their wives. A similar, more complete code is found in Col 3:18–4:1 and in Eph 5:21–6:9, where the formal structure is obvious:

1. wives *be subject* to husbands ----------------husbands love your wives
2. children *obey* parents ---------------------fathers do not anger children
3. slaves *obey* masters---------------------------masters treat slaves justly

Six social classes are involved, and they are arranged in three pairs of relationships. The primary interest is in the submission of wives, children, and slaves, who are mentioned first in the pairs. There is similar material, though not so precisely organized, in 1 Tim 2:8–15; 5:1–2; 6:1–2; Titus 2:1–10; 3:1. 1 Peter has only one of the three pairs in Colossians (wives-husbands, 3:1–7). Only slaves are exhorted (2:18–25), not masters, and the children-fathers pair drops out completely. There are two additional features in 1 Peter: the code is introduced by an additional injunction to be submissive "to every human institution," to the emperor and his governors (2:13–14), and second, the code is followed by commands to "all of you" (3:8–9).[1]

It would be difficult to trace the origin of the stress in the NT on the subordination of wives if this balanced pattern had not been used; most cultures in the history of the world have assumed the inferiority of women. The first part of this study will attempt to discover which culture first used this balanced pattern of submissiveness. A survey of previous research on these NT codes will introduce the study.

Previous Research on the New Testament Codes of Household Ethics

Alfred Seeberg did the first serious research on the codes; he stressed virtue and vice catalogues, the "domestic code," and doctrinal elements.[2] He was the first to insist that standardized ethical material is traditional in nature and so cannot be understood as a reflection of the situation in particular churches. This ethic was taught by Jesus and John the Baptist, in his opinion. His construction has generally been rejected as an artificial attempt to associate material which is quite diverse. For example, the household pattern of submissiveness does not appear early in the Pauline letters; it appears only in the later Pauline traditions and in 1 Peter, although Seeberg thought it had been taught by all Christian missionaries.[3]

Seeberg was followed by Dibelius, who gives more detailed attention to the household code itself.[4] The Colossians code is a lightly Christianized version of a code borrowed from the Stoics. The motivations "as is fitting" (3:18) and "acceptable" (3:20) are common in Stoic literature. The phrase "in the Lord" (3:20) Christianizes a Stoic ethic.[5]

This thesis was taken up by his student, Weidinger,[6] who discusses the code in the context of early Christian paraenesis. Hellenistic Judaism had already appropriated this ethic without developing the Stoic conceptions in any original way. In texts like Tobit 4 and 12, such paraenesis is unrelated to nearby verses.[7] Another example of such material is pseudo-Phocylides, *Maxims* 175–227.[8] Weidinger also cites eight texts in Philo, the last and most important of which is *The Decalogue* 165–167. Josephus, *Against Apion* II.189–209 is also an example.[9]

When Weidinger presented examples of the schema in Hellenism, he used Hierocles, an early second-century A.D. Stoic, as his first and most important example.[10] Hierocles' list of duties is closely related to the Stoic conception of "duty." Such a list was probably the basis of Brutus' work on duties mentioned by Seneca.[11] The Stoic concept of duty is itself but an adaptation of the ancient Greek "unwritten law": fear of the gods, honor toward parents, proper care of the dead, love of friends, and fidelity toward country.[12] This material is so uniform that sources from the third century B.C. to the fourth century A.D. reflect essentially the same ethic.[13] So Weidinger polemicizes against those who use the material to draw conclusions about the actual situation of the church to whom it was addressed.[14] Such material would have been taken over by the Christians only when the immediate expectation of Jesus' coming on the clouds had receded.[15]

Hierocles is so important for Weidinger, and therefore for the subsequent discussion, that I will give a short summary. The first section, "How to Conduct Oneself Towards the Gods,"[16] is concerned with the immutability of the gods, drawing the practical conclusion that "there is no probability that the punishments which divinity thinks proper to inflict can be remitted."[17]

The second section of Hierocles, "How to Conduct Oneself Towards the Fatherland,"[18] presents the fatherland as a secondary god, our greatest parent, to be "honored" before either parent separately. Hierocles opposes the recent introduction of new customs into the country.[19]

The third section concerns "How to Conduct Oneself Towards Parents."[20] Parents are terrestrial gods, to be "honored more" than the gods themselves.[21] We owe them "duties" as they are images of the gods for us, the guardian gods of the house, our greatest benefactors, our nearest kindred, our creditors, our lords, and friends.[22] Children should provide food, a bed, sleep, unction, a bath, and garments for them.[23]

The fourth section, "On Fraternal Love,"[24] opens in a striking way:

> Act by every one, in the same manner as if you supposed yourself to be him, and him to be you. For he will use a servant well who considers with himself, how he would think it proper to be used by him, if indeed he were the master, and himself the servant. The same thing also must be said of parents with respect to children, and of children with respect to parents; and in short, of all men with respect to all. This admonition, however, is transcendently adapted to the alliance of brothers to each other. . . .[25]

This is true even if the brother is rough and stupid,

> for no great thanks are due to those who conduct themselves moderately towards worthy and benign men; but to render him more mild who is stupid, and whose manners are rough, is the work of a man and deserves great applause.[26]

In a certain sense a brother is a part of oneself, just like eyes, legs, and hands. Brothers should work together; no one will then be alone.[27]

Fifth is a section concerning "How to Conduct Oneself Towards Other Kindred."[28] One is related to all mankind just as the center point is related to a series of concentric circles. The inner circle includes one's own mind and body, the next circle one's parents, brothers, wife, and children, the third circle other relatives, etc. The sixth circle includes all citizens; the ninth and largest circle includes the whole human race.

Sixth, there is a section on "Economics" or "Household Management"[29] which is concerned with the proper work of husband and wife:

> These therefore are to be divided after the accustomed manner; rural, forensic and political works are to be attributed to the husband; but to the wife, such works as pertain to spinning wool, making of bread, cooking, and in short everything of a domestic nature.[30]

However, he then contradicts this assumption: "Nevertheless, it is not fit that the one should be entirely exempt from the works of the other."[31] Men who are in danger of being considered effeminate should not do women's work, but

> what should hinder the man from partaking of works which pertain to a woman, whose past life has been such as to free him from all suspicion of absurd and effeminate conduct? For in other domestic works, is it not thought that more of

them pertain to men than to women? For they are more laborious, and require
corporeal strength, such as to grind, to knead meal, to cut wood, to draw water from
a well, etc.[32]

Correspondingly the wife ought not to be engaged only with her maid servants
in spinning wool but ought to gather grapes, collect olives, and work beside
her husband in the field sowing and plowing.

For when a house is governed after this manner by the husband and wife, so far as
pertains to necessary works, it appears to me that it will be conducted in this respect in
the best manner.[33]

The seventh section, "Concerning Marriage,"[34] begins by asserting that
"cities could not exist without a household."[35] The second fragment begins
with a reference to a treatise *On Families* which we do not have.[36] There are
other indications that some sections of Hierocles have been lost.[37] One
sentence in the section "Concerning Marriage" begins, "I say therefore that
marriage is likewise advantageous,"[38] and there is no antecedent for the
"likewise." There is also a reference to the duties of parents, brothers, *wives,
and children*,[39] as well as the assertion:

We have summarily shown how we ought to conduct ourselves towards our kindred,
having before taught how we should act towards ourselves, our parents, and brothers;
and besides these, towards our wife and children. . . .[40]

The italicized references to a discussion of the duties with respect to wives and
children refer to lost portions of Hierocles, a loss which is especially
regrettable in light of the purpose of this study.

To return to the summary of the section "Concerning Marriage," the
third fragment is worth quoting:

Hence he will not err, who says that a house is imperfect without wedlock. For it is not
possible to conceive of a governor without the governed, nor of the governed without a
governor. And this reason appears to me to be very well calculated to make those
ashamed who are adverse to marriage.[41]

Weidinger's summary of this fragment[42] did not point out Hierocles'
assumption that the husband governs and the wife submits, nor is it noted in
subsequent modern discussions. For Hierocles it is such an obvious
assumption that it can form the basis for another argument, that the house is
incomplete without a wife. Further, when we remember that Hierocles applies
the golden rule to the relationships of master-slave and parents-children (see
above p. 3), it is clear that Hierocles mentions the three reciprocal
relationships found in the codes in Colossians and Ephesians.

The husband works outside the house;[43] he is concerned with external,
she with internal, affairs.[44] She does not allow the house to be without a ruler;

she pays attention to the domestics.[45] In view of 1 Peter 3, the following text is especially important:

> I also think that a married life is beautiful. For what other thing can be such an ornament to a house, as is the association of husband and wife? For it must not be said that sumptuous edifices, walls covered with marble plaster, and piazzas adorned with stones, which are admired by those who are ignorant of true good, nor yet painting and arched myrtle walks, nor any thing else which is the subject of astonishment to the stupid, is the ornament of a family. But the beauty of a household consists in the conjunction of man and wife, who are united to each other by destiny, and are consecrated to the gods who preside over nuptials, births, and houses, and who accord, indeed, with each other, and have all things in common, as to their bodies, or rather their souls themselves; who likewise exercise a becoming authority over their house and servants; are properly solicitous about the education of their children; and pay attention to the necessaries of life, which is neither excessive nor negligent, but moderate and appropriate. For what can be better and more excellent, as the most admirable Homer says, "Than when at home the husband and wife unanimously live."[46]

To be sure, some men destroy themselves by marrying wives who are tyrants and have to contend for the chief authority.[47] The final fragment insists on the value of numerous offspring both for parents and for the city.

Such an outline is basic to one part of Stoic ethics. This summary indicates that Hierocles says more about the submissiveness of the wife and the proper place of slaves and children than has been recognized, although these are not exhortations to wives, children, and slaves but rather assumptions with which Hierocles is so comfortable that they need no argument. Hierocles does suggest a modification in the social role of the wife; she should be allowed to work outside the house. But it does not occur even to this "liberal" popular philosopher to doubt that she should "be governed" by her husband.

Lohse[48] stated his essential agreement with the Dibelius-Weidinger hypothesis, repeating the citation of Phil 4:8 ("Whatever is . . . just, whatever is pure, . . . if there is any virtue, if there is anything worthy of praise, think about these things") as an attitude conducive to such use of Hellenistic paraenesis.

Lohmeyer[49] objected to the thesis of the Hellenistic origin of the code, insisting rather that it was Jewish. Special interest was given in Jewish tradition to those persons who were not full members of the religious community, i.e., women, slaves, and minors, who were not required to fulfill all cultic obligations. Rejecting Lohmeyer's view, Crouch notes that his examples deal with release from cultic duties, not with positive moral exhortation.[50]

According to Rengstorf[51] the code was specifically Christian. Sufficient differences exist between Hellenistic and Jewish parallels, on the one hand, and the Christian household codes, on the other, to enable him to deny that the latter are slightly Christianized versions of the former. The major impulse

in the formation of these codes was the early Christian interest in the "house";
therefore the central interest was in the father as the head of the entire
household. Further, "to be submissive" as a designation of the duty of the wife
was specifically Christian.

Schroeder believes that there was an ethical tradition going back to Jesus
which was taught in all the early Christian churches no matter who founded
them.[52] The schema found in the NT codes is not to be found in the OT or in
rabbinic Judaism, but rather in Stoicism. The Stoic duty list is clearest in
Epictetus (c. A.D. 55–135),[53] who states that there are three fields of study (*Dis.*
III.2.1):

> The second field of study deals with duty; for I ought not to be unfeeling like a statue,
> but should maintain my relations, both natural and acquired, as a religious man, as a
> son, a brother, a father, a citizen. (III.2.4. Trans. Oldfather)

Epictetus' chief goal is to make his will correspond to fate (god), but there is
the problem of reconciling this goal with the maintenance of the social
"duties" just mentioned:

> Under our control are moral purpose and all the acts of moral purpose; but not under
> our control are the body, the parts of the body, possessions, parents, brothers,
> children, country—in a word, all that with which we associate. Where then shall we
> place the "good"? (I.22.10–11)[54]

Another list of things not under our control includes the body, a farm, slaves,
clothes, a house, horses, children, a wife, brother, friends (IV.1.66–67). In
III.24 Epictetus argues for an individualistic self-sufficiency without
dependence on these relationships.[55]

Schroeder is also quite concerned with the *order* of the terms in the list.[56]
The order of terms in the Stoic lists is not traditional but rational; the same
order rarely recurs.[57] These lists are exhortations directed to individuals, not
to groups (e.g. not to slaves).[58]

But Schroeder finds the parallels in first-century Hellenistic Judaism,
especially in Philo, *The Decalogue* 165, more important[59] for three reasons:
(1) the *order* of the Colossians and Ephesians codes—wife, children, slaves—
occurs in Philo but not in Stoicism, (2) the duties are mentioned in *pairs*—
wives and husbands, children and parents, slaves and masters—in Philo but
not in Stoicism, and (3) Philo is concerned that one member of each of these
pairs is to be *subordinate* to the other member of the pair, a concern absent
from and even alien to Stoicism.[60] Hellenistic Judaism developed this ethic
out of the Decalogue (Exod 20:12, "Honor your father and your
mother. . . .") as it was interpreted with Leviticus 18–19.[61] The special stress
on submission in the NT results from the writers' opposition to a social
actualizing of Gal 3:27–28 ("There is neither Jew nor Greek, there is neither
slave nor free, there is neither male nor female. . . ."), which caused problems

like those in 1 Corinthians 7, where women insisted on emancipation.[62] One new element in the NT household codes is that the "submission" required of the wife is tied to the "love" of the husband, whereas in pagan texts the verb would express the "power" of the man.[63]

Crouch gives a comprehensive survey and evaluation of previous studies:[64] Against Schroeder's suggestion that this ethic was developed out of the Decalogue, he argues that the exhortations to wives and slaves are actually the most important, for they are the only ones common to all NT codes. In 1 Peter the exhortation to fathers and children is absent. Further, the content of the children-fathers unit reflects the influence of the more prominent exhortations; the exhortation to "obey," characteristic of the slave section, has displaced the duty to "honor" parents (Col 3:20; Eph 6:1; cp. Exod 20:12 and Deut 5:16). Thirdly, Crouch suggests that the insistence that children obey parents "in all things" (Col 3:20) has a parallel in the Hellenistic Jewish statements[65] about the submission of women.

I doubt whether this last point can be maintained, for other authors stress the unlimited obedience which children owe their parents. The child is to obey even if the parent is insane, according to the Neopythagorean Perictione, *On the Harmony of a Woman*;[66] and in Epictetus, *Manual* 30, the child is to obey, to endure revilings, whether the father is good or evil. Musonius even has a diatribe on the subject (*Must One Obey One's Parents Under All Circumstances? Or.* XVI), but his opinion that the child may in certain circumstances do other than what the father wishes is unusual.[67] So in this case the influence may go from the traditional assertion that the child must obey the parent in all things to the exhortation in 1 Pet 2:18 that the slave must submit to the master whether he is gentle or harsh. This suggests that the framer of the code in 1 Peter concentrated attention on the slave section.

Crouch carefully studied the proposed Stoic parallels to the NT codes, concluding that this influence, while not to be denied, should be minimized and that a greater role should be attributed to the Oriental-Jewish background of the code's form.[68] This is so for two of the three reasons which Schroeder had already given:

> Serious among Weidinger's errors was his failure to note certain unique factors in the Hellenistic Jewish usage of the Stoic schema. Discussion of social duties in reciprocal terms and the distinction between subordinate and superior persons are non-Stoic features which characterize Hellenistic Jewish codes. At the same time, his [Weidinger's] failure to examine the content of the Haustafel exhortations caused him to overlook the fact that exhortation to women and slaves conform neither to the concerns of the Stoic schema nor to the presuppositions of Stoic philosophy.[69]

There are two exceptions to this general rule.[70] As related by Seneca, the Stoic Hecaton refers to the mutual duties of father and son, husband and wife; duty is not to be that which makes one "self-sufficient" but is reciprocal. Hecaton doubts that a slave can give a "benefit" to his master or that he can perform a "duty," a moral ability reserved for a son, a wife, or related persons. Rather the slave, for Hecaton, can only perform a "service." Seneca disagrees by affirming that a "willing" slave can also perform a "benefit" inside the household.[71]

The second text showing an interest in reciprocity is also in Seneca, *Ep.* 94.1–3. Seneca discusses the refusal of Ariston[72] to use any form of casuistry including precepts concerning "how a husband should conduct himself towards his wife, or how a father should bring up his children, or how a master should rule his slaves." Ariston maintained that the only legitimate interest of a philosopher is to define the Supreme Good; one having this knowledge would automatically know how to live with wife and children. So Ariston disapproved of his teacher Zeno's willingness to incorporate these domestic ethical matters into the Stoic system. Crouch understands Seneca's reference to Ariston to be the first time in which the schema is limited to the relationships in a household.[73]

After surveying the Stoics' lists of duties, Crouch observes that only Epictetus (*Dis.* II.14.9) and Seneca assume that a woman is capable of performing duties. He understands this as a tendency in late Stoicism away from Stoic individualism toward an interest in marriage and the family.[74] Of all the Stoic texts using this schema, only in Ariston is there a clear reference to the treatment of slaves.[75]

In treating Hellenistic Judaism, Crouch notes that the schema is used in ps.-Phocylides 175–227 but that the form there is merely the framework for other material. He repeats Schroeder's emphasis on Philo, *The Decalogue* 165–167, noting the reciprocity and the concern for the duties of the inferior position.[76] He adds Philo, *Special Laws* II.226–227, but finds his most important parallels in Philo, *Apology for the Jews* 7.14, and Josephus, *Against Apion* II.190–219. These last two texts, along with ps.-Phocylides, are panegyrics on the Jewish law.[77] Positing a common source for the three texts, Crouch suggests[78] that such panegyrics were used by Jewish missionaries in an effort to convert Gentiles. The function of these three texts is a significant issue, for the closest parallel to the Colossians household code is in Philo, *Apology for the Jews* 7.14. Philo's statement—husbands, fathers, and masters are to provide wives, children, and slaves with a knowledge of the law—differs from Colossians in that (a) there is no reference to the responsibilities of wife, children, and slaves, and (b) the husband-father-master has the same duty in each instance.[79] Nevertheless, he explains the reciprocity which he sees in this text on the basis of the observation[80] that social duties in Egypt and Israel in antiquity were often understood in reciprocal terms, especially the relationship between rich and poor.[81] So reciprocity is a "Jewish-Oriental" characteristic of the codes. However, it is a very broad jump from the reciprocal relations of rich and poor in society to the reciprocal relations of husband and wife in a household. I doubt whether Crouch has discovered the source of the reciprocity in the NT codes.

Crouch contrasts the gradual emancipation of women in Greco-Roman culture with the intensification of the inferiority of women in Judaism during the Roman period.[82] On the one hand, the Stoic Musonius proclaimed the ethical equality of the sexes with all its consequences, while, on the other hand, the rabbinic view concerning women constituted a regression from the status women had in the OT. And Hellenistic Jewish writers were even more one-sided than the rabbis. In Philo and Josephus there is a "low view" of women: they are inferior and are to be submissive to their husbands. The same exhortation in the NT is indisputably the result of Hellenistic Jewish propaganda, not of Stoicism or popular philosophy.[83] The rigid attitude of Hellenistic Jews in this respect was due to their reaction against Hellenistic religiosity and against the license allowed women in the cults of Dionysus, Isis, and Cybele.[84] So the NT codes are the result of tension between Jewish morality, which the codes mirror, and Hellenistic religiosity, which found expression within some Christian circles through a stress on Gal 3:28 (". . . there is neither male nor female. . . ."), a stress which caused unrest among Christian slaves and women who desired emancipation.[85] In this, Crouch agrees with Schroeder. In Christianity the household code became one aspect of a nomistic tendency in Pauline churches.[86]

In some respects Crouch's analysis of the domestic code in Stoicism is very successful. If Cynicism is taken as the essence of Stoicism (as in Ariston), then it is correct that a concern for women, children, or slaves would be alien to the effort of the individual wise man to become self-sufficient. The tension between social duties and individual self-sufficiency within Stoicism tends to confirm the assertion that a concern for household duties is alien to Stoicism, something introduced from another source. Crouch refers to Zeller's suggestion[87] that these duties, derived from the popular "unwritten law," were added to the Stoic system in an effort to tone down the more radical elements of Stoic dogma and appeal to the law and order Roman mentality, making Stoicism more capable of responding to the criticism of Carneades and others. The introduction of this popular ethic is precisely what produced the protest of Ariston referred to above.

Klaus Thraede has suggested an alternative source for the stress on these social, household duties: the Greek discussions of household management.[88] He notes that both Aristotle (*Pol.* I 1259a 37–39) and some of the NT household duty codes have a three-part form concerned with mastership, fatherhood, and marriage.[89] The only later writings "concerning household management" ($\pi\epsilon\rho\grave{\iota}$ $o\grave{\iota}\kappa o\nu o\mu\acute{\iota}\alpha\varsigma$), besides Xenophon, he suggests, are three pseudo-Aristotelian works and Neopythagorean fragments. The latter mix a Peripatetic stress on subordination with a Stoic stress on equality.[90] He argues that the NT codes are more closely related to Peripatetic discussions of domestic science than to Stoic lists of duties (*Pflichtenschema*) because the former are concerned about social life whereas the latter are concerned about individual ethics.[91] Thraede agrees with Schroeder and Crouch that the source

of this domestic ethic is not Stoicism, although Thraede disagrees with the
other two authors over whether that source is ultimately Greek or Jewish. For
Thraede, Philo represents the Jewish status quo.[92] He thinks that wives,
children, and slaves were discriminated against in Judaism and asks whether
Christianity altered this inheritance in the direction of the emancipated Greek
views.[93]

Summary and Conclusions

I conclude that Schroeder, Crouch, and Thraede have successfully
criticized the Dibelius-Weidinger hypothesis that Stoicism offers the most
important parallels to the NT *Haustafeln*. Especially Crouch's thorough and
careful investigation of the proposed Stoic parallels has convinced me that
such influence "should be minimized."[94] This does not mean that the Stoic
parallels are irrelevant. A few will be cited in the following pages, but the
origin of the form seems to lie elsewhere.

This survey has shown that the origin of the pattern of submissiveness is
still problematic. There are some hints of reciprocal duties in Stoic texts, but
no exhortations to *pairs* in a household. There are close parallels to such pairs,
as Crouch suggests, in Hellenistic Judaism, but the suggestion that this is a
"Jewish-Oriental" influence on Philo has not been demonstrated. Should
Thraede's suggestion of a Peripatetic origin for the form of the NT household
codes be accepted? There are close parallels to the central interest in the
submission of one member of the pair to the other in Aristotle and in Philo.
The submission of the poor to the rich in oriental society is not an adequate
explanation of the source of this ethic. So the question of influences on Philo
at this point is still open, as is the question of the origin of the form of the NT
codes.

There have been three suggestions about the *function* of this ethic.
Dibelius and Weidinger emphasized its paraenetic use, its use as general
ethical exhortation unrelated to any specific situation. Second, Schroeder and
Crouch argued that the code was used to repress social unrest within the
church among Christian slaves and wives, unrest stimulated by the baptismal
formula in Gal 3:28 (see above pp6–7,9).Third, Schroeder, appealing to 1 Pet
3:1–7, 1 Tim 2:1–4, and Titus 2:5, suggested that this ethic was a part of the
church's mission.[95] A major part of the discussion in chapter VI will evaluate
these suggestions in relation to 1 Peter. Is the household code in that document general paraenesis so that nothing can be determined about the social
situation of the church to which it is addressed? Can it be determined whether
there is social unrest among the Christian slaves and wives being addressed? Is
Schroeder correct that the whole household ethical code in 1 Peter (not just
3:1–7) has a missionary intent?[96] What purpose does the code have?

Previous Research on 1 Peter

Recent research has produced several competing hypotheses not only
about the origin of the pattern of submissiveness in 1 Peter but also about the

nature of the book itself. A brief survey of recent studies of 1 Peter should clarify the questions and problems.[97]

From the time of Harnack,[98] many scholars have been of the opinion that 1 Peter is not a letter but a sermon. The idea was further developed with much originality by Perdelwitz.[99] From the references to baptism (3:21; cp. 1:3, 23; 2:2) and from the phrases which seem to point to its recent reception ("now" in 1:12; 2:10, 25; 3:21; "at the present time" in 1:6, 8; and especially "like newborn babes" in 2:2), Perdelwitz urged that 1:3–4:11 should be understood as a baptismal homily. Somewhat later, Bornemann[100] defended Harnack against hostile criticism. 1 Peter is, he argued, a baptismal sermon delivered by Silvanus to a church in Asia Minor around 80–90 A.D., a sermon which follows the outline of Psalm 34 and corresponds to 1:3–5:11 of our present text. Windisch[101] agreed with the hypothesis of a baptismal homily, assuming however that some elements of traditional exhortation were added (2:18–3:7; 4:7–11).

In the third edition of Windisch's commentary, H. Preisker developed Windisch's brief remarks into an elaborate theory.[102] Before 4:11 persecution was a possibility, but after 4:11 it was an actual experience. Persecution had broken out before the writing of the final section. "Homily" is not a satisfactory designation; rather the text was an actual liturgy. 1:3–4:11 was the baptismal liturgy (the oldest extant), and 4:12–5:11 was a concluding liturgical service for the whole congregation. The actual rite of baptism occurred after 1:21. A charismatic sang the hymn in 2:1–10 (with all its OT references!), after which a different preacher exhorted the congregation in 2:11–3:12; then an apocalyptist revealed the coming persecution (3:13–4:7a).

Cross[103] accepted Preisker's thesis and added that the text was the part of the celebrant in the baptismal rite at Easter time. Noting the occurrence in 1 Peter of the verb "to suffer" and the noun "suffering," he suggested that this was due to the popular etymological relation between "to suffer" (*paschō*) and the "passover" (*pascha*), found in Melito of Sardis, *Homily on the Passion*, and Hippolytus, *Apostolic Constitution*. The many references in 1 Peter to "suffering" are simply a reflection of typical language of an Easter liturgy (near the time of Passover), not of persecution.[104]

> Moral teaching such as is given to various groups in society in 2:3–3:7 must always have been incidental to the preparation for Baptism; and some recapitulation of it at the actual Baptism would be very natural. It may be added that if we are right in supposing that we have an actual Baptismal text before us, then we can at once explain the seemingly arbitrary choice of groups in 1 Peter (only servants, wives and husbands). This selection would be readily explained if we may suppose that only these three classes presented themselves for Baptism on this particular occasion.[105]

The prohibition of women's adornments in 3:3 was a typical preparation for baptism.[106]

M.-E. Boismard[107] took a cautious approach to these theories. 1 Peter itself is not a baptismal homily or liturgy, but it contains a number of fragments of a primitive baptismal liturgy, an assertion based on comparisons with passages in Titus, 1 John, Colossians, and James. His articles were followed by a book[108] in which he concluded that there are four baptismal hymns in 1 Peter dating to before 56–57 A.D., hymns similar to those found in Romans. However, he did not find hymns in that pericope which contains the exhortation to wives.

W. C. van Unnik[109] produced an independent thesis: the letter was written before 70 by Peter to people who had been God-fearers in the synagogue but who were converted to Christianity. Peter wrote to assure them that through Christ they had been taken into the covenant as true proselytes, and he exhorted them to live as children of obedience.

In the process of this discussion, two important commentaries appeared, one by Beare[110] and the other by Selwyn.[111] Beare was very sympathetic toward the views of Perdelwitz. He denied the Petrine authorship of the book and dated it in the reign of Trajan during the persecution referred to by Pliny (A.D. 111–112). The section of the epistle containing the baptismal discourse (1:13–4:11) is complete in itself; it does not need the epistolary setting.[112]

> Its principal theme is not steadfastness under the pressure of persecution, but an exposition of the significance of baptism as the sacrament of regeneration, a body of instruction and exhortation respecting the character and conduct which should accompany and flow from their profession of Christian faith.[113]

So the references to baptism are not incidental, nor is the real theme found in the encouragement of suffering Christians.[114]

Selwyn, on the other hand, insisted that Peter, with the counsel of Silvanus, wrote from Rome in 63, and that the letter was probably read in Asia Minor at the Easter festival the following year. One of Selwyn's major contributions was his discussion of the traces of a baptismal catechism in 1 Peter, comparing them with those in other NT epistles. In this he declares his debt to Carrington,[115] who had drawn a parallel between religious instruction among the Jews and catechetical material in the NT. The instructions to Jewish proselytes were based on Leviticus 17–19, and these Levitical conditions were also primary in the Christian mission.[116] There is a pattern in the catechetical material common to Colossians, Ephesians, 1 Peter, and James, a pattern which includes exhortations (1) to put off all evil, (2) to submit to . . . , (3) to watch and pray, and (4) to resist the devil.[117] The household ethical code is included in section (2). Thus it is part of a larger body of material.

Selwyn took up Carrington's four points, emphasizing the use of Leviticus 17–19. A common catechetical pattern current in the early church, he thought, is especially clear in 1 Thessalonians, 1 Peter, and Acts 15.[118] 2 Thess 2:13–17 and 1 Peter 1 contain a summary of this catechetical pattern, which Selwyn would attribute to Silvanus: (1) God in love and mercy called believers, which evokes the community's thanksgiving, (2) they are sanctified by the Spirit, (3) their objective is salvation and glory at the Parousia, (4) their life now is lived in hope.[119] Romans, Colossians, Ephesians, 1 Peter, and James have the baptismal catechism in an advanced second form which involves six points: (1) rebirth through the word, (2) renunciation of sins ("abstain," ἀπέχεσθαι, is replaced by the stronger "put away," ἀποθέσθαι), (3) worship, (4) be subject, (5) watch (pray and be sober), (6) stand fast (especially in persecution).[120] In this scheme, the domestic codes fit in the fourth section (see Selwyn's Tables X–XIII), although they do not actually occur in Romans or James (where Selwyn cites instead Romans 13 on obedience to authority and James 4 on humility). The parallels, Selwyn demonstrates, are not the result of coincidence, but in the case of the domestic codes, he is actually appealing to only two examples, Colossians (on which Ephesians is dependent) and 1 Peter.

Lohse rejects the hypothesis of a baptismal liturgy.[121] He doubts that the succession of psalms, teaching hymns, exhortation, and apocalyptic in 1 Peter would be found, as Preisker suggested, in a worship service. Nor is baptism the primary theme, for baptismal references are found almost exclusively in the first part of the letter (1:3–2:10; also 3:21). Further, he expresses general skepticism about Selwyn's attempt to reconstruct an early Christian catechism.[122] Rather, the theme of the whole letter is that, by doing good, suffering Christians will silence the ignorance of foolish men (2:15; cp. 2:12).[123] In the domestic code, the exhortations to slaves and women correspond to this theme. The exhortation to husbands is so short precisely because it is unrelated to the theme of suffering. Its presence indicates that traditional material was adapted to the situation faced by the churches receiving the letter.[124] Though not dependent on any Pauline letters, 1 Peter has contacts with Pauline theology. It was written in Rome, for only this explains the close relationship to 1 Clement.[125]

Hill has taken a similar position.[126] 1 Peter is concerned with actual physical and mental suffering. The virtually continuous harrying of Christians by local opponents led to loss of civil rights, arrest, imprisonment, and even death.[127] According to Hill,

> the link between baptism and suffering (such as would befall Christians in a hostile environment) may be accounted for simply and adequately by assuming that, since baptism was the occasion and the sign of voluntary self-commitment to the Christian way, those who offered themselves for the rite were aware, through their knowledge of what Christians endured, that this way on which they were embarking would inevitably involve suffering.[128]

To treat the letter as a baptismal homily or liturgy is to treat as explicit and prominent what is only implicit, presupposed, and subsidiary; 1 Peter is paraenetical, not catechetical.[129]

Goppelt, in a commentary on 1 Peter, is primarily concerned about the relation of the Christian to the institutions of society.[130] Writing from Rome in 65–80, the author exhorts congregations in light of a growing persecution which has its source not in police action but in popular slander (1 Pet 2:12; 3:16; 4:4, 14).[131] Christians did not conform to the life style of Hellenistic society, and this refusal to conform was the decisive basis of conflict (see 1 Pet 4:3–4).[132] However, the author's thought does not begin from the crisis situation in which the world is persecuting the church but from Christ's call to discipleship.[133] 1 Peter is not opposing a Zealot rebellion against superiors but opposes an ascetic-pneumatic emigration out of one's social station (cp. 1 Corinthians 7).[134] A person who believes becomes a stranger to society but at the same time is placed in the social institutions of society. Conformity is avoided by "doing good" in the structure of society. This determines the structure of the letter: (1) 1:1–2:10 grounds the social difference of Christians in their Christian existence; (2) 2:11–4:11 develops the paradox that being a stranger in the society involves Christian participation in the institutions of society; (3) 4:12–5:14 closes the letter declaring that repression by society is unavoidable for Christians and is a participation in the sufferings of Christ.[135]

This survey demonstrates that there are two basically different interpretations of 1 Peter by modern exegetes. Some interpreters think 1 Peter is centrally concerned with baptism; the book is a baptismal sermon or an entire liturgy. The references to suffering are either liturgical or of secondary importance. Lohse, Hill, van Unnik, and Goppelt oppose this formerly dominant interpretation. They understand 1 Peter in a context of persecution. The traditional paraenesis was modified to address that situation. In the first interpretation, the household duty code in 1 Peter was a traditional part of catechesis in preparation for baptism; in the second interpretation, the code was traditional ethical exhortation modified to address the problem of persecution. The understanding of the function of the domestic code reached in this study should help clarify the nature of 1 Peter.

A Different Approach

Weidinger observes[136] that much of the Stoic material is a repetition of earlier material in Plato and Aristotle. The neglect of this material until Thraede's recent discussion of the NT codes of household ethics has led to unnecessary confusion. Investigation of it yields rich results and sheds new light on the Stoic material itself.

In approaching this material, I have found two observations to be of basic importance, observations which will be clarified in the course of the discussion. The first was made by Friedrich Wilhelm,[137] who observed that the three topoi "concerning the constitution" ($\pi\epsilon\rho\grave{\iota}$ $\pi o\lambda\iota\tau\epsilon\acute{\iota}\alpha\varsigma$), [138] "concerning household management" ($\pi\epsilon\rho\grave{\iota}$ $o\grave{\iota}\kappa o\nu o\mu\acute{\iota}\alpha\varsigma$), and "concerning marriage" ($\pi\epsilon\rho\grave{\iota}$ $\gamma\acute{\alpha}\mu o\nu$) were so combined and interrelated that it is difficult to distinguish them clearly. Second, I observe that the second of these three topoi is nearly identical with the topos which often is referred to by the German word *Haustafel*, the NT pattern of household submissiveness. Plato and

Aristotle, as well as other Greek political theorists, were interested in the relation between the "city" and the "house," a relation expressed in these topoi. Whether the concern with the "household" which appears in these discussions is relevant to the NT codes will be the subject of the following inquiry.

NOTES TO CHAPTER I

[1]See the more complete comparison and contrast of the NT codes by J. Paul Sampley, "and the two shall become one flesh." A Study of Traditions in Ephesians 5:21-31 (SNTSMS 16; Cambridge: Cambridge University, 1971) 17–27.

[2]Alfred Seeberg, Der Katechismus der Urchristenheit (Leipzig: A. Deichert, 1903) 37–39; Das Evangelium Christi (Leipzig: A. Deichert, 1905) 125–127 on the Haustafel in 1 Peter; Die beiden Wege und das Aposteldekret (Leipzig: A. Deichert, 1906), in which Seeberg notes that a vice list of sins prohibited in the Decalogue was commonly combined with the golden rule in the traditional interpretation of Lev 18–19; Die Didache des Judentums und der Urchristenheit (Leipzig: A. Deichert, 1908), in which Seeberg discusses the "Hausmission" (p. 86). For criticism see James E. Crouch, The Origin and Intention of the Colossian Haustafel (FRLANT 109; Göttingen: Vandenhoeck and Ruprecht, 1972)13–16.

[3]Seeberg, Katechismus 41.

[4]Martin Dibelius, An die Kolosser, Epheser, an Philemon (Tübingen: Mohr, 1913), esp. the excursus following Col 4:1.

[5]Martin Dibelius, Geschichte der urchristlichen Literatur 2 (Berlin and Leipzig: Walter de Gruyter, 1926) 68.

[6]Karl Weidinger, Die Haustafeln, ein Stück urchristlicher Paraenese (UNT 14; Leipzig: J. C. Heinrich, 1928). He profitably used Rudolf Hirzel, Agraphos Nomos (Abhandlungen der philologisch-historischen Classe der königlich sächsischen Gesellschaft der Wissenschaften 20; Leipzig: B. G.Teubner, 1903) and Karl Praechter, Hierokles der Stoiker (Leipzig: T. Weicher, 1901) with its excursus (pp. 121–150) on the topos peri gamou and the 19 authors who used this topos. Praechter emphasized the Stoic connections of the topos "concerning marriage" (pp. 122, 128) and denied its Aristotelian origin. Since then Aristotle seems to have been ignored, but see Weidinger, Haustafeln 46, 53, who is quoted by Crouch, Colossian Haustafel 118.

[7]Weidinger, Haustafeln 14–15.

[8]Ibid., 15–16, 23–25. Ps.-Phocylides was edited, with commentary, by Jacob Bernays, Gesammelte Abhandlungen 1 (ed. H. Usener; Berlin: Wilhelm Hertz, 1885) 192–261. There is an English translation by B. S. Easton in ATR 14 (1932) 222–228.

[9]Weidinger, Haustafeln 25–27.

[10]Ibid., 27–33, 41–43.

[11]Ibid., 42–43. The reference is to Seneca, Ep. 95.4; the list of duties was a part of philosophy according to Seneca, Ep. 94.1.

[12]Weidinger, Haustafeln 46. He cites Hirzel, Agraphos Nomos 47 and Praechter, Hierokles.

[13]Weidinger, Haustafeln 19–20, 42. It will be argued below that the fourth century B.C. should be included in this generalization.

[14]Ibid., 3–4. See Martin Dibelius, From Tradition to Gospel (New York: Charles Scribner's Sons, 1935) 238; idem, Der Brief des Jacobus (MeyerK; Göttingen: Vandenhoeck and Ruprecht, 1957) 7–9.

[15]Weidinger, Haustafeln 6–9.

[16]Stob. I.3.53–54; I.63,6–64,14 Wachsmuth; also Stob. II.9.7; II.181,8–182,30 Wachsmuth. Hierocles' work is preserved in excerpts made by Stobaeus (=Stob.) in his philosophical handbook written in the early fourth century A.D. I have used the edition of Wachsmuth (vols. I–II) and O. Hense (vols. III, IV, V), Stobaeus, Anthologium (1958), 5 vols. I will cite Stobaeus'

book, chapter, and excerpt-number, then the volume, pages, and lines in Wachsmuth-Hense. When I refer to one particular fragment of Hierocles' work in several, immediately successive footnotes, I will not repeat the reference to Stobaeus but I will specify the volume, page(s), and line(s) in Wachsmuth-Hense. There is an old translation of Hierocles by Thomas Taylor, *Political Fragments of Archytas . . . and Other Ancient Pythagoreans Preserved by Stobaeus and also Ethical Fragments of Hierocles* (London: C. Whittingham, 1822) 75–115, which is quoted below.

[17]I.63,13–15 Wachsmuth.

[18]Stob. III.39.34–36; III.730,17–734,10 Hense.

[19]III.734,2–6 Hense.

[20]Stob. IV.25.53; IV.640,4–644,15 Hense.

[21]IV.640,8–10 Hense.

[22]IV.641,3–21 Hense.

[23]IV.642,9–12 Hense.

[24]Stob. IV.27.20; IV.660,15–664,18 Hense.

[25]IV.660,17–661,7 Hense.

[26]IV.661,21–662,3 Hense; cp. 1 Pet 2:18.

[27]IV.663,1–4 and 15; 664,7 Hense.

[28]Stob. IV.27.23; IV.671,3–673,18 Hense.

[29]Stob. IV.28.21; V.696,21–699,15 Hense.

[30]V.696,23–697,3 Hense.

[31]V.697,4–5 Hense.

[32]V.698,13–20 Hense.

[33]V.699,13–15 Hense.

[34]Stob. IV.22.21–24; IV.502,1–507,5 Hense; also Stob. IV.24.14; IV.603,8–24 Hense.

[35]IV.502,5 Hense.

[36]περὶ οἴκων; IV.502,9 Hense.

[37]See Praechter, *Hierokles* 8–9, 74.

[38]Stob. IV.22.24; IV.503,18 Hense.

[39]Stob. IV.27.23; IV.671,4–5 Hense.

[40]Stob. IV.27.23; IV.672,11–14 Hense (my emphasis).

[41]τῷ μήτε τὸ ἄρχον ἄνευ τοῦ ἀρχομένου δύνασθαι νοηθῆναι μήτ᾽ ἄνευ τοῦ ἄρχοντος τὸ ἀρχόμενον. Stob. IV.22.23; IV.503,12–16 Hense.

[42]Weidinger, *Haustafeln* 32.

[43]IV.504,2 and 10 Hense.

[44]ἐκτός and ἔνδον; IV.504,14–15 Hense.

[45]οἰκετοί; IV.504,19–20 Hense.

[46]Stob. IV.22.24; IV.505,5–22 Hense.

[47]IV.506,19–21 Hense.

[48]Eduard Lohse, *A Commentary on the Epistles to the Colossians and to Philemon* (Hermeneia; Philadelphia: Fortress, 1971) 154–163.

[49]Ernst Lohmeyer, *Die Briefe an die Philipper, an die Kolosser und an Philemon* (MeyerK; Göttingen: Vandenhoeck and Ruprecht, 1954) 152.

[50]Crouch, *Colossian Haustafel* 105.

[51]Karl Heinrich Rengstorf, "Die neutestamentliche Mahnungen an die Frau sich dem Manne unterzuordnen" in W. Foerster ed., *Verbum Dei Manet in Aeternum, Festschrift Otto Schmitz* (Wittenberg: Luther, 1953) 131–145. Idem, *Mann und Frau im Urchristentum* (Arbeitsgemeinschaft für Forschung des Landes Nordrhein-Westfalen. Abhandlungen Geisteswissenschaften 12; Köln: Westdeutscher, 1954) 25–46.

[52]David Schroeder, *Die Haustafeln des neuen Testaments (ihre Herkunft und theologischer Sinn)* (Diss. Hamburg: Mikrokopie, 1959) 18, 21, 23. However, he criticizes Seeberg, preferring to say that Paul had a διδαχή but no catechism. He observes (p. 8) that Seeberg's case is finally based only on Rom 6:17, 16:17.

[53]Ibid., 34.

[54]Ibid., p. 37 with nn. 43 and 44; pp. 42 and 117 with nn. 167–171.

[55]Ibid., p. 117, n. 167. But see the diatribe II.10.

[56]Schroeder's second appendix contains the 38 lists which he has found in Epictetus, as well as 12 other lists, in chart form.

[57]Ibid., 41–43.

[58]Ibid., 38.

[59]However, he finds Weidinger's reference to Josephus, *Against Apion*, of doubtful value (ibid., 70).

[60]Ibid., 69, 74, 80, 83–84, 117. However, both Hierocles (see above p. 3–4) and Seneca (see below p. 7–8) discuss reciprocal duties.

[61]Ibid., 69–70, 74, 92, 97 (with n. 72), 124. This relation between the *Haustafel* and the Decalogue is stressed, with observations about the theological use of the *Haustafeln* in Colossians, Ephesians, and the Pastorals, by Peter Stuhlmacher, "Christliche Verantwortung bei Paulus und seinen Schülern," *EvT* 28 (1968) 165–186.

[62]Schroeder, *Haustafeln* 89, 90.

[63]Ibid., 122–123.

[64]Crouch, *Colossian Haustafel* 13–36.

[65]Josephus, *Against Apion* II.199–201; Philo, *Apology for the Jews* 7.3.

[66]Holger Thesleff, ed., *The Pythagorean Texts of the Hellenistic Period* (Acta Academiae Aboensis Ser. A., Humaniora 30; Abo: Abo Akademie, 1965) 145,13.

[67]*Musonius Rufus, The Roman Socrates*, edited and translated C. Lutz (Yale Classical Studies 10; New Haven: Yale University, 1947) 100,17–106,16. Contrast Dionysius Hal., *Rom. Ant.* II.26. The stress on the "obedience" of children comes from the Hellenistic diatribe, influenced by the Roman *patria potestas*. But see Deut 21:18 and Mal 1:6.

[68]Crouch, *Colossian Haustafel* 146–147.

[69]Ibid. Crouch (72) found the order wives, children, slaves in Seneca, *Ep.* 94 and in ps.-Plutarch, *The Education of Children* 10.

[70]Crouch, *Colossian Haustafel* 52–53, 55–56, 59–60.

[71]Seneca, *On Benefits* 2.18.1–2; 3.18.1–2; 3.22.1–2. Hecaton was a student of Panaetius in the early first century B.C. Crouch (56) cites Max Pohlenz, review of Heinz Gomoll, *Der stoische Philosoph Hekaton* in *Göttingische gelehrte Anzeigen* 197 (1935) 104–111, who argued that Hecaton represents a school of thought within Stoicism which based its *kathekon* on the four cardinal virtues rather than a list of duties. Crouch observes that Hecaton uses both.

[72]See Hans von Arnim, "Ariston (56)," *PW* 2 (1895) 957–959. Also Eduard Zeller, *Die Philosophie der Griechen in ihrer geschichtlichen Entwicklung* 3 (5th ed.; Leipzig: O. R. Reisland, 1923) 56–58, 279–281. He was one of the two most influential philosophers in Athens c. 250 B.C. He was a major source for Plutarch, *On Curiosity*; he opposed meddling in others' household affairs as this would lead to a neglect of one's own individual virtue. Instead of dealing with external affairs, one should manage one's inner life. See Otto Hense, "Ariston bei Plutarch," *RhM* 45 (1890) 541–554.

[73]Crouch, *Colossian Haustafel* 66.

[74]Ibid., 66, 71, 72, 147. He denies (66) that the list in Epictetus is an example of reciprocity, observing that even ἄρχων and ἀρχόμενος theoretically could describe the same person in two different relationships.

[75]Ibid., 70. Later he adds ps.-Plutarch, *The Education of Children* 10, but he sees the "women, children and slaves" as a late addition to an early Stoic (Chrysippian) list.

[76]Crouch, *Colossian Haustafel* 79–80.

[77]Following P. Wendland, "Die Therapeuten und die philonische Schrift vom beschäulichen Leben," *Jahrbücher für classische Philologie* 22 (1896) 693–770, esp. 709–712.

[78]Following Gottlieb Klein, *Der älteste christliche Katechismus und die jüdische Propaganda-Literatur* (Berlin: B. Reimer, 1909).

[79]Crouch, *Colossian Haustafel* 106–107; 82 n. 30.

[80]By Hendrik Bolkestein, *Wohltätigkeit und Armenpflege im vorchristlichen Altertum* (Utrecht: A. Oosthoek, 1939) 6–11, 14–17, 45.

[81]Crouch, *Colossian Haustafel* 78, 103.

[82]Ibid., 107, 111.

[83]Ibid., 109, 111, 119.

[84]Ibid., 144 (with n. 108), 149.

[85]Ibid., 122–145, esp. 126 on Gal 3:28.

[86]Ibid., 144, 151. But Crouch (117–118) admits that the Jews were no more interested than non-Jews in listing the social duties of slaves. He cites only Philo, *The Decalogue* 167, and *Sibylline Oracles* II.278. Crouch here repeats Weidinger's reference to Plato (*Laws* VI.776D–778A) and Aristotle (*Pol.* I 1360b 6) and points further to Seneca, *Ep.* 47.

[87]Ibid., 49, 52. Zeller, *Philosophie* 3: 288–289. Stoic attitudes toward sexual relationships, women's clothing, the relation of parents to children, and rites for the dead were especially offensive. See e.g. Sextus Empiricus, *Outlines of Pyrrhonism* I.145, 160; III.200, 205, 210, 245–249; *Against the Ethicists* [*Against the Mathematicians* XI] 190–199.

[88]Klaus Thraede, "Ärger mit der Freiheit. Die Bedeutung von Frauen in Theorie und Praxis der alten Kirche," in Gerta Scharffenorth, ed., "*Freunde in Christus werden . . .*" *Die Beziehung von Mann und Frau als Frage an Theologie und Kirche* (Berlin: Burckhardthaus, 1977) 31–181, esp. 53, 63, 119–120. This view of the source of the NT domestic codes was the basis of my dissertation, completed at Yale University in 1974.

[89]Ibid., 53.

[90]Ibid., 63.

[91]Ibid., 120.

[92]Ibid., 89.

[93]Ibid., 116, 118.

[94]Crouch has done very careful, at points brilliant, work (a) in evaluating previous studies of the *Haustafeln* and (b) in discussing the Stoic texts. The criticisms of some of his conclusions which will occur in the following pages are necessary in light of additional texts, but they are not intended to obscure my appreciation of a good book.

[95]Schroeder, *Haustafeln* 138, 158–159. Crouch, *Colossian Haustafel* 89–99, 148, characterizes the purposes of the summary of the Jewish Law in ps.-Phocylides, *Maxims*, Philo, *Apology for the Jews*, and Josephus, *Against Apion*, as missionary, although he nowhere claims that the Colossian *Haustafel* has a similar missionary intent. For him it seems to have only the first and second functions listed above.

[96]Schroeder's suggestions that the ethic functioned both to suppress social unrest within the church and as a mission thrust outward seem incompatible.

[97]See the recent survey by John H. Elliott, "The Rehabilitation of an Exegetical Step-Child: I Peter in Recent Research," *JBL* 95 (1976) 243–254. See also R. P. Martin, "The Composition of I Peter in Recent Study," *Vox Evangelica* (London Bible College, 1962) vol. 1, 29–42.

[98]Adolf von Harnack, *Geschichte der altchristlichen Literatur bis Eusebius*: Vol. II. *Die Chronologie der altchristlichen Literatur bis Eusebius* (Leipzig: J. C. Heinrich, 1897) 451–465.

[99]R. Perdelwitz, *Die Mysterienreligionen und das Problem des I Petrusbriefes. Ein literarischer und religionsgeschichtlicher Versuch* (Religionsgeschichtliche Versuche und Vorarbeiten 11; Giessen: Alfred Töpelmann, 1911). He also argued that the author and the recipients of 1 Peter might have been devotees of the mystery cult of Cybele before they became Christians.

[100]Wilhelm Bornemann, "Der erste Petrusbrief—eine Taufrede des Silvanus?" *ZNW* 19 (1919–1920) 143–165.

[101]Hans Windisch, *Die katholischen Briefe* (HNT; Tübingen: Mohr, 1951).

[102]Ibid., 156–162.

[103]Frank Leslie Cross, *I Peter. A Paschal Liturgy* (London: A. R. Mowbray, 1954). For criticism see C. F. D. Moule, "The Nature and Purpose of I Peter," *NTS* 3 (1956–1957) 1–11, and esp. T. C. G. Thornton, "I Peter, A Paschal Liturgy?" *JTS* 12 (1961) 14–26. Cross was given weak

support by A. R. C. Leaney, "1 Peter and the Passover: An Interpretation," *NTS* 10 (1963-1964) 238-251.

[104]Cross, *1 Peter* 12-17.

[105]Ibid., 31.

[106]Ibid., 34.

[107]M.-E. Boismard, "Une liturgie baptismale dans la Prima Petri," *RB* 63 (1956) 182-208; 64 (1957) 161-183.

[108]M.-E. Boismard, *Quartre hymnes baptismales dans la première Épître de Pierre* (Paris: Les Éditions du Cerf, 1961). The third hymn he isolates is 1 Pet 2:22-25, underlying which is Isaiah 53; but as it is in that part of the *Haustafel* dealing with slaves, I will not be concerned with it in detail.

[109]Willem Cornelis van Unnik, *De verlossing 1 Petrus 1:18-19 en het probleem van den eersten Petrusbrief* (Mededulingen der Nederlandsche Akademie van Wetschappen. Afd. letterkunde. Nieuwe reeks, deel 5, no. 1; Amsterdam: Noor-hollandische uitg. mij, 1942). He notes that the verb προσάγω (3:18) is a translation of הקריב, a technical term for "to make proselytes." See W. C. van Unnik, "Christianity according to 1 Peter," *Exp Tim* 68 (1956) 79-83, at p. 81. F. W. Danker, *CTM* 38 (1967) 331, n. 2 adds προσερχόμενοι (2:4) as a word for proselytes, and 1:14, 18 as pointing to Gentile converts.

[110]Francis Wright Beare, *The First Epistle of Peter* (2nd ed.; Oxford: B. Blackwell, 1958).

[111]Edward Gordon Selwyn, *The First Epistle of St. Peter* (2nd ed.; London: Macmillan, 1958).

[112]Beare, *First Epistle* 52.

[113]Ibid.

[114]Ibid., 196.

[115]Phillip Carrington, *The Primitive Christian Catechism. A Study in the Epistles* (Cambridge: Cambridge University, 1940).

[116]Ibid., chap. 2.

[117]Ibid., chaps. 4-6.

[118]Selwyn, *First Epistle* 369-375.

[119]Ibid., 382-384.

[120]Ibid., 386-389.

[121]Eduard Lohse, "Paraenese und Kerygma im 1.Petrusbrief," *ZNW* 45 (1954) 68-89. See p. 70.

[122]Ibid., 72, 85.

[123]Ibid., 74; cp. 80.

[124]Ibid., 74, 78.

[125]Ibid., 83-85.

[126]David Hill, "On Suffering and Baptism in I Peter," *NovT* 18 (1976) 181-189. Cp. Elliott in his survey, *JBL* 95 (1976) 252.

[127]Hill, "On Suffering," 182.

[128]Ibid., 184-185.

[129]Ibid., 189.

[130]Leonhard Goppelt, *Der Erste Petrusbrief* (MeyerK; Göttingen: Vandenhoeck and Ruprecht, 1978) 6, 41, 59, 177.

[131]Ibid., 40, 58.

[132]Ibid., 59.

[133]Ibid., 41, 57.

[134]Ibid., 176.

[135]Ibid., 42.

[136]Weidinger, *Haustafeln* 46, 53.

[137]Friedrich Wilhelm, "Die Oeconomica der Neupythagoreer Bryson, Kallikratidas, Periktione, Phintys," *RhM* 70 (1915) 163-164, 222. Wilhelm's observation has been developed recently by Thraede, "Ärger mit der Freiheit."

[138]Translating the term *politeia* is difficult; terms such as constitution, form of government, and state have been used. I will use the first of these, despite its inadequacy. See Heinrich Ryffel, *Metabole Politeion. Der Wandel der Staatsverfassungen; Untersuchungen zu einem Problem der griechischen Staatstheorie* (Bern: P. Haupt, 1949) 3–6. The English term "constitution" is inadequate because it suggests a set of written laws, so is much narrower than the Greek term, which included all the unwritten customs according to which a particular people lived. Ryffel observes that in the Greek term the ethical is primary; the social and legal elements are always secondary. The *politeia* is the soul of the city, its manner of life (Isocrates, *Areopagiticus* 14; Aristotle, *Pol.* IV 1295b 1). The success or failure of a city, her development or decline, is grounded in her *politeia* in the famous text in Polybius: "Now the chief cause of success or the reverse in all matters is the form of a state's *politeia*; for springing from this, as from a fountainhead, all designs and plans of action not only originate, but reach their consummation." (Polybius, *History* VI.2.9–10; cp. Dionysius Hal., *Rom. Ant.* II.3.5).

PART I

PHILOSOPHICAL DISCUSSIONS "CONCERNING THE CONSTITUTION" AND "CONCERNING HOUSEHOLD MANAGEMENT"

Chapter II

Plato, Middle Platonists, and Stobaeus

At the end of chap. I, it was observed that classical Greek political theorists were interested in household ethics. In the following chapters we will investigate what Plato, Aristotle, and later philosophers had to say about household relationships in order to determine whether this has any relation to NT attitudes about wives, children, and slaves. The discussion will begin with the *Republic*, probably written in the period 384–370 B.C., where Plato sometimes mentions the relationship between the "city" and the "house."

A. Plato, Republic

The question whether the main subject of Plato's *Republic* (*Politeia*) is justice or the city-state has never been settled. The work begins with the question of whether the just life is the happy one for the individual.[1] Since this question is difficult to answer, Plato suggests that there is an analogy between an individual man and a whole city, and that whether a just life is the best one would be easier to determine in the case of the larger object, the city (II 368E). Through characters in the *Republic*, Plato contrasts the ideal city with a sick (luxurious) one (II 372E; 399E; IV 427D). Justice in the city brings love and oneness of mind, but injustice produces factions, hatreds, and internecine conflicts (I 351D).[2] This applies to injustice in a city, family, or camp (I 351E). The disputants then try to determine whether a healthy city exhibits the four virtues of being wise, brave, sober, and just (IV 427E; 428B; 429A; 430D; 432B). The object of the whole of Plato's dialogue is to discover the "justice" of the city (IV 430D). It is just for each person to have a social place and duty.

Each one must perform one social service in the state for which his nature was best adapted. Yes, we said that. And again that to do one's own business and not to be a busybody is justice. . . . If we were required to decide what it is whose indwelling presence will contribute most to making our city good, it would be a difficult decision whether it was the unanimity of rulers and ruled, or the conservation in the minds of the soldiers of the convictions produced by law as to what things are or are not to be feared, or the watchful intelligence that resides in the guardians, or whether this is the

chief cause of its goodness, the principle embodied in *child, woman, slave,* free,
artisan, *ruler,* and *ruled,* that each performed his one task as one man and was not a
versatile busybody. (IV 433A,C–D)[3]

It is centrally important for Plato that child, woman, slave, etc., perform his
or her assigned function without trying to perform the function of members of
a different class. It is clear from IV 431C[4] that the place of "children and
women and slaves" is one of submission; they are to be ruled just as the
"appetites" in a man must be ruled by the "reason." Plato thinks that the rulers
must be older and the ruled younger (III 412C).[5] It is "fitting" for the young to
be silent in the presence of their elders and to serve their parents (IV 425B).[6]
Reason must rule the appetites, and pleasures must not be allowed to usurp
the rule improperly (442B), enslaving the better part; the rule of reason will
produce friendship and concord (442D) instead of faction in both city and
individual (IV 441C–445B).[7]

Plato's own summary of the *Republic* appears in *Timaeus* 17C–19A.
Two topics which appear in this short summary are "concerning women,"
who must be in accord with the men, and "concerning child-production"
(18C).[8]

B. Plato, Laws

Plato's *Laws,* written not long before his death in 347 B.C., is also
centrally concerned with the discussion of the best "constitution" and "laws."[9]
One of the opening observations is that each of us has a superior part and an
inferior part and that the same condition exists in house, village, and city
(627A).[10] Exactly what this means is spelled out in a striking passage:

Very well then: what and how many are the agreed rights or claims (ἀξιώματα) in the
matter of ruling and being ruled, alike in States [cities], large or small, and in
households? Is not the right of father and mother one of them? And in general would
not the claim of parents to rule over offspring be a claim universally just? Certainly.
And next to this, the right of the noble to rule over the ignoble; and then, following on
these as a third claim, the right of older people to rule and of younger to be ruled. To be
sure. The fourth right is that slaves ought to be ruled, and masters ought to rule.
Undoubtedly. And the fifth is, I imagine, that the stronger should rule and the weaker
be ruled. A truly compulsory form of rule, . . . being "according to nature. . . ." The
most important right is, it would seem, the sixth, which ordains that the man without
understanding should follow, and the wise man lead and rule. . . . This is the natural
rule of law, without force, over willing subjects. . . . Heaven's favour and good-luck
mark the seventh form of rule, where we bring a man forward for casting of lots, and
declare that if he gains the lot he will most justly be ruler, but if he fails he shall take his
place among the ruled. Very true. Seest thou, O legislator—it is thus we might
playfully address one of those who lightly start on the task of legislation, how many
are the rights pertaining to rulers, and how they are essentially opposed to one
another? Herein we have now discovered a source of factions, which thou must
remedy. (III 690A–D)[11]

These thoughts are not originally Platonic; this quotation refers to "agreed rights" or axioms. The "house" is similar to the "city" in that both must have a "ruler" and those who "are ruled." Further, these relationships are expressed in pairs, which in XI 917A includes the man-woman pair.[12] So in the *Laws* these relationships include the three pairs which appear later in Col 3:18–4:1. It seems obvious that these pairs result from the concern for "ruling": the _____ must "rule" and the _____ must "be ruled"; Greek authors filled in these blanks with various pairs. Further, the legislator for the city is concerned with all seven relationships, including those within the house, for they are a source of potential political problems.[13]

"Contempt for law" originated in modern music, according to Plato,[14] in not being satisfied with the old style (701A).

> Next after this form of liberty would come that which refuses to be subject to rulers; and, following on that, the shirking of submission to one's parents and elders and their admonitions; then, as the penultimate stage, comes the effort to disregard the laws; while the last stage of all is to lose all respect for oaths or pledges or divinities. . . . (III 701B)

Here one's "submission," or rather the lack of it, in one relationship spills over into other relationships. In IV 713E–714A Plato pictures the disastrous consequences of disregarding law in "house and city" and living according to pleasures and lusts.

There is an isolated reference to marriage in IV 720E–721C.[15] Plato insists that the "first law to be laid down by the lawgiver" will regulate the "starting-point of generation in the States," that is, the "union and partnership of marriage." Those who refuse to marry should be punished by the state. This is said while Plato and the other disputants seek to "build up by arguments the framework of a state" (III 702D).[16]

In general terms, the whole section VI 771E to VII 824C concerns "household management." The first part of it concerns marriage (771E, 772D, 773A–775E, 779D; cp. 802A–806C); *within* this part of the discussion, the last element is an extensive discussion concerning slaves (776B–777E, 793E).[17] Then there is a discussion of the birth (VI 783B–785B), nurture, and education of children (VII 788A–824C).[18]

Many of the ideas expressed in this large section reappear in later discussions. This is partially because of Plato's dominating influence in later thought, but that is not an adequate explanation. This topos is not originally Platonic, as III 690 and VI 769A, among other texts, indicate. Plato is simply giving his version of topics commonly discussed in Greek politics, using the topoi "concerning the constitution," "concerning household management," "concerning marriage," and several others.[19] Plato was neither the first nor the last to ask "What ought we to do about our own country, in regard to the owning of slaves and their punishment?" (777B; cp. 776D) or to ponder:

Suppose that women do not share with men in the whole of their mode of life, must they not have a different system of their own? They must. Then which of the systems now in vogue shall we prescribe in preference to that fellowship which we are now imposing upon them? Shall it be that of the Thracians? . . . Or that which obtains with us [Athenians]? . . . Or again, shall we prescribe for them, Megillus, that midway system, the Laconian? (VII 805D–E)

I conclude that Plato's discussion about the constitution (the whole state) relates the "city" to the "house." Plato is concerned with the woman's place in society, the use of slaves, the education of children, and many other topics. Marriage is the "first" concern of a city legislator. There is a concern for relationships of rule and submission; seven such relationships are "axioms" (*Laws* III 690A–D). Those household relationships which we normally consider private, individual matters are here part of a social-political, philosophic ethic.

C. The Middle Platonists

According to Giusta,[20] there are three sources for tracing the later interpretation of Platonic ethics: Albinus, *Introduction to the Doctrines of Plato*; Apuleius, *On the Doctrines of Plato*; and Diogenes Laertius, *Lives and Opinions of Eminent Philosophers* III. All three discuss Plato's politics and ethics, but it is especially Laertius and Albinus who have interpretations which are relevant to this study and which show that the ideas being discussed here remained alive in the later Platonic school, the Academy. Laertius summarizes Plato's views on the constitution in several places (III.82, 83, 86, 103, 104), but it is especially III.91–92 on "ruling" which recalls Plato, *Laws* III 698E–699C.

Rule has five divisions, one which is according to law, another according to nature, another according to custom, a fourth by birth, a fifth by force. Now the magistrates in cities when elected by their fellow-citizens rule according to law. The natural rulers are the males, not only among men, but also among the other animals; for the males everywhere exert wide-reaching rule over the females. Rule according to custom is such authority as attendants exercise over children and teachers over their pupils. Hereditary rule is exemplified by that of the Lacedaemonian kings. . . . Others have acquired power by force or fraud, and govern the citizens against their will; this kind of rule is called forcible. Thus rule is either by law, or by nature, or by custom, or by birth, or by force. (Trans. Hicks)

In the early third century A.D. when Laertius probably lived, Plato was interpreted as teaching that women are to be ruled by men and children by attendants, and this was still done in the context of thought about "cities." It is, of course, an inaccurate interpretation, but Laertius records as Plato's doctrine that men "by nature" rule women; such a view is Aristotelian.[21] Slaves are not mentioned in this text, but what Plato taught about their chastisement was not forgotten either (see Diog. Laert. III.38–39).

Albinus (fl. c. A.D. 151), *Introduction to the Doctrines of Plato* 27–33, discussed Plato's moral and political thought, especially his views on constitutions (including his laws about women). But it is an introductory observation in chap. 3, a summary of the ethical part of Plato's philosophy, that is most noteworthy:

> Practical (science) is concerned about things to be done. . . . Of Practical science one part is seen to be concerned about the care of morals, and another about the regulation of a household, and another relating to the state, and its safety. Of these, the first is called Moral; the second Oeconomical (οἰκονομικόν); the third, Political.[22]

Albinus never expanded this; one wonders how he would have interpreted Plato's "household" regulations.

Apuleius, born in A.D. 123, discussed Plato's moral philosophy in *On the Doctrines of Plato* II.[23] In chap. 24 he observes:

> Respecting the constitution of the states, and the preservation of commonwealths to be ruled over, Plato thus ordains. At the very commencement he defines the form of a state after this fashion. A state is the union of very many persons amongst themselves, where (some) are rulers, others inferiors, bringing, when united, aid and assistance to each other in turn, and regulating their duties by the same correct laws. . . .

Then in chap. 25 Apuleius discussed Plato's *Republic* and in chap. 26 his *Laws*, in both cases noting his regulations about marriages and the rearing of children. He was more accurate than Albinus in observing that

> Plato wished (male and female) to be united in all arts, that are thought to be peculiar to men, and even in those of war; since to both there is the same power, as their nature is one. . . . (II.25)

From these texts in Diogenes Laertius, Albinus, and Apuleius, I conclude that Plato's political thought which dealt with ruling and being ruled in city and house was referred to but was not a dominant element in the Middle Platonists. Laertius referred to the necessity of "rule" over women, and Albinus hinted at it. Apuleius discussed Plato's regulations about women and children without any relation to the topic of ruling and being ruled, although in the same context Apuleius stressed that some are rulers in the "state" and others are inferior.

D. Plato in Stobaeus

Many of the passages of Plato discussed above were excerpted centuries later by Stobaeus in his anthology (see notes 1–8, 11, 15, 17–18). The passage from Plato, *Laws* III 689E–690C about "ruling" and "being ruled" in house and city appears in Stobaeus, as does *Laws* VI 777B–778A about masters and slaves, and the *Republic* III 412C on elders ruling and the

younger being ruled.[24] No writer in the NT used Plato, so these citations in
Stobaeus are important in determining the availability of such texts and ideas.
Stobaeus apparently made his collection of texts for his son in the early fourth
century A.D.,[25] excerpting texts from authors as early as the fourth century
B.C.[26] In selecting excerpts he was often dependent on earlier handbooks like
the *Opinions* (*Placita*) of Aetius and the *Epitome* of Areius Didymus (in
Stobaeus, books I and II).[27] Other examples of older handbooks used by
Stobaeus are an Euripidean gnomology, probably arranged alphabetically by
titles of the dramas, and perhaps a handbook of Neopythagorean
documents.[28] Many of the excerpts from Plato, the immediate concern here,
were made by Stobaeus himself from his own reading, since they are often
added at the end of a chapter.[29] This, of course, reduces the probability that
exactly those Platonic excerpts which appear in Stobaeus were taken by him
from handbooks current earlier in the Hellenistic and Roman ages.

The chapter titles in Stobaeus were apparently supplied by Stobaeus
himself, and not later by Photius.[30] They are more valuable the more closely
Stobaeus followed his sources. Diels' reconstruction of Aetius[31] showed that
in his *Opinions* the chapter titles were more exact than in Stobaeus. However,
Stobaeus was less independent after the first book. Many of his chapter titles
correspond to the titles of books written by ancient philosophers,[32] as a
comparison with the titles cited by Diogenes Laertius shows.[33] Among the
examples of these titles which Hense lists are precisely those with which I am
concerned: "Concerning Justice" (III.9), "Concerning the Constitution"
(IV.1), "Concerning Laws" (IV.2), "Concerning Marriage" (IV.22),
"Concerning Household Management" (IV.28). Greek culture was not
continually creative in the sphere of ethics. These were topoi in Plato's time,
and 700 years later in Stobaeus' time they were still topoi, having been
repeated in many treatises and Hellenistic sermons in the intervening
centuries.[34] Hense concludes that the Stobaean chapter titles present us with
generally known topoi, widely used for hundreds of years in ethics and
popular philosophy.[35] The three Platonic extracts mentioned above are taken
from chapters in Stobaeus entitled "Concerning Laws and Customs" (IV.2),[36]
"Concerning Masters and Slaves" (IV.19), and "Concerning the
Constitution" (IV.1). The chapter "Concerning Laws and Customs" is
demonstrably a topos used widely over several centuries by many wandering
Cynic-Stoic preachers in the Hellenistic-Roman world (see n. 36). That the
second, "Concerning Masters and Slaves," is also such a topos is not so easily
demonstrable from our remaining literary evidence, but the fact that it is
discussed by Plato and that it appears as a chapter title in Stobaeus in itself
points to that conclusion. That the Stobaean chapter "Concerning Household
Management" was a topos is clear from Dio Chrysostom's oration with that
same title, even though only six short fragments of it have survived.[37] These
few sentences indicate that Dio discussed how to be a master of slaves, a wife's
piety and love of her husband, and the rearing of children. I suggest that this
lost oration corresponds to "ordering the household," which Dio says

philosophers and orators concerned with the constitution would discuss in advising and legislating for the state (*Or.* 22.1–2; cp. 69.2). And Dio lived near the time and place 1 Peter was written! Since Dio's works reflect popular ideas, the topoi would have been available to early Christian writers and preachers. As noted above, this may not mean that the specific citations from Plato were widely known, but the topoi they represent were, precisely in the period with which I am concerned, the Roman imperial age.

NOTES TO CHAPTER II

[1]See e.g. I 347E, 352D, II 358; this includes the assertion that obedience to rulers is just (I 339D; cp. III 389D) in cities where the form of government may be either a tyranny, a democracy, or an aristocracy (I 338D). Elders rule and the younger are ruled (III 412C) (excerpted in Stobaeus IV.1.157; IV.106,11–109,20 Hense). On the manner of citing Stobaeus, see p. 15. n. 16 above. The meaning of these excerpts in Stobaeus will be discussed below, pp.27–29.

[2]This text is excerpted in Stob. III.9.60; III.386,3–5 Hense. Cp. ps.–Plato, *Cleitophon* 408E–410B (an excerpt in Stob. III.9.64; III.405,10–407,26 Hense). Also ps.–Plato, *Alcibiades* I 126B–127D (an excerpt in Stob. IV.1.151; IV.98,3–100,6 Hense), in which the pairs parents-son, brother-brother, husband-wife (126E) appear.

[3]Trans. Shorey. My emphasis. An excerpt in Stob. IV.1.100; IV.43,4–44,21 Hense.

[4]An excerpt in Stob. IV.1.99; IV.41,17–18 Hense.

[5]An excerpt in Stob. IV.1.57; IV.106,13–14 Hense.

[6]An excerpt in Stob. IV.1.97; IV.38,12–14 Hense.

[7]An excerpt in Stob. III.9.61; III.390,13–397,18 Hense (in Stobaeus' chapter "Concerning Justice").

[8]An excerpt in Stob. IV.2.9; IV.117,10–120,2 Hense.

[9]Plato, *Laws* I 625A, 631C, 634D, 636A, 641D and passim. Plato refers to this kind of discussion as "the ancients' game of reason" (VI 769A). See IV 714B on the relation of the concepts of *politeia* and "law."

[10]Several texts relate the "house" to the "city": I 626E–628A, III 690A–D (cp. 714E, 917A), II 665C, 680B, IV 713E–714A, VI 779B, VII 790B, X 890B, 910B.

[11]Trans. Bury. An excerpt in Stob. IV.2.31; IV.166,2–167, 4 Hense. Cp. *Laws* 714E.

[12]Earlier in *Rep.* V (e.g. 451D–E, 455D–E, 456A, 466C–D), Plato had argued that some men and women have the same nature, except that the men are stronger, the women weaker. Some women should go with men to war and some should share guardianship of the state. So in the *Republic* (unlike the *Laws*), the stronger-weaker distinction does not necessitate the conclusion that all men rule and all women are ruled. For an explanation of Plato's change from the more egalitarian *Republic* to the stricter *Laws*, see Anne Dickason, "Anatomy and Destiny: The Role of Biology in Plato's Views of Women," in C. C. Gould and M. W. Wartofsky, eds., *Women and Philosophy. Toward a Theory of Liberation* (New York: G. P. Putnam's Sons, 1976) 45–53. Plato's speculations in the *Republic* were rejected by Xenophon, *Concerning Household Management*, e.g., 7.3, 22–25, 35–36, 41 (written in 362–361 B.C.).

[13]One problem is discussed in III 694C: Plato accuses Cyrus of paying no attention to "household management." According to Thomas Alan Sinclair, *A History of Greek Political Thought* (London: Routledge and Paul, 1951) 190, n. 5, this is polemic against Xenophon's *The Education of Cyrus* or against Antisthenes (on whom see n. 19 below).

[14]Elsewhere, discussing music, Plato notes: "It is the duty of every man and child—bond and free, male and female—and the duty of the whole State, to charm themselves unceasingly with the chants we have described" (II 665C). Two of these three pairs occur in VIII 838D.

[15]An excerpt in Stob. IV.2.33; IV.168,5–169,14 Hense.

[16]Note the summary statements about this effort in IV 724A, V 730B, VI 768E, 783B, VIII 842E, XI 917A; also I 631D to 632E.

[17]Stob. IV.18.52; IV.431,14–433,14 Hense excerpts 777B–778A (in the chapter "Concerning Masters and Slaves").

[18]On young reverencing the old see IX 879B–C (an excerpt in Stob. IV.2.44; IV.179,14–180,4 Hense). On children honoring parents as gods see XI 930E–931A (an excerpt in Stob. IV.25.34; IV.625,8–626,2 Hense); and further IV 717B–718A (an excerpt in Stob. IV.25.49; IV.629,16–631,3 Hense).

[19]Plato's contemporary Antisthenes wrote a treatise on "household management" (περὶ νίκης οἰκονομικός; Diog. Laert. VI.16). For hypotheses about the title and content, see Karl Joël, *Der echte und der Xenophontische Sokrates* 2/1 (Berlin: R. Gartners Verlagsbuchhandlung, 1901) 261 and 370, n. 2; also 2/2, 989–991 and 1078. Sinclair, *Greek Political Thought* 52–53 notes that Protagoras was the first to entitle a work περὶ πολιτείας (Diog. Laert. IX.55), the title later made famous by Plato's *Republic*.

[20]Michelangelo Giusta, *I dossografi di etica* 1 (Università di Torino, Pubblicazioni della Facoltà di lettere e filosofia 15/3; Torino: G. Giappichelli, 1964) 13. See vol. 2 (15/5; 1967) 523–527 on the relation of these works to the section in Areius Didymus on Peripatetic politics.

[21]See Plato, *Laws* III 690B and n. 12 above. The Middle Platonic presentations of Plato's philosophy are highly eclectic. For the tripartite Peripatetic and Stoic form in which Plato's thought is given, see Abraham J. Malherbe, "The Structure of Athenagoras, 'Supplicatio pro Christianis'," *VC* 23 (1969) 3–4.

[22]*Epitome*, ed. by P. Louis (Paris: Société d'édition "Les Belles Lettres," 1945) 9,13–16. The translation is by George Burges, *The Works of Plato* (London: George Bell and Sons, 1891), vol. 6 in *The Bohn Classical Library*.

[23]The work is of disputed authenticity; see Josef Redfors, *Echtheitskritische Untersuchung der apuleischen Schriften De Platone und De Mundo* (Lund: Akademisk avhandling, 1960). It was edited by P. Thomas (Stuttgart: B. G. Teubner, 1908) and translated by G. Burges, *Works of Plato*, vol. 6. I quote from Burges' translation.

[24]See nn. 11, 17, and 5 respectively.

[25]Otto Hense, "Ioannes Stobaios," *PW* 9 (1916) 2549. See Karl Praechter, *Hierocles der Stoiker* (Leipzig: T. Weicher, 1901) 2.

[26]See Hense, "Ioannes Stobaios," 2549–2586. Also Wilhelm von Christ, Wilhelm Schmid, and Otto Stählin, *Geschichte der griechischen Literatur* 2/2 (6th ed.; Munich: O. Beck, 1924) section 838, p. 1088: "Stobaeus took nearly all the excerpts from older collections." (my trans.)

[27]Hense, "Ioannes Stobaios," 2561, 2564–2580. See John Burnet, *Early Greek Philosophy* (4th ed.; London: A. and C. Black, 1930) 33–38 on doxographers. And on Areius Didymus see Eduard Zeller, *Philosophie* 3/1:635–639.

[28]Hense, "Ioannes Stobaios," 2573 on Euripides; 2570 and 2580 on the Neopythagoreans. On pre-Christian Neopythagorean doxography see Henry Chadwick, "Florilegium," *RAC* 7 (1969) 1153–1154; also in general, I. Opelt, "Epitome," *RAC* 5 (1962) 944–973.

[29]Hense, "Ioannes Stobaios," 2569. On the problem of Platonic doxographies earlier than Stobaeus see Chadwick, "Florilegium," 1142–1143 and Malherbe, "Athenagoras," 4.

[30]Hense, "Ioannes Stobaios," 2556. The content of many or most of the chapters has been lost, but a list of the original chapter titles as listed by Photius is given by Wachsmuth-Hense in their edition of Stobaeus, *Anthologium*, vol. 1, 3–10.

[31]Hermann Diels, *Doxographi Graeci* (Berlin and Leipzig: Walter de Gruyter, 1929) 273–444.

[32]Hense, "Ioannes Stobaios," 2557–2558.

[33]For Diog. Laert.'s use of handbooks and other sources see Eckart Mensching, *Favorin von Arelate I. Der erste Teil der Fragmente* (Berlin: Walter de Gruyter, 1963) 8 with n. 6.

[34]The titles of Seneca's essays, Plutarch's *Moralia*, the diatribes of Musonius, Epictetus, and Dio Chrysostom, among others, allow us to see what topoi were discussed with some regularity. See André Oltramare, *Les origines de la diatribe romaine* (Lausanne: Librairie Payot, 1926) 301–306 for a list.

[35]Hense, "Ioannes Stobaios," 2559.

[36]Against Schroeder, *Haustafeln* 74 with n. 300, it does not necessarily follow from the fact that a writer mentions νόμοι καὶ ἔθη that the material is exclusively Jewish. See Dio Chrysostom, *Or. 75 On Law* and *Or. 76 On Custom.*

[37]The six fragments in Stobaeus are collected by H. Lamar Crosby in his *LCL* edition of Dio (1964), vol. 5, 348-351. For a discussion of these rhetorical, political topoi see Aristotle, *Rhetoric* I.4 and 8. "The most important and effective of all the means of persuasion and good counsel is to know all the forms of *politeiai* and to distinguish the manners and customs, institutions, and interests of each" (I.8.1-2). Aristotle observes that this has been discussed in his *Politics* (*Rhet.* I.8.7). In this context the character of the women is also considered: the character of Spartan women is unsatisfactory, so the state is only half-happy (ibid., I.5.6). A similar concern for rhetorical treatment of the *politeiai* is found in ps.-Aristotle [Anaximenes?], *Rhetoric to Alexander* 2 (1424a 9-1424b 25).

These topoi are mentioned by Heinrich Ryffel, "Anhang IV: Die Metabole der Verfassungen als Topos der symbuleutischen Rede," *Metabole Politeion* 243-247. Ryffel's views are evaluated by Kurt von Fritz, *The Theory of the Mixed Constitution in Antiquity. A Critical Analysis of Polybius' Political Ideas* (New York: Columbia University, 1954) 50, n. 36; 61, n. 2. For a characterization of the political topoi found in Aristotle, *Rhetoric* I.4 see George Kennedy, *The Art of Persuasion in Greece* (Princeton: Princeton University, 1963) 100, 118. These political topoi are "particular topics" which belong to a specialized study, not "common topics."

Chapter III

Aristotle, the Peripatetics, and Three Dependent Writers

Modern historians rarely refer to Aristotle when discussing the NT pattern of submissiveness. But he discusses women, children, and slaves, and the exact outline he gives the topos "on household management" in his *Politics* I, written c. 335 b.c.,[1] is quite important in determining the origin of the NT codes.

A. Aristotle

Aristotle does not like the comparison between a "house" and a "city." He complains that if this analogy is made directly, then several different kinds of authority and rule are confused (*Pol.* I 1252a 7-9). However, he agrees with Plato that one must begin the discussion of this topic with marriage (1252a 24-28), which is the union of natural ruler and natural subject. When a slave is added, this is called a "house" (1252b 9-10). Several households make a "village" (1252b 16), and several villages compose a "city-state," which can be called "self-sufficient" (1252b 28-31; cp. III 1280b 35). This city-state is natural, because man is by nature a political animal (1253a 2-3; cp. III 1278b 18-20), and one who is cityless is either low in the scale of humanity or above it. So the city is prior by nature to the individual (1253a 25). "Justice," he notes, "is an element of the state" (1253a 37).

> Now that it is clear what are the component parts of the state, we have first of all to discuss household management (οἰκονομία); for every state is composed of households (ἐξ οἰκιῶν). Household management falls into departments corresponding to the parts of which the household in its turn is composed; and the household in its perfect form consists of slaves and freemen. The investigation of everything should begin with its smallest parts, and the primary and smallest parts of the household are *master and slave, husband and wife, father and children* (δεσπότης καὶ δοῦλος, καὶ πόσις καὶ ἄλοχος, καὶ πατὴρ καὶ τέκνα); we ought therefore to examine the proper constitution and character of each of these *three* relationships, I mean that of mastership (δεσποτική), that of marriage (γαμική) . . . , and thirdly the progenitive relationship (τεκνοποιητική). . . . There is also a department which some people

> consider the same as household management and others the most important part of
> it . . . : I mean what is called the art of getting wealth. (I 1253b 1–14. Trans. Rackham.
> Emphasis added.)

This is the most important parallel to the NT codes.[2] It demonstrates that the pattern of submissiveness (cp. the three pairs in Col 3:18–4:1) was based upon an earlier Aristotelian topos "concerning household management"; the discussion of these three relationships in a household was not a Jewish or Christian innovation.[3] The topos is so well defined that there were disagreements about its exact relation to the discussion of the art of getting wealth.

Aristotle discussed these relationships 17–20 years earlier than his *Politics* according to Moraux, who concentrates attention on *Pol.* III 1278b, where these three pairs are also discussed. The phrase "the several recognized varieties of government" ($\tau\hat{\eta}s\ \dot{\alpha}\rho\chi\hat{\eta}s\ \tauo\dot{v}s\ \lambda\epsilon\gammao\mu\dot{\epsilon}\nuo\nu s\ \tau\rho\dot{o}\pio\nu s$) is interpreted by the more difficult one $\dot{\epsilon}\xi\omega\tau\epsilon\rho\iota\kappao\grave{\iota}\ \lambda\dot{\epsilon}\gammao\iota$, sometimes translated "external discourses."[4] This latter expression, he argues, refers to dialogues which Aristotle published in his youth, in which his views were worked out in opposition to Plato. Aristotle worked out his suggestions about these three forms of rule—despotic, economical (domestic), political—as they relate to the three relationships in the house in his lost dialogue *Concerning Justice*, which was written shortly after 352 B.C.[5]

Aristotle begins his discussion of these three relationships in *Pol.* I with the master-slave pair (1253b 15–1254a 17; see VII 1330a 32–33), which he discusses at much greater length than he does the other two pairs.[6] Some think that such mastership is contrary to nature, because only convention (law) makes one man a slave and the other free (1253b 20–24). Aristotle here refers to a position like that of the sophist Alcidamus, a student of Gorgias, who asserted, "God has set all men free; nature has made no man a slave,"[7] one of the three or four criticisms of slavery in all of extant Greek literature. Aristotle counters by arguing that property is a part of the house (1253b 23); further,

> Authority and subordination ($\tau\grave{o}\ \ddot{\alpha}\rho\chi\epsilon\iota\nu\ \kappa\alpha\grave{\iota}\ \ddot{\alpha}\rho\chi\epsilon\sigma\theta\alpha\iota$) are conditions not only
> inevitable but also expedient; in some cases things are marked out from the moment of
> birth to rule or to be ruled. (1254a 22–24)

After this discussion, Aristotle considers the art of getting wealth, since slaves are one division of property (1256a 1–4); then he returns to the three pairs (1259b 22). He asks about the virtue of a slave and how it differs from that of a free man (1259b 22–1260b 25), whether their temperance, courage, and justice are the same or not. The same question is raised with respect to the woman and the child:

> Hence there are by nature various classes of rulers and ruled. For the free rules the
> slave, the male the female, and the man the child in a different way. And all possess the

various parts of the soul, but possess them in different ways; for the slave has not got the deliberative part at all, and the female has it, but without full authority, while the child has it, but in an undeveloped form. (1260a 9–14)

Authority and subordination are necessary for Aristotle because the man is the most rational, the woman is less rational, the child immature, and the slave irrational. So the virtue of each of these classes is different, not the same as Socrates taught.[8] The virtue of a woman is silence (1260a 31).

The form of rule in the household is related to the form of the constitution in the state. At the end of his discussion in *Pol.* I, Aristotle promises to discuss this elsewhere:

It will be necessary to follow up in the part of our treatise dealing with the various forms of a constitution. For since every household is part of a state, and these relationships are part of the household, and the excellence of the part must have regard to that of the whole, it is necessary that the education both of the children and of the women should be carried on with regard to the form of the constitution, if it makes any difference as regards the goodness of the state for the children and the women to be good. And it must necessarily make a difference; for the women are a half of the free population, and the children grow up to be the partners in the government of the state. (1260b 12–21)[9]

Aristotle does compare various forms of authority in the household with authority in the state in *The Nicomachean Ethics*. Both assume that man is a political animal who is happy and develops his capacities only in a correctly organized society. While discussing the various forms of constitution, he notes,

One may find likenesses and so to speak models of these various forms of a constitution in the household. The relationship of father to sons is regal in type, since a father's first care is for his children's welfare. This is why Homer styles Zeus "father," for the ideal of kingship is paternal government. Among the Persians paternal rule is tyrannical, for the Persians use their sons as slaves. The relation of master to slaves is also tyrannic, since in it the master's interest is aimed at. The autocracy of a master appears to be right, that of the Persian father is wrong; for different subjects should be under different forms of rule. The relationship of husband to wife seems to be in the nature of an aristocracy: the husband rules in virtue of fitness, and in matters that belong to a man's sphere; matters suited to a woman he hands over to his wife. When the husband controls everything, he transforms the relationship into an oligarchy, for he governs in violation of fitness, and not in virtue of superiority. And sometimes when the wife is an heiress it is she who rules. In these cases then authority goes not by virtue but by wealth and power, as in an oligarchy. . . . Democracy appears most fully in households without a master, for in them all the members are equal; but it also prevails where the ruler of the house is weak, and everyone is allowed to do what he likes. Under each of these forms of government we find friendship existing between ruler and ruled, to the same extent as justice. (*NE* VIII 1160b 23–1161a 10. Trans. Rackham)[10]

Here Aristotle goes beyond merely asserting that the authority of men is natural and necessary. Some ways of ruling are right, others wrong. It is wrong for a father to be tyrannical. (Compare the Neopythagorean Callicratidas and Col 3:21.) However, hierarchical authority itself is right and just. He argues this in a way that is in high tension with modern egalitarian, democratic thought.

> Justice between master and slave and between father and child is not the same as absolute and political justice, but only analogous to them. For there is no such thing as injustice in the absolute sense towards what is one's own; and a chattel [i.e. a slave] or a child till it reaches a certain age and becomes independent, is, as it were, a part of oneself, and no one chooses to harm himself; hence there can be no injustice towards them, and therefore nothing just or unjust in the political sense. For these, as we saw, are embodied in law, and exist between persons whose relations are naturally regulated by law, that is, persons who share equally in ruling and being ruled. Hence justice exists in a fuller degree between husband and wife than between father and children, or master and slaves; in fact, justice between husband and wife is domestic justice in the real sense, though this too is different from political justice. (*NE* V 1134b 9–18)

When the more rational, self-controlled men do not assert their authority but allow women to gain equality and authority, the government degenerates and wars are lost.

> Again, the freedom in regard to women is detrimental both in regard to the purpose of the constitution and in regard to the happiness of the state. For just as man and wife are part of a household, it is clear that the state also is divided nearly in half into its male and female population, so that in all constitutions in which the position of women is badly regulated one half of the state must be deemed to have been neglected in framing the law. And this has taken place in the state under consideration [Sparta], for the lawgiver [Lycurgus] wishing the whole community to be hardy displays his intention clearly in relation to the men, but in the case of the women has entirely neglected the matter; for they live dissolutely in respect of every sort of dissoluteness, and luxuriously. So that the inevitable result is that in a state thus constituted wealth is held in honour, especially if it is the case that the people are under the sway of their women. . . . Hence this characteristic existed among the Spartans, and in the time of their empire many things were controlled by the women; yet what difference does it make whether the women rule if the rulers are ruled by the women? The result is the same. And although bravery is of service . . . even in this respect the Spartans' women were most harmful. . . . But as for the women, though it is said Lycurgus did attempt to bring them under the laws, yet since they resisted he gave it up. So the Spartan women are, it is true, to blame for what took place then and therefore manifestly for the present defect; although we are not considering who deserves excuse or does not, but what is right or wrong in the constitution as it is. But as was also said before, errors as regards the status of women seem not only to cause a certain unseemliness in the actual conduct of the state but to contribute in some degree to undue love of money. (*Pol.* II 1269b 12–1270a 15; cp. V 1313b 33–36; 1314b 26; VI 1319b)[11]

This very passage is mentioned by Plutarch, *Lycurgus* xiv. 1, who disagrees with Aristotle in insisting that Lycurgus did "carefully regulate marriages," and "even to the women Lycurgus paid all possible attention." I take Plutarch's reference to indicate a continuing interest in this topic in the first century A.D.[12] That women's freedom in Sparta was debated in classical times is apparent in Plato, *Laws* I 637B.

It is possible that Aristotle did fulfill his stated intent to complete his treatment of the three pairs of a household in a work *Concerning the Association of Husband and Wife*.[13] Four of the six references to this work given by Rose list four pairs: father-children, husband-wife, master-slave, and the relation of income to expenditure. If this work is genuine, Aristotle probably treated the husband-wife relationship at greater length in it than in the *Politics*, just as Moraux suggests he did in the early work *Concerning Justice*.

We do have fragments of forty of Aristotle's *Constitutions*, because they were excerpted by Heraclides Lembus, a statesman and scholar living in Alexandria during the second century B.C.[14] These fragments, varying from one sentence to one page in length, briefly characterize a people, and the nature of the characterization is relevant to the study of the NT codes. In the *Constitution of the Lacedaemonians*, Aristotle mentions the founder Lycurgus. He describes some institutions of government and says the Lacedaemonians honor a certain singer and do not sell land. Then he observes,

> Women in Lacedaemon are not allowed to wear ornaments, to let their hair grow long, or to wear gold. They bring up their children on empty stomachs to train them to be able to endure hunger. They also train them to steal.[15]

Here Aristotle includes a description of the life of the women and children in his summary of the Spartan constitution. The *Constitution of the Aetans* mentions that the city is hospitable to strangers (cp. the *Constitution of the Tyrrhenians*).[16] The *Constitution of the Lycians* reads as follows:

> The Lycians spend their lives as brigands. They don't employ laws, but customs, and from ancient times they have been ruled by women. They sell those convicted of perjury and confiscate their possessions.[17]

In these examples, the form "concerning the constitution" is reduced to a few sentences which characterize the way of life of a certain nation, and these few words include descriptions of the life of the women and children.

But there is a basic problem with citing texts from Aristotle: he had very little influence for two centuries after his death. His ideas were not important in the Hellenistic age, although later in the time of the Romans, especially in the late first century B.C., his writings again became available.[18] The story of the odyssey of Aristotle's library gives some impression of the availability, or unavailability, of his ideas. Strabo[19] tells the famous story of Aristotle's bequest of his library to Theophrastus, who in turn left both his and

Aristotle's libraries to Nelsus of Scepsis (in Asia Minor). Nelsus' heirs, in order to keep the libraries from being appropriated by the Attalid kings of Pergamum, hid the books underground, and much later they were sold to Apellicon of Teos (c. 150–86 B.C.), after whose death Sulla carried the library to Rome. Von Fritz[20] observes that, while the story deserves no credit, its wide acceptance shows clearly that Aristotle's works were not read by the educated public before the time of Apellicon and that it must have been very difficult to obtain copies of them. However, there was a revival of the Peripatetic school in 40–20 B.C. when Andronicus of Rhodes published a new edition of Aristotle's treatises brought to Rome by Sulla. Andronicus reestablished the school.

B. The Peripatetics

Theophrastus, Aristotle's successor as head of the school, wrote a work *Concerning Laws*,[21] in which he compared and evaluated laws and customs in various cities and countries. Theophrastus' work is quoted by Josephus, *Against Apion* I.22, the work which Weidinger and Crouch suggest has close parallels to the NT codes of household submission. Theophrastus also wrote about marriage, a fragment of which is in the Christian writer Jerome, *Against Jovian* I.47.[22]

One of Aristotle's most famous students in political theory was Dicaearchus.[23] He is credited with a work entitled *Mixed Constitution (Tripoliticus)*, in which he tried to show that the best constitution was a mixture of monarchy, aristocracy, and democracy. He seems to have discussed the Spartan constitution as an example.[24] If Sparta was Dicaearchus' ideal, he differed in this from Aristotle. His works were highly praised by Panaetius (in Cicero, *Concerning the Ends of Goods and Evils* IV.28.79) and Cicero (*Letters to Atticus* II.2) and criticized by Polybius (in Strabo, *Geography* II 4, 104–105).[25] Again, it has been argued that there are clear traces of Dicaearchus' work *On Greek Life* in Josephus, *Against Apion* I.10 and 63.[26]

The topos "concerning household management" with its three pairs was used in the pseudo-Aristotelian *Great Ethics* (I 1194b 5–28), a witness for the Peripatetic use of the form.[27] As Dirlmeier originally suggested, this work is probably a compendium of Peripatetic doctrine produced in the second half of the second century B.C.

Many of these concerns are reflected in the first of the three pseudo-Aristotelian works entitled *Concerning Household Management (Oeconomicus)*.[28] According to Philodemus, the Epicurean contemporary of Cicero, this book was written by Theophrastus,[29] and Armstrong agrees that it is the work of an early Peripatetic, uninfluenced as yet by Stoicism and dependent on Xenophon, *Concerning Household Management*, and Aristotle, *Politics* (esp. book I). The author agrees with Aristotle that there are differences between "housecraft" and "statecraft" (1.1 1343a). A "house" consists of human beings and goods and chattels, as Hesiod says (1.2 1343a 22). It is part of housecraft to order the relation between man and woman (1.2 1343a 23–24). Men beget children because of nature and in order to receive a benefit (1.3 1343b 21–22). Laws for a man's treatment of his wife and her treatment of him are then given (1.4 1344a 8–18). "Adornment" is disparaged (1.4 1344a 19–23). Concerning property, the first step is to obtain good slaves (1.5 1344a 23–28), who are to be given work, punishment, and food (1.5 1344a 35). Freedom is to be set before a slave; then he will put his heart into his work (1.5 1344b 16). Aristotle, *Pol.* VII 1330a 32–33, is similar.

This pseudo-Aristotelian work, *Concerning Household Management*, is an early Peripatetic discussion of the topos with its concern for husband and wife, their slaves, children, and household income. The other Peripatetic texts from Theophrastus, Dicaearchus, and the unknown author of the *Great Ethics* demonstrate that the discussion of constitutions and of household management remained alive in the school. The author of the *Great Ethics* refers to exactly the three relationships dealt with in the NT codes, although his denial that "justice" can be discussed in relation to these three pairs differs from Col 4:1 and 1 Pet 2:19, 23.

C. Three Dependent Writers

Philodemus

Because of its relation to the first of the three pseudo-Aristotelian works *Concerning Household Management*, I will discuss the Epicurean Philodemus' (c. 110–35 B.C.) work *Concerning Household Management*.[30] He first polemicizes against the treatment of the topos by Xenophon, Theophrastus, and the Cynics. According to Philodemus, Xenophon's work *Concerning Household Management* discussed "ruling and child-rearing" (23, 1–2 Jensen).[31] Philodemus complains about the continuity of the topos when he observes that Theophrastus' treatment is derived from Xenophon's, and the other writers who have treated the subject have also adopted Xenophon as superior (26, 3–9).[32] Philodemus himself, at the end of his treatise, observes that he has discussed the subject in general terms according to the "tradition" (75, 14–17).[33]

Philodemus' objections to Theophrastus' treatment of the topos reveal the status of the discussion in the first century B.C. He disagrees with Theophrastus' opinions about wives. Philodemus objects: Why is it that man must first be concerned about marriage when one can live a happy life without a wife (29,7–11)? Why does Theophrastus think that the manner of living with a wife (τρόπον γαμετῆι) properly belongs to the topic of household managing (29,12–15)?

Philodemus says little about raising children, but he does object to Theophrastus' discussion of slaves (30,6–34,4). Should a man first obtain slaves, instead of, as Hesiod says, a house and a wife (30.13–18 [21–26])? But Philodemus thinks Theophrastus correctly said that one should not allow slaves to be insolent or burdensome (30,18–31,2). It is a common concern, not limited to philosophers, that slaves' work, food, and punishment be kept moderate (32,3–7). It is proper not to use an unreasonable punishment (32,7–8).

Philodemus objects to Theophrastus' treatment of how to handle property (34,7). He then presents his own views on the topos (38,2–73,20). Philodemus is not concerned about how to live well at home (οὐχ ὡς ἐν οἴκωι καλῶς ἐστιν βιοῦν) but about how to use and keep one's property (38,5–9). The philosopher should be concerned about riches (38,17–19), an assertion which Philodemus spends the rest of his treatise discussing.

In rejecting the Peripatetic concern for "the manner of living with a wife" and for "how to live well at home," Philodemus was following his teacher Epicurus, who rejected Aristotle's positive evaluation of the political life.[34] Epicurus criticized Aristotle for giving up philosophy and taking up political rhetoric.[35] Aristotle incorrectly insisted that politics was part of philosophy.[36] Typically, Epicurus asserted:

> Nor, again, will the wise man marry and rear a family. . . . Nor will he take part in politics. . . . He will have regard to his property and to the future. (Diog. Laert. X.119–120. Trans. Hicks)[37]

> The wise man does everything for his own sake; he refers all things which he does to his own advantage. . . . There is no society among men.[38]

The last citation rejects the concern for "justice" in Plato and Aristotle. For Aristotle, politics included household management, but for the Epicureans, neither politics nor relationships within the household were part of philosophy.

For clear reasons, the Epicurean Philodemus rejected the discussion of three of the four parts of the Aristotelian form. The later NT writers do the opposite: they discuss only these three relationships, not moneymaking. However, Philodemus' treatise demonstrates that the topos on household management with its concern for ruling, for the functions of wife and slaves in the house, for the art of child-rearing, for acquiring and maintaining money for the support of the house, was widely known in the first century B.C. It would be interesting to know which "other" (26,7–8) writers besides Xenophon, Theophrastus, and Zeno were known by Philodemus.

Areius Didymus

Philodemus' younger contemporary, Areius Didymus,[39] a Stoic who was Augustus Caesar's friend and philosophical teacher, wrote an *Epitome* of Aristotle's ideas, including a summary of his ethics.[40] In his study of this epitome, von Arnim argued[41] against the prevailing opinion that these Aristotelian ideas were influenced by the Stoicism of Antiochus of Ascalon (c. 120–68 B.C.), insisting rather that Areius drew on a Peripatetic handbook from the third century which was based exclusively on Aristotle and

Theophrastus. However, Regenbogen notes that von Arnim overlooked an important fact. There is a polemic against Critolaus' (fl. 156 B.C.) definition of "happiness" in Areius' handbook (Stob. II.7.14; II.126,15 Wachsmuth) which destroys the hypothesis of an older Peripatetic handbook.[42] Regenbogen denies that Areius Didymus' handbook is simply Stoic material; rather it contains material newly thought through within the Peripatetic system. Regenbogen[43] is undecided whether this rethinking arose independently within Aristotle's school or whether it was motivated by a need to oppose the Stoics.

There may be texts which prove that Philo used Areius Didymus. Philo of Alexandria often relied on Eudorus of Alexandria[44] (fl. c. 25 B.C.) for philosophical summaries rather than on the convenient handbook of Areius Didymus (also of Alexandria). However, in his study of this section of Areius, Giusta[45] has pointed to several striking parallels with Philo. According to Giusta, Philo, *On Joseph* 38, paraphrases Areius Didymus (Stob. II.7.26; II.148,7–12 Wachsmuth); both say that a house is a small city, so relate "economics" to politics.[46] Philo, *Who is the Heir* 161–163 and *Special Laws* IV.237, says that "equality" brings peace while "inequality" produces "factions" and evil, repeating Areius Didymus (II.151,10–12 Wachsmuth) according to Giusta. Giusta posits the *literary* dependence of a whole series of authors (including Philo) on Areius Didymus' ethical work, because they all preserve traces of the arrangement of Eudorus' "headings"[47] included by Areius Didymus in the epitome. However, his reviewers reject the suggestion.[48] For example Kerferd says,

> I am left with the impression that Giusta has also made out a case for a broad general similarity of treatment. . . . But this broad pattern is departed from too frequently, and requires too much reinterpretation of individual passages before it can be seen to apply in individual cases, for any cogent conclusions to be drawn from it. . . . May this not be the way Greeks and Romans were trained to present discussions of ethics through attendance at standardized lectures and through reading standardized manuals and text books?[49]

I agree with Giusta's critics, who see the references he collects as demonstrating a "broad general similarity of treatment" rather than widespread literary dependence on Areius Didymus. But that alone is an important conclusion! Areius Didymus' epitome outlines the Aristotelian topos on household management, which is quite similar to the NT codes of household ethics. Kerferd suggests that Greeks and Romans were taught this ethic through standardized lectures and textbooks.

A translation of this section in Areius (Stob. II.7.26; II.147, 26–149,11 Wachsmuth), with references to the parallels in Aristotle pointed out by Henkel and Wachsmuth, follows:

147,26   When the virtues have adequately been defined and, I dare say, the
         many headings of the topos on ethics have been taken up, it is

necessary in succession to go through in detail both household
management (οἰκονομικός) and civic affairs (πολιτικός), since man
148,5   is by nature a political animal. (cp. *Pol.* I 1253a 2–3) There is a
primary constitution (πολιτεία) in the union of a man and a woman
according to law for the begetting of children and for community of
life. This is called a house (οἶκος), which is the beginning (source) of a
city, concerning which we must also speak. (cp. *Pol.* I 1252a 27–28;
1252b 10) For the house is like a small city, if as is ideal, the marriage
148,10   increases and children come; and if the first house is coupled with
others, the other house stands as a support, and so a third and a
fourth, and out of these grows a village and a city. For a city is
produced after many villages have come into existence. (cp. *Pol.* I
1252b 15–16, 28) So just as the house provides for the city the seeds of
its birth, so does it provide the seeds of the constitution. For the
148,15   house is also a pattern for monarchy as well as aristocracy and
democracy. For the relation (κοινωνία) of parents to children has
monarchic character; of men to women, aristocratic; of children to
one another, democratic. (cp. *NE* VIII 1160b 23–25, 32–33; 1161a 3–
4) For the male is joined to the female by a desire to beget children
148,20   and to continue the race. For each of them aims at producing
children. (cp. *Pol.* I 1252a 26–30) When they come together and take
149,1   for themselves a helper in partnership—either a slave by nature
(strong in body for service, but stupid and unable to live by himself,
for whom slavery [τὸ ἄρχεσθαι] is beneficial), or a slave by law—a
house is organized in consequence of the union and the forethought
of all for one thing that is profitable. (cp. *Pol.* I 1254b 19–23, 27–29;
149,5   1254a 14–15; 1255a 5) The man has the rule (ἀρχή) of this house by
nature. For the deliberative faculty in a woman (τὸ βουλευτικόν) is
inferior, in children it does not yet exist, and it is completely foreign
to slaves. Rational household management, which is the controlling
of a house and of those things related to the house, is fitting for a
149,10   man. (cp. *Pol.* I 1260a 9–14; III 1278b 37–38) Belonging to this are
fatherhood (τὸ πατρικόν), the art of marriage (τὸ γαμικόν), being a
master (τὸ δεσποτικόν), and moneymaking (τὸ χρηματιστικόν).
(cp. *Pol.* I 1259a 37–39; 1253b 6–14)

Areius continues discussing moneymaking. His opinion is similar to
Philodemus' when he asserts, "Clearly this division of household management
is the most important." (II.149,17–18 Wachsmuth) The next three pages
outline the topos on civic affairs (II.150,1–152,25 Wachsmuth); Areius
mentions the founding of cities, the best constitution, seditions, magistrates,
laborers, establishing temples for the gods, public education of the children,
and abortion, among other items.

When outlining the topos "concerning household management," Areius
does not present the household relationships by pairs, a contrast with the NT

household codes. However, the two elements which produce those pairs are present: (1) there is a concern for authority in the household, and (2) the classes which constitute a household are listed. Men—not women, children, or slaves—have the authority (II.149,5-8 Wachsmuth). Further, "women, children, and slaves" are mentioned in the same order as in Colossians and Ephesians, an important point in the discussion of the origin of the NT codes. In Areius' epitome, the topos "concerning household management" retains its Aristotelian structure; it still has four parts: fatherhood, marriage, mastership, and moneymaking (II.149,10-12 Wachsmuth; cp. Aristotle, *Pol.* I 1253b 6-8). The nature of the authority exercised within these relationships is still a concern (II.148,15-16 Wachsmuth). And finally, the house is still related to the city (II.148,6-7 Wachsmuth).

Diogenes Laertius' summary of Aristotle's philosophy should be compared with Areius Didymus' summary. Laertius notes that Aristotle's philosophy is divided into practical and theoretical parts:

> The practical part includes ethics and politics, and in the latter not only the doctrine of the state but also that of the household is sketched (. . . πολιτικόν, οὗ τά τε περὶ πόλιν καὶ τὰ περὶ οἶκον ὑπογεγράφθαι). (Diog. Laert. V.28. Trans. Hicks)

Similarly, Seneca observes:

> Certain of the Peripatetic school have added a fourth division, "civil philosophy," because it calls for a special sphere of activity and is interested in a different subject matter. Some have added a department for which they use the Greek term "economics," the science of managing one's own household. (*Ep.* 89.10-11. Trans. Gummere)

Despite the fact that the age was eclectic, Areius Didymus, Diogenes Laertius, and Seneca remembered that these ideas on household management were Aristotelian.

Cicero

Cicero, *Concerning the Ends of Goods and Evils* IV,[50] gives a criticism of Stoicism from a Peripatetic perspective:

> For the present I only say that the topic of what I think may fitly be entitled Civic Science (the adjective in Greek is πολιτικόν) was handled with authority and fullness by the early Peripatetics and Academics, who agreed in substance though they differed in terminology. (IV.2.5; cp. IV.22.61 and V.4.10-11. Trans. Rackham)

> This whole field Zeno and his successors were either unable or unwilling to cover; at all events they left it untouched. (IV.3.7)

Cicero (or the source, his teacher Antiochus of Ascalon) thought that Plato and Aristotle (and Theophrastus and Dicaearchus) were interested in "politics" in a way that the Stoics were not. This supports Crouch's position that the Stoics were not the source of the political concern for household duty.

According to Cicero, Aristotle and others taught the following:

> They further divided the nature of man into soul and body. (IV.7.16)
>
> The goods of the body, they held, required no particular explanation, but the goods of the soul they investigated with more elaboration, finding in the first place that in them lay the germs of Justice; and they were the first of any philosophers to teach that the love of parents for their offspring is a provision of nature; and that nature, so they pointed out, has ordained the union of men and women in marriage, which is prior in order of time, and is the root of all the family affections. Starting from these first principles they traced out the origin and growth of all the virtues. (IV.7.17; cp. III. 19.62; 20.68)
>
> There Cato, I said, is the scheme of the philosophers of whom I am speaking. Having put it before you, I should be glad to learn what reason Zeno had for seceding from this old-established system. (IV.7.19)

Cicero mentions the Stoic Ariston (e.g. III.3.11).

> And therefore (since my discourse must now conclude) this is the one chief defect under which your friends the Stoics seem to me to labour,—they think they can maintain two contrary opinions at once. How can you have a greater inconsistency than for the same person to say both that Moral Worth is the sole good and that we have a natural instinct to seek the things conducive to life? Thus in their desire to retain ideas consonant with the former doctrine they are landed in the position of Ariston; and when they try to escape from this they adopt what is in reality the position of the Peripatetics, though still clinging tooth and nail to their own terminology. (IV.28.78; cp. IV.18.49; 25.68–27.72)

As noted earlier (p. 8), Ariston rejected (see Seneca, *Ep.* 94.1–3) the Aristotelian pattern of household submissiveness. Cicero observes that Ariston, in a parallel dispute, was opposed by a member of his own school, the Stoic Chrysippus, when he insisted that individual virtue and vice were the only real values (*Concerning the Ends of Goods and Evils* III.50; IV.43, 68). Indeed Chrysippus, perhaps following Aristotle, listed duties toward wives, children, and slaves[51] (in his dispute with Ariston?). These texts in Cicero show that there was a dispute in early Stoicism about the nature of virtue, and this may have included a dispute about whether to retain the Aristotelian concern for civic science (including a concern for the household). The outline of the classical discussions was remembered, even in the first century B.C.

D.   Summary and Conclusions

Classical Greek philosophers were concerned about authority and subordination in the household and in the city. Plato, *Laws* III 690A–D, lists seven pairs of relationships "in the matter of ruling and being ruled alike in cities and in households" which he refers to as agreed rights or axioms. Aristotle worked out his own ideas on this subject over against his teacher Plato. Aristotle specified that household management involved proper authority in three relationships—master and slave, husband and wife, father and children—as well as properly balancing income and expenditure.

These ideas were available to persons who were not technical philosophers as late as the Roman period. The Academy remained interested in Plato's household regulations. The middle Platonists Albinus and Apuleius mention the subject, but they do not spell out their impression of the content of Plato's household ethic in relation to authority and subordination. Laertius reports as Plato's opinion that men by nature rule women. In the fourth century A.D., Stobaeus excerpted a number of Platonic texts because they expressed popular topoi "concerning justice," "concerning the constitution," and "concerning household management." These three topoi were chosen as titles for several treatises written in the time between Plato and Stobaeus, which suggests the popularity and continuity of the topoi. That the topos "concerning household management" was popularly known is indicated by the fact that Dio Chrysostom wrote a treatise with this title (see above p. 28); we do not know the exact form of his discussion. He was an itinerant preacher-philosopher, who spoke in the public assemblies of his fellow Greeks, at the court of the emperor, and among semi-barbarians in frontier regions.[52]

The earliest post-Aristotelian reference to the *three* pairs is in the Peripatetic *Great Ethics*, probably from the second half of the second century B.C. The fourth element of the topos, the relationship of income to expenditure, is not mentioned in this work, just as it remains unmentioned in the NT. All four elements of the Aristotelian topos are mentioned in the first century B.C. by the eclectic Stoic Areius Didymus in his popular handbook. Men, not women, children, and slaves, have authority in the household. This reference is crucial because, according to Kerferd, it probably represents the way Greeks and Romans were trained to present discussions of ethics through attendance at standardized lectures and through reading standardized manuals such as Areius produced. References in Seneca and in Diogenes Laertius to Aristotle's concern for properly managing the household strengthen Kerferd's suggestion. Some Stoics such as Chrysippus continued the discussion of the duties of wives, children, and slaves; other Stoics such as Ariston denied that philosophical ethics should deal with such relationships. The Epicureans also rejected Aristotle's concern for the three relationships in the household. In the first century B.C., Philodemus regarded only the discussion of household finances as philosophically worthwhile, not the discussion of how to live well at home. So Philodemus stressed the one element of the topos which the *Great Ethics* and the NT authors drop.

The continuity of the Aristotelian topos is demonstrated by the references in the *Great Ethics*, Areius Didymus, and perhaps Chrysippus. Its popular availability is suggested by both Areius Didymus and Dio Chrysostom, although we do not know the form of the latter writer's treatise.

NOTES TO CHAPTER III

[1]Willy Theiler, "Bau und Zeit der Aristotelischen Politik," *Museum Helveticum* 9 (1952) 65–78 argues that *Pol.* VII–VIII closely parallel Plato's *Laws* and were composed in 345, soon after Plato's death; *Pol.* I, III, VII.2–3 were added in 335; *Pol.* IV–VI in 329–326; and finally *Pol.* I, III, IV were expanded about 325. See Peter Steinmetz, ed., *Schriften zu den Politika des Aristoteles* (Hildesheim: Georg Olms, 1973).

[2]This text is important in the article by Gerhard Delling, "Zur Taufe von 'Häusern' im Urchristentum," *NovT* 7 (1965) 289. See André Jean Voelke, *Les rapports avec autrui dans la philosophie grecque d'Aristote à Panetius* (Paris: J. Vrin, 1961) 52–59. And most important, see Paul Moraux, *Le dialogue "Sur la justice": à la recherche de l'Aristote perdu* (Louvain: Publications universitaires, 1957) 15–62, whose hypothesis is accepted by Ingemar Duering, "Aristoteles," PWSup 11 (1968) 299, and by Anton-Hermann Chroust, "Aristotle's *On Justice*," *Aristotle. New Light on His Life and on Some of His Lost Works* (Notre Dame: University of Notre Dame, 1973) 2:71–85, at 77–79. The evaluation of this text by James Crouch, *Colossian Haustafel* 106 is inadequate.

[3]*Pace* Goodspeed, who wrote, "As for the haustafeln [*sic*] idea, we at Chicago were never able to find any such 'haustafeln' idea as it is claimed anciently existed." From a personal letter cited by F. W. Beare, *First Epistle of Peter* 195.

[4]Paul Moraux, *Le dialogue* 7–21, 23, 27–28. See also Moraux, "From the Protrepticus to the Dialogue *On Justice*," *Aristotle and Plato in the Mid-Fourth Century*, ed. Ingemar Düring and G. E. L. Owen (Göteborg, 1960) 113–132.

[5]Moraux, *Le dialogue* 56, 58. Chroust, "Aristotle's *On Justice*" 79, agrees, although he would date it in 355 B.C. For a discussion which relates three forms of rule—here despotic, domestic, and political, elsewhere tyrannic, aristocratic, and monarchical—to the three household relationships, see *NE* VIII 1160b 23–1161a 10 (quoted p. 35)

[6]Expansion of this same section occurs later in Colossians and 1 Peter, but the author of Ephesians stresses the husband-wife section.

[7]See W. K. C. Guthrie, *A History of Greek Philosophy* (Cambridge: Cambridge University, 1969) 3:157, 159, and 311–313; Guthrie omits the similar statements in Philo discussed p. 55. below. Also Olof Gigon, "Die Sklaverei bei Aristoteles," in *La "Politique" d'Aristote* by Rudolf Stark et al. (Entretiens sur l'antiquité classique 11; Geneva: Fondation Hardt, 1965) 245–276; also R. Schlaifer in M. I. Finley, ed., *Slavery in Classical Antiquity* (Cambridge: W. Heffer, 1960) 93–132.

[8]See VII 1325b 1–14 and Plato, *Meno* 71E, 72D–73D.

[9]Cp. p. 31, n. 37 above on *Rhetoric* 1.5.6. But as H. Rackham, the editor in *LCL*, notes, in books VII–VIII, which deal with the best constitution, this subject is not reached. But cp. *NE* VIII 1160b 23–1161a 10, quoted below.

[10]See *NE* VIII 1161a 16–1162a 34 on the "friendship" between these pairs, and esp. VIII 1162a 16–34 on friendship between husband and wife. On the evil aspects of democracy in the household, esp. on the conduct of wives and slaves, see *Pol.* V 1313b 34–37, VI 1319b 17–33, and n. 50 below. Also M. I. Finley, *Democracy Ancient and Modern* (New Brunswick: Rutgers University, 1973).

[11]See Egon Braun, *Die Kritik der lakedaimonischen Verfassung in den Politika des Aristoteles* (Kärntner Museumsschriften 12; Klagenfurt: Landesmuseums für Kärntner, 1956) 21–24. This text is cited by Claude Vatin, *Recherches sur le mariage et la condition de la femme mariée a l'époque héllenistique* (Paris: E. de Boccard, 1970) 26.

[12]Dionysius Hal., *Rom. Ant.* II.24.6 agreed with Plutarch. But see Plutarch, *Agis* 7.3.

[13]περὶ συμβιώσεως ἀνδρὸς καὶ γυναικός in V. Rose, *Aristotelis qui ferebantur librorum fragmenta* (Leipzig: B. G. Teubner, 1885, 1967) 138–139.

[14]Mervin R. Dilts, ed. and trans., *Heraclides Lembus, Excerpta Politarum* (Greek, Roman and Byzantine Monograph 5; London: William Clowes and Sons, 1971) 7–8.

[15]Ibid., 18,3–5.

¹⁶Ibid., 19,29 and 28,6.

¹⁷Ibid., 29,1–3.

¹⁸For bibliography and discussion of this question see Fritz Wehrli, *Die Schule des Aristoteles* (10 vols.; Basel: B. Schwabe, 1944–1959) 10: 96 with n. 2; 128; K. L. Brink, "Peripatos," PWSup 7 (1940) 939–940; Kurt von Fritz, *Mixed Constitution* 49 with n. 32; 422 with n. 3. Von Fritz asserts that it is improbable that Polybius knew Aristotle's *Politics*, although he probably knew the works of some of Aristotle's disciples on political theory. O. Regenbogen, "Theophrastos," PWSup 7 (1940) 1518 thinks Polybius knew Theophrastus' works and Plutarch knew Aristotle's political writings only through Theophrastus. See also Horst Braunert, "Staatstheorie und Staatsrecht in Hellenismus," *Saeculum* 19 (1968) 47–66, esp. 52–53, 58–59. The few citations of Aristotle's *Politics* by later Greek authors are given by A. Dreizehnter, ed., *Aristoteles Politik* (Studia et testimonia antiqua 7; Munich: Wilhelm Fink, 1970) 227.

¹⁹Strabo, *Geography* XIII.1.54 609; see Plutarch, *Sulla* 26; Diog. Laert. V.52. See Felix Grayeff, *Aristotle and His School* (New York: Barnes and Noble, 1974) chap. 4 on the library of the Peripatos and its history.

²⁰von Fritz, *Mixed Constitution* 49.

²¹See Regenbogen, "Theophrastos," 1519–1520. The fragments were edited by H. Hager, "Theophrastus περὶ νόμων," *Journal of Philology* 6 (1876) 1–27.

²²See Ernst Bickel, *Diatribe in Senecae philosophi fragmenta I: Fragmenta De matrimonio* (Leipzig: B. G. Teubner, 1915) 388,11–390,14. Also Regenbogen, "Theophrastos," 1487. Bickel says it is not a separate work but part of the work *On Various Schemes of Life* (Diog. Laert. V.42). Regenbogen, against Bickel, sees Seneca as Jerome's source for this fragment, and Seneca used Theophrastus directly.

²³See Wehrli, *Schule des Aristoteles* 1, *Dikaiarchos*; Heinrich Edgar Martini, "Dikaiarchos," *PW* 5, 550–551; Carl Schneider, *Kulturgeschichte des Hellenismus* 2 (Munich: C. H. Beck, 1969) 496 with n. 1; Gerhard Jean Daniels Aalders, *Die Theorie der gemischten Verfassung im Altertum* (Amsterdam: A. M. Hakkert, 1968) 72–81, 84–86, 111 with n. 19, 126–128.

²⁴See Wehrli, *Schule des Aristoteles* 1: 28–30 and 65 for further bibliography. See also Werner Jaeger, "Über Ursprung und Kreislauf des philosophischen Lebensideals," *Sitzungsberichte der preussischen Akademie der Wissenschaften, philosophisch-historische Klasse* 25 (Berlin: Akademie der Wissenschaften, 1928) 390–421, translated in the 2nd ed. (only) of Werner Jaeger, *Aristotle* (London: Oxford University, 1948), appendix II, 426–461. See esp. 450–461 on Dicaearchus, 455–459 on Pythagoras. He suggested that Dicaearchus was the *first* to describe Pythagoras as a "lawgiver." This has been proved incorrect by Cornelia Johanna de Vogel, *Pythagoras and Early Pythagoreans* (Assen: Van Gorcum, 1966) 92 with n. 2, 134–135, 140, 141 with n. 2, 142 with n. 1, 151 with n. 1.

²⁵Wehrli, *Schule des Aristoteles* 1: 65. He even states that Polybius' interpretation of Rome as the mixing of the three constitutions was stimulated by Dicaearchus. Whether that is true or not, Polybius' criticism of Dicaearchus assumes some knowledge on his part of Peripatetic political theory. On whether Cicero used Dicaearchus as a source for *De re publica*, see Wehrli, ibid., 52, 66.

²⁶Alfred von Gutschmid, *Kleine Schriften*, ed. Franz Ruhl (Leipzig: B. G. Teubner, 1893) 4: 389 and 415. His argument is accepted by Martini, "Dikaiarchos," 549.

²⁷Its authenticity was denied by Werner Jaeger and his student Richard Walzer in an acrimonious debate with Hans von Arnim. See Walzer, *Magna Moralia und Aristotelische Ethik* (Neue philologische Untersuchungen 7; Berlin: Weidmann, 1929) and von Arnim, *Der neueste Versuch die Magna Moralia als unecht zu erweisen* (Akademie der Wissenschaften in Wien, philosophisch-historische Klasse 211/2; Vienna: Hölder-Pichler-Tempsky, 1929). Wehrli, *Schule des Aristoteles* 10:108, assumes that it reflects the time after Theophrastus, as does Regenbogen, "Theophrastos," 1488–1492. Strong arguments against authenticity were given by Franz Dirlmeier, "Die Zeit der 'Grossen Ethik'," *RhM* N. F. 88 (1939) 214–243. Despite the fact that Dirlmeier later reversed himself and argued for authenticity, his former arguments remained convincing to most. See D. J. Allen, "Magna Moralia and Nicomachean Ethics," *JHS* 77 (1957)

7-11; also Allen's review of Dirlmeier's edition of the *Eudemian Ethics* in *Gnomon* 38 (1966) 138–149. Allen made the interesting suggestion that the Magna Moralia is "a selective version of Peripatetic ethics that . . . is designed to make converts from Stoicism" ("Magna Moralia," 7).

[28]Ed. and trans. G. C. Armstrong in LCL (1935) and recently by B. A. van Groningen and André Wartelle (1958) in the Collection Budé. The continuing influence of this Aristotelian ethic was traced in an essay by Otto Brunner, "'Das ganze Haus' und die alteuropaische 'Oekonomik'," *Neue Wege der Sozialgeschichte* (1956) 33–61.

[29]See O. Regenbogen, "Theophrastos," 1521 and 1488. Theophrastus' authorship was accepted by Hermann Mutschmann in his review of Willy Kraemer, *De Aristotelis, qui fertur, Oeconomicorum libro primo* (1910) in *Wochenschrift für klassische Philologie* 5 (1912) 118–123.

[30]Ed. by Christianus Jensen, *Philodemi Περὶ οἰκονομίας qui dicitur Libellus* (Leipzig: B. G. Teubner, 1906). See also Johann Adam Hartung, *Philodem's Abhandlungen über die Haushaltung und über den Hochmut und Theophrast's Haushaltung und Charakterbilder, Griechisch und Deutsch mit kritischen und erklärenden Anmerkungen* (Leipzig: Wilhelm Engelmann, 1857) 1–12, 21–61, who (10–11) accepts Theophrastus' authorship of the first pseudo-Aristotelian book on household management. By discussing Philodemus here, I do not imply that he was dependent exclusively on Peripatetic sources for his discussion of the topos. Besides Xenophon's treatise, he also knew Zeno's *Politeia*. See Max Pohlenz, *Die Stoa. Geschichte einer geistigen Bewegung* 2 (2nd ed.; Göttingen: Vandenhoeck and Ruprecht, 1955) 74; also Wilhelm Crönert, *Kolotes und Menedemos, Text und Untersuchungen zur Philosophen- und Literaturgeschichte* (Studien zur Palaeographie und Papyruskunde; Leipzig: Eduard Avenarius, 1906) 53–67 on Philodemus, Περὶ τῶν Στωικῶν. In his *Politeia*, Zeno apparently discussed "ruling" and "being ruled" in the context of discussing justice, oratory, and the *politeia*; see Hans von Arnim, *Stoicorum Veterum Fragmenta* 1 (Leipzig: B. G. Teubner, 1921) n. 262 (from Plutarch, *On Stoic Self-Contradictions* 1033B).

[31]Xenophon also discussed "ruling" in *Memorabilia* III.1–7. As was the case with Plato, Stobaeus excerpted certain of Xenophon's remarks because he thought they corresponded to well-known topoi. See Stob. IV.1.53; 2.22 and 23; 5.108; 25.24.

[32]Hartung's emended text (p. 28,15) is: . . . ὥσπερ οὐδὲν μετηλλάχασιν, "having changed nothing."

[33]Cp. Philodemus' *Rhetoric*, ed. Siegfried Sudhaus, *Philodemi Volumina Rhetorica* 2 (Leipzig: B. G. Teubner, 1896) p. 291, frag. XVI:

> If the rhetor cannot guide his own household, consisting of wife, children, slaves and free servants (τὴν ἑαυτῶν οἰκίαν ἐκ τέκνων καὶ γυναικὸς καὶ δούλων καὶ ἐλευθέρων συγκειμένην), how can he control the greater ship, the state (τὴν πόλιν), consisting of more children and women?

This is the trans. of H. M. Hubbell, "The Rhetorica of Philodemus," trans. and commentary, in *Transactions of the Connecticut Academy of Arts and Sciences* 23 (1920) 362.

[34]See S. Sudhaus, "Aristoteles in der Beurteilung des Epikur und Philodem," *RhM* 48 (1893) 552–564; Cyril Bailey, *The Greek Atomists and Epicurus* (Oxford: Clarendon, 1928) 515–517, 521–522; Werner Liebich, *Aufbau, Absicht und Form der Pragmateiai Philodems* (Dissertation Ost-Berlin: Photokopie von der Autor, 1956, 1960) 107–110; André Tulier, "La notion de φιλία dans ses rapports avec certains fondements sociaux de l'épicurisme," *Actes du VIIIᵉ Congrès*, Association Guillaume Budé (Paris: Les Belles Lettres, 1969) 318–329; Benjamin Farrington, *The Faith of Epicurus* (New York: Basic Books, 1967) chap. 2.

[35]See Cicero, *On the Nature of the Gods* I.33.93; *Letters to Atticus* 14.20.5; Plutarch, *Pyrrus* 20.

[36]Liebich, *Aufbau* 108, citing Philodemus, *Rhetoric* (II. 50 and 57 Sudhaus).

[37]Epicurus does refer to "household duties" (Cyril Bailey, *Epicurus: The Extant Remains* [Oxford: Clarendon, 1926] p. 112, nr. xli), but in view of Philodemus' opinion, this may refer primarily to attending to household income, although Epicurus does comment on friendship to slaves (Diog. Laert. X.118).

[38]Cited by Bailey, *The Greek Atomists* 511, from Lactantius, *Divine Institutes* 3.17.42.

[39]I owe this crucial reference to Areius Didymus to Prof. Abraham J. Malherbe's knowledge of Hellenistic philosophy. See Eduard Zeller, *Philosophie* 3/1: 635-639. Augustus' admiration of Areius is noted by Dio Cassius, *Roman History* 51.16.4; Suetonius, *Augustus* 89.1; Plutarch, *Antony* 80.1.

[40]In Stob. II.7.13-26; on politics and "economics": Stob. II.7.26; II.147,26-152,25 Wachsmuth. See Hermann Henkel, "II. Der Abriss der peripatetischen Oekonomik und Politik bei Stobaios und die Politik des Aristoteles," *Gymnasium zu Seehausen in der Altmark* (Stendal: Franzen und Grosse, 1875) 10-17; also Walzer, *Magna Moralia* 257; von Arnim, *Der neueste Versuch* 50-53 and *Arius Didymus' Abriss der peripatetischen Ethik* (Akademie der Wissenschaften in Wien, philosophisch-historische Klasse 204/3; Vienna: Hölder-Pichler-Tempsky, 1926) 119. However, in the second work listed von Arnim does not discuss Areius' epitome of Peripatetic *politics*, only referring to Henkel. See also Regenbogen, "Theophrastos," 1492-1494; Willy Theiler, "Philo von Alexandria und der Beginn des kaiserzeitlichen Platonismus," *Parusia, Studien zur Philosophie Platons und zur Problemgeschichte des Platonismus, Festgabe für Johannes Hirschberger*, ed. Kurt Flasch (Frankfurt/Main: Minerva, 1965) 213-217; A. A. Long, "Aristotle's Legacy to Stoic Ethics," *Institute of Classical Studies (University of London), Bulletin* 15 (1958) 83, nn. 8-10.

[41]von Arnim, *Arius Didymus* 7-12.

[42]Regenbogen, "Theophrastos," 1494. On Critolaus' definition see H. von Arnim, "Kritolaos," PW 11 (1922) 1931, who cites Clement of Alexandria, *Stromata* II.xxi.316D, and Cicero, *Tusculan Disputations* V.51.

[43]"Theophrastos," 1493.

[44]Theiler, "Philo von Alexandria," 215. See Zeller, *Philosophie* 3/1:633-635; Heinrich Doerrie, "Der Platoniker Eudoros von Alexandria," *Hermes* 79 (1944) 25-39, esp. 38-39 on Eudoros and Philo; Michelangelo Giusta, *I dossografi di etica* 1:11-14, 151-174.

[45]Giusta, *I dossografi di etica* 2:529.

[46]Cp. Philo, *On Flight and Finding* 36.

[47]διαιρέσεις; in Stob. II.7.2; II.42,7-45,10 Wachsmuth; also Seneca, *Ep.* 89.

[48]Pierre Boyance in *Latomus* 26 (1967) 246-249; Robert Joly in *L'antiquité classique* 35 (1966) 289-290 and 38 (1969) 308-309; G. B. Kerferd, "Ethical Doxographers," *The Classical Review* 81 (1967) 156-158 and 85 (1971) 371-373.

[49]Kerferd, "Ethical Doxographers," 157. He notes the chronological difficulty of supposing that Areius, still writing in 9 B.C., was Cicero's source for *Tusculans* and *Concerning the Ends of Goods and Evils* c. 50 B.C. Joly in *L'antiquité classique* 38 (1968) 308 allows an undefined literary relation between Areius Didymus, Diogenes Laertius, and Albinus, though he excludes Cicero from the list.

[50]See Regenbogen, "Theophrastos," 1494-1495; Moraux, *Le dialogue* 71-74; Giusta, *I dossografi di etica* 1:13. Note also the criticism of democracy in Cicero, *Republic* I.67: it produces anarchy among slaves and wives, leaving private houses without a master (a paraphrase of Plato, *Republic* VIII 562C-563E). Cp. n. 10 above.

[51]Adolf Dyroff, *Die Ethik der alten Stoa* (Berliner Studien für classische Philologie und Archaeologie, N. F. 2; New York: Arno, 1979, originally published 1897) 283-294, understood Chrysippus to be the main source for ps.-Plutarch, *The Education of Children* 7E, which lists these duties: "to be chaste with women, to be affectionate with children, and not to be overbearing with slaves" (cited by Crouch, *Colossian Haustafel* 70, n. 69). Dyroff (250, 260) denies that Chrysippus' terminology as found in ps.-Plutarch is Peripatetic. However, the Aristotelian origin of the form of the domestic code in Ariston, Chrysippus' opponent, means that Crouch may be incorrect in maintaining that the reference to "women, children and slaves" is a "late addition" to Chrysippus' list.

[52]Hans von Arnim, *Leben und Werke des Dio von Prusa mit einer Einleitung: Sophistik, Rhetorik, Philosophie in ihrem Kampf um die Jugendbildung* (Berlin: Weidmann, 1898). C. P. Jones, *The Roman World of Dio Chrysostom* (Loeb Classical Monographs; Cambridge, Mass.: Harvard University, 1978).

Chapter IV

The Topos "Concerning Household Management" in Eclectic Stoics, Hellenistic Jews, and Neopythagoreans

The preceding chapters trace the origin of the structured discussion of household governance. In this chapter, I will argue that this Aristotelian form was used by philosophers close in time and place to the writers of the NT books. These later writers include eclectic Stoics, Hellenistic Jews, and Neopythagoreans.

A. Ariston, Hecaton, Seneca, and Hierocles

That department of philosophy which supplies precepts appropriate to the individual case, instead of framing them for mankind at large—which, for instance, advises how a husband should conduct himself towards his wife, or how a father should bring up his children, or how a master should rule his slaves—this department of philosophy, I say, is accepted by some as the only significant part, while the other departments are rejected on the ground that they stray beyond the sphere of practical needs. . . . But Aristo the Stoic, on the contrary, believes the above-mentioned department to be of slight import. . . . (Seneca, *Ep.* 94.1–2. Trans. Gummere)

Crouch commented, "For the first time we have before us a schema which is limited to the relationships within the household."[1] On the contrary, Seneca (first century A.D.) and Ariston (fl. c. 250 B.C.) referred to a form which, with these three pairs, was exactly outlined by Aristotle (*Pol.* I 1253b 6–8). And Ariston's fellow Stoic, Chrysippus, may have debated him about whether the school should retain an interest in the virtues of wives, children, and slaves.[2] Further, Seneca also referred to Hecaton's (early first century B.C.) discussion of this same department of philosophy:[3]

Every obligation (*officium*) that involves two people makes an equal demand upon both. When you have considered the sort of person a *father* ought to be, you will find that there remains the not less great task of discovering the sort that a *son* should be; it is true that a *husband* has certain duties, yet those of the *wife* are not less great. In the

exchange of obligations each in turn renders to the other the service that he requires,
and they desire that the same rule of action should apply to both, but this rule, as
Hecaton says, is a difficult matter. . . . (*On Benefits* 2.18.1–2. My emphasis. Trans.
Basore)

Seneca argued against Hecaton that a slave must be included in these
reciprocal household relationships (ibid., 3.18.1–4). In discussing this division
of philosophy, Ariston, Hecaton, and Seneca used the topos "concerning
household management" and retained its Aristotelian outline. Despite the
fact that the age was eclectic, several philosophers who used the topos showed
an awareness of its Aristotelian origin, philosophers such as Areius Didymus,
Diogenes Laertius, Cicero, and Seneca himself (see above p. 43). Whether this
was also the case with respect to the Stoics Ariston and Hecaton cannot be
determined. The topos in Ariston, Hecaton, and Seneca had the same outline
as in Aristotle, however indirect the relationship might have been.

Hierocles has been central to the discussion of the NT pattern of
submissiveness since Weidinger's study. There is a text in Hierocles which
indicates the continuing influence of the topos outlined by Aristotle (Stob.
IV.22.24; IV.505,5–22 Hense, quoted above p. 5). This text discusses the
association of husband and wife, their authority over their house and
servants, the education of their children, and their use of the household
income. Compare the four elements of the topos "concerning household
management" in Aristotle, *Pol.* I 1253b 1–14.[4]

B. Philo and Josephus (and Dionysius of Halicarnassus)

Such Platonic-Aristotelian ideas of political science influenced not only
Roman Stoics but also Hellenistic Jews. Philo, *On Joseph, That Is, The Life
of the Statesman*, related that Joseph was sold into Egypt where his nobility
was recognized, and he was placed in charge of a household.

> So, while in outward appearance it was his purchaser who appointed him steward of
> his household, in fact and reality it was nature's doing, who was taking steps to procure
> for him the command of whole cities and a nation and a great country. For the future
> statesman (πολιτικόν) needed first to be trained and practised in house management
> (οἰκονομίαν); for a house is a city compressed into small dimensions, and household
> management may be called a kind of state management (πολιτεία), just as a city too is
> a great house and statesmanship the household management of the general public. All
> this shows clearly that the household manager is identical with the statesman, however
> much what is under the purview of the two may differ in number and size. (38–39.
> Trans. Colson. Cp. 54 and *On Flight and Finding* 36)

Philo agreed with Plato on the identity of city and house management, against
Aristotle's view that a ruler in the state governed differently from the master of
a household. *Special Laws* III.169–171, discussing women's modesty, is
similar:

The women are best suited to the indoor life which never strays from the house, within which the middle door is taken by the maidens as their boundary, and the outer door by those who have reached full womanhood. Organized communities are of two sorts, the greater which we call cities and the smaller which we call households. Both of these have their governors; the government of the greater is assigned to men, under the name of statesmanship (πολιτεία), that of the lesser, known as household management (οἰκονομία), to women. A woman then, should not be a busybody, meddling with matters outside her household concerns, but should seek a life of seclusion. She should not show herself off like a vagrant in the streets before the eyes of other men, except when she has to go to the temple. (Trans. Colson)[5]

It is against this background that one must consider the centrally important text in *The Decalogue* 165–167, which has been seen[6] as the closest parallel to the NT codes:

In the fifth commandment on honouring parents we have a suggestion of many necessary laws drawn up to deal with the relations of old to young, rulers to subjects, benefactors to benefited, slaves to masters. For parents belong to the superior class of the above mentioned pairs, that which comprises seniors, rulers, benefactors and masters, while children occupy the lower position with juniors, subjects, receivers of benefits and slaves. And there are many other instructions given, to the young on courtesy to the old, to the old on taking care of the young, to subjects on obeying their rulers, to rulers on promoting the welfare of their subjects, to recipients of benefits on requiting them with gratitude . . . , to servants on rendering an affectionate loyalty to their masters, to masters on showing the gentleness and kindness by which inequality is equalized. (Trans. Colson)

Special Laws II.225–227 is very similar:

For parents are midway between the natures of God and man, and partake of both. . . . Parents are to their children what God is to the world. . . . For in the judgment of those who take account of virtue, seniors are placed above juniors, teachers above pupils, benefactors above beneficiaries, rulers above subjects, and masters above servants. Now parents are assigned a place in the higher of these two orders, for they are seniors and instructors and benefactors and rulers and masters; sons and daughters are placed in the lower order, for they are juniors and learners and recipients of benefits and subjects and servants. (Trans. Colson)

Philo then expanded on this. In a very similar list, Hierocles gave instructions about child-parent relationships (see above p. 3): children owe parents duties because they are images of the gods for them, the guardian gods of the house, their greatest benefactors, their nearest kindred, creditors, lords, and friends.[7] But the *pairs* in Philo and the interest in one member of the pair being *obedient* to the other were not organically developed out of the Decalogue, as Schroeder suggested. Neither are the hierarchically related pairs a "Jewish-Oriental" characteristic of social codes developed in analogy to the reciprocal relations of rich and poor in Egypt and Israel in antiquity, as Crouch suggested. Rather Philo was interpreting the Decalogue in light of Platonic and Aristotelian political ethics (see Plato, *Laws* III 690A–D, quoted above p. 24). Philo's suggestion that the relations between parents and children were analogous to those between masters and slaves (cp. *Special Laws* II.231; IV.184) was *denied* by Aristotle (*NE* VIII 1160b 25–32, quoted above p. 35), who suggested that such an understanding of parenthood is inappropriately tyrannical. But neither was Philo's suggestion originally Jewish; rather, the Roman *patria potestas* increased the stress on the obedience of children already present in the Platonic-Aristotelian discussions of household management.[8] Within this form, Philo assumed that not only masters but also slaves must be exhorted (*Special Laws* II.67–68 and 90; III.137–143) [9]

Philo combined elements of the topos "concerning household management" and "concerning the constitution" in *The Posterity and Exile of Cain* 181, when he criticized Onan (Gen 38:9):

> Will you not—so I would say to him—by providing only your individual profit, be doing away with all the best things in the world, . . . honor paid to parents, loving care of a wife, bringing up of children, happy and blameless relations with domestic servants, management of a house, leadership in a city, maintaining of laws, guardianship of customs, reverence towards elders, respect for the memory of the departed, fellowship with the living, piety in words and actions towards the Diety?[10]

There is a similar rejection of practices which destroy the state and home in Epictetus, *Dis.* III.7.19–22, there directed against Epicureans. But every element in Philo's list has a parallel in Platonic-Aristotelian political ethics.

Both Weidinger and Crouch understood Josephus, *Against Apion* to contain close parallels to the NT codes of household submission.

> The woman, says the law, is in all things inferior to the man. Let her accordingly be submissive, not for her humiliation, but that she may be directed, for the authority has been given by God to the man. (II.199. Trans. Thackeray)

Josephus then discusses "honour to parents" (II.206) as well as the law and punishment for slaves (II.216). Similarly, in his *Apology* Philo said,

> Wives must be in servitude to their husbands, a servitude not imposed by violent ill-treatment but promoting obedience in all things. Parents must have power over their children. . . . The same holds of any other persons over whom he [a man] has authority. . . . (*Apology for the Jews* 7.3 and 5. Trans. Colson)

I have shown elsewhere[11] that Josephus in *Against Apion* II closely followed the Hellenistic rhetorical outline for an encomium as given by Menander of Laodicea. He was praising the Jews' lawgiver and "constitution" according to set rules for which the Greeks had detailed and elaborate directions; and originality was unscholarly. His description of the social roles of women, children, and slaves have very close parallels in rhetorical handbooks of the period, and most importantly, in the encomium of Rome given 100 years earlier by Dionysius of Halicarnassus in *Roman Antiquities* I.9–II.29 (written 30–7 B.C.). In Greek political writing and rhetoric, the discussions of the "constitution" and of the "household" were very closely related (see p. 31, n. 37). Dionysius, too, observed in his rhetorical encomium that "cities" are composed of many "houses" (*Rom. Ant.* II.24.2), so that the constitution must regulate marriages (II.24.14) or the whole state will come to ruin. So Romulus, founder of Rome, passed a law that

> obliged both the married women, as having no other refuge, to conform themselves entirely to the temper of their husbands, and the husbands to rule their wives as necessary and inseparable possessions. Accordingly, if a wife was virtuous and in all things obedient to her husband, she was mistress of the house to the same degree as her husband was the master of it. . . . (II.25.4–5. Trans. Cary)

He followed this with the laws respecting "reverence and dutifulness of children towards parents, to the end that they should honour and obey them in all things, both in their words and actions. . . ." (II.26.1). The punishments ordained for disobedience in children were very severe (II.26.3), so severe that the Greeks regarded the Romans as cruel and harsh (II.27.1). Romulus gave "greater power to the father over his son than to the master over his slaves" (ibid.). So in praising Roman household relationships, Dionysius used the Aristotelian three pairs—wives and husbands, children and parents, master and slaves (in the same order as the pairs in Colossians). Further, duties of wives precede those of husbands (II.25.4), and those of children precede those of fathers (II.26.1 and 4), as in the NT. Dionysius does not expand on the relationship of masters and slaves. Aristotle's outline of household submissiveness was adapted by Hellenistic rhetoric; and Josephus and Philo assimilated it to the extent that it was used to praise Moses' laws! Both Philo and Josephus claimed that Plato read and copied Moses' ideas, but in this case the reverse was true: Philo and Josephus were reading Aristotle (or Plato) into the Pentateuch. Instead of maintaining Moses' protective attitude toward slaves,[12] Hellenistic Judaism assimilated Aristotle's repressive ideas about them.

Philo did cite the opinion that "servants are free by nature, no man being naturally a slave."[13] He ascribed this opinion to the Therapeutai and to the Essenes.[14] The difference between the sophist Alcidamus and Aristotle (above p. 34) demonstrates that this debate belongs to classical Greek political ethics. Neither the Essenes nor the Therapeutai were the origin of this philosophical opinion. And Philo himself saw slaves as "indispensable." They were not excluded from Moses' commonwealth, "for the course of life contains a vast number of circumstances which demand the ministrations of slaves."[15]

We cannot ascertain the immediate source of Philo's ideas on household management. Giusta's effort to demonstrate widespread literary dependence on the handbook of Areius Didymus has failed. Unquestionably the closest parallels to the texts quoted above from Seneca, Hierocles, Philo, and

Josephus are found in Plato and Aristotle, though in authors of the first and
second centuries A.D., these ideas almost certainly were mediated through a
handbook similar to that of Areius Didymus. Classical Greek thought
generated these ethical ideas about society, and they were common as late as
the first and second centuries A.D. They were even taken over by Hellenistic
Judaism and used to interpret the Decalogue.[16]

C. The Neopythagoreans

The ethical-political fragments of the Neopythagoreans were dependent
especially on Peripatetic sources, and they are also strikingly similar to NT
statements about marriage and household ethics.[17] Recently there have been
convincing arguments that these Neopythagorean authors belong to the first
centuries B.C. and A.D.; they used terminology which was an eclectic mixture
of Platonic, Aristotelian, and Stoic doctrines impossible before the first
century B.C. The Neopythagorean documents are similar in terminology and
date to Areius Didymus' *Epitome*.[18] This means that the following quotations
represent ideas known and available in the culture of imperial Rome, the time
of the writing of the NT.

The Aristotelian form constituted the outline for the extensive treatise by
the Neopythagorean Bryson, *On Household Management*. The first sentence
reads, "He says, the topos 'household management' is complete in four things;
the first of them concerns money, the second slaves, the third the wife, and the
fourth children."[19] Plessner observes[20] that this outline reflects Aristotle, *Pol.*
I 1253b 6–8.

The Neopythagorean authors continued the concern for the relationship
between the "house" and the "city." Callicratidas, *On the Happiness of
Households*, says, "A house however and a city are an imitation according to
analogy of the government of the world" (p. 105,23–24).[21] Occelus, *On the
Nature of the Universe*, says that man "is part of a house and a city" (135,20–
21).

These two authors and the other Neopythagoreans were also concerned
about the subordination of wives, children, and slaves. I will quote some of the
examples:

> Every system consists of certain dissimilar contraries, and is coarranged with reference
> to one certain thing, which is the most excellent. . . . Thus too a house, being a system
> of kindred communion, consists of certain dissimilars, which are its proper parts, and
> is coarranged with a view to one thing which is best, the father of the family. . . .
> (Callicratidas, *On the Happiness of Households* 103,21–23 and 103,28–104,3. Trans.
> Taylor)

> The husband governs, but the wife is governed, and the offspring of both these is an
> auxiliary. (Ibid., 105,8–9)

> Since therefore the husband rules over the wife, he either rules with a despotic, or with
> a guardian, or in the last place, with political power. But he does not rule over her with
> a despotic power: for he is diligently attentive to her welfare. Nor is his government of

her entirely of a guardian nature; for this is itself a part of the communion [between man and wife]. It remains, therefore, that he rules over her with a political power, according to which both the governor and the thing governed establish [as their end] the common advantage. Hence also wedlock is established with a view of the communion of life. Those husbands therefore that govern their wives despotically, are hated by them, but those that govern them with a guardian authority are despised by them. For they appear to be, as it were, appendages and flatterers of their wives. But those that govern them politically are both admired and beloved. (Ibid., 106,1–10)

Those who marry a woman above their condition have to contend for the mastership, for the wife, surpassing her husband in wealth and lineage, wishes to rule over him. But he considers it to be unworthy of him, and preternatural to submit to his wife. (Ibid., 106,17–19; cp. Aristotle, *NE* VIII 1160b 23–1161a 9).

Moraux argues that the material in Callicratidas is dependent on Aristotle's work *On Justice*, noting the similarity to ideas in *Pol.* I. Callicratidas, *On the Happiness of Families*, has a number of specifically Aristotelian conceptions and terms.[22] Occelus, *On the Nature of the Universe* 136,17–25, says something very similar to Callicratidas 106,17–19.

There are also examples of the exhortation to children to be subordinate:

Parents ought not to be injured either in word or deed; but it is requisite to be obedient to them, whether their rank in life is small or great. . . . It is necessary to be present with, and never to forsake them, and almost to submit to them even when they are insane. (Perictione, *On the Harmony of a Woman* 145,8–13)

Everyone therefore endued with intellect should honour and venerate his parents. . . . (Pempelus, *On Parents* 142,4–5)

Wilhelm[23] noted long ago that slaves are treated in every Neopythagorean discussion of household management (οἰκονομικός). In this generalization, Wilhelm refers to the works of Bryson, Callicratidas, Perictione, and Phintys, which, although their titles vary, belong to the topos on household management. Slaves are also regularly treated in the NT household codes (Col 3:22–25; Eph 6:5–8; 1 Pet 2:18–25; 1 Tim 6:1–2; Titus 2:9–10). In contrast, among the Stoics only Seneca, *Ep.* 94.1–3, and ps.-Plutarch, *The Education of Children* 10, refer to masters' treatment of slaves as part of the list of duties.[24] As argued above (pp. 44, 51), Seneca quotes Ariston and ps.-Plutarch relies on Chrysippus, who debated each other c. 250 B.C., perhaps about retaining the Aristotelian concern for wives, children, and slaves as a part of Stoic philosophy. And "the Jews were no more interested than the non-Jews in listing the social duties of slaves."[25] The *Sibylline Oracles* ii.278 and Philo, *The Decalogue* 167, are unusual examples. Again it seems probable that the Aristotelian tradition is the source of the concern for the duties of slaves.

Callicratidas, *On the Happiness of Households* 105,10–15, thinks that the rule of master over slave should be despotic, for the master's advantage, not that of the slave. Theano's letter to Callistona gives advice to wives

governing slaves (τῶν οἰκετῶν ἄρχειν), discussing household management
(περὶ τῆς οἰκονομίας; 197,25-28 Thesleff).[26] Married women have the rule of
the house (ἀρχὴ . . . οἴκου; 197,31). Refractory behavior of servants is not to
be met with cruelty (198,7-9), but too much relaxation produces disobedience
(198,25-26). Eccelus, On Justice, makes a remarkable reference to "the
benevolence (εὔνοια) [cp. Eph 6:7] of the servant towards the master, and the
anxious care of the master for the welfare of the servant" (78,10-11) in the
context of discussing justice in house and city. Bryson, Concerning Household
Management, has a long section concerning slaves. There are three classes:
slaves by law, slaves of their own passions, and slaves by nature (II.56-57).
Slaves by nature have a strong body but only enough understanding to obey
another person; like house animals, they are unable to govern themselves.
When he needs correction, a slave should first be warned, then beaten (II.64);
the same punishment is to be used for a child (II.65). Younger slaves are the
best, for they are the most obedient (II.71).

NOTES TO CHAPTER IV

[1]James Crouch, Colossian Haustafel 59.

[2]See above p. 44; also p. 17, nn. 72, 75.

[3]On Seneca's debate with Hecaton, see C. E. Manning, "Seneca and the Stoics on the
Equality of the Sexes," Mnemosyne 26 (1973) 174-175.

[4]Michelangelo Giusta, I dossografi di etica 2:522, compares Areius Didymus on οἰκονομικός
(II.148, 2 Wachsmuth) with Hierocles περὶ οἴκων (IV.502,9 Hense). Ibid., 529 compares Philo,
Joseph 56-57 with Areius Didymus (II.149,7-10 Wachsmuth). See E. R. Goodenough, The
Politics of Philo Judaeus (New Haven: Yale University, 1938) 49-50 on this text in Philo with
parallels to Plato, Xenophon, and Aristotle.

[5]Cp. Plato, Rep. IV 433A and D (quoted above p. 23-24). E. R. Goodenough, The
Jurisprudence of the Jewish Courts in Egypt (New Haven: Yale University, 1929) 130-131 argues
that Philo's source here is the Neopythagorean Phintys (154,1-11 Thesleff). They do have a
common source: both Philo and Phintys are influenced by Platonic, Aristotelian political ideas.
See Franz Geiger, Philon von Alexandria als sozialer Denker (Tübinger Beiträge zur Altertumswissenschaft 14; Stuttgart: W. Kohlhammer, 1932) 42-47, 69, 73 on Philo's view of wives and
slaves.

[6]David Schroeder, Haustafeln 69, 74, 80, 84.

[7]IV.641,3-21 Hense.

[8]Cp. Dionysius Hal., Rom. Ant. II.27.1-2. K. Thraede, "Ärger mit der Freiheit" 89, 116,
118 mistakenly says that Philo's stress on the wife's subordination is Jewish paraenesis typical of
the attitude toward women, children, and slaves, social groups discriminated against in Judaism.
Actually, Thraede's own analysis shows that Philo is using Greek material. Cp p. 149, n. 34.

[9]Schroeder, Haustafeln 73.

[10]Karl Weidinger, Haustafeln 25; Schroeder, Haustafeln 68, n. 253; and Crouch, Colossian
Haustafel 77 all refer to this text. Note the order: wife, children, servants, the same as the order in
Colossians.

[11]See my paper on "Josephus, Against Apion II.145-295," in the Society of Biblical
Literature 1975 Seminar Papers (Missoula: Scholars Press, 1975) 1:187-192 and my forthcoming
article, "Two Apologetic Encomia: Dionysius on Rome and Josephus on the Jews," JSJ (1981).

[12]Shalom M. Paul, Studies in the Book of the Covenant in Light of Cuneiform and Biblical
Law (VTSup 18; Leiden: E. J. Brill, 1970) 40 says that "all laws pertaining to slaves are concerned
with furthering his protection and preserving his human dignity. . . ."

[13]Philo, *Special Laws* II.69; III.137. John Stuart Mill, *The Subjugation of Women*, used exactly the argument which Philo gives in the last text: a man who practices tyranny at home would do so in the larger society if he had enough power. See Alice S. Rossi, ed., *Essays on Sex Equality by John Stuart Mill and Harriet Taylor Mill* (Chicago: University of Chicago, 1970) 173–175: "The family [at present] is a school of despotism. . . . The family, justly constituted, would be the real school of the virtues of freedom."

[14]Philo, *The Contemplative Life* 70 and *Every Good Man Is Free* 79.

[15]Philo, *Special Laws* II.123. See Geiger, *Philon* 69, n. 229; and above p. 34

[16]It is regrettable that we can no longer determine the form of Dio Chrysostom's lost treatise on the topos (see above p. 28).

[17]The following is a summary of my article, "The Neopythagorean Moralists and the NT," in *Aufstieg und Niedergang der römischen Welt*, Teil II, Band 26, ed. H. Temporini and W. Haase (Berlin-New York: Walter de Gruyter, forthcoming).

[18]See K. Praechter, "Metopos, Theages und Archytas bei Stobaeus," *Philologus* 50 (1891) 29–57; F. Wilhelm, "Die Oeconomica der Neupythagoreer Bryson, Kallikratidas, Periktione, Phintys," *RhM* 70 (1915) 161–223; Walter Burkert, "Hellenistische Pseudopythagorica," *Philologus* 105 (1961) 16–43 and 226–246; idem, "Zur geistesgeschichtlichen Einordnung einiger Pseudopythagorica," *Pseudepigrapha*, ed. K. von Fritz (Entretiens sur l'antiquité classique 18; Geneva: Fondation Hardt, 1972) 23–55.

[19]Martin Plessner, *Der Oikonomikos des Neupythagoreers 'Bryson' und sein Einfluss auf die islamische Wissenschaft. Edition und Übersetzung der erhaltenen Versionen* (Orient und Antike 5; Heidelberg: C. Winter, 1928) 214.

[20]Ibid., 40, n. 5.

[21]Unless otherwise noted the following references will be to the page(s) and line(s) of the edition of Holger Thesleff, *The Pythagorean Texts of the Hellenistic Period* (Acta Academiae Aboensis Ser. A., Humaniora 30; Abo: Abo Akademi, 1965). I have used the translation by Taylor cited p. 15, n. 16 above. See also Kenneth Sylvan Guthrie, trans., *The Life of Pythagoras and Pythagorean Library* (2 vols. in 1; Alpine: The Platonist, 1919).

[22]Paul Moraux, *Le dialogue 'Sur la justice'* 82–86. For the idea in the last quotation from Callicratidas, see *NE* VIII 1161a 1.

[23]Friedrich Wilhelm, "Die Oeconomica der Neupythagoreer" 165.

[24]Crouch, *Colossian Haustafel* 70–71, 118.

[25]Ibid., 117.

[26]Thraede, "Ärger" 67, overlooks this letter when he affirms that Neopythagoreans nowhere refer to wives governing household slaves. See also Perictione, *On the Harmony of a Woman* 144,20 and 25.

Conclusion to Part I

The NT pattern of subordination in the household with its pairs and its interest in the submission of the inferior member of each pair does exist outside Judaism and Christianity. Chapter II demonstrated that this ethic was developed in classical Greek discussions of the constitution in which the "city" and the "house" were hierarchically ordered. Plato thought it was "axiomatic" that there must be a "ruler" in such relationships (the most important text in Plato is *Laws* III 690A–D, quoted above   p. 24): parents are to rule children, masters rule slaves, the stronger rule the weaker,etc. This topic was not prominent among Middle Platonists, but they mentioned it, e.g., in the summary of Plato's thought in Diogenes Laertius III.91–92 (quoted p.   26 above). The chapter titles in Stobaeus indicate that such ideas were popular topoi in the Roman period; two of these topoi are "concerning the constitution" and "concerning household management" (see above p. 28). And Stobaeus excerpted some of the very texts in Plato which give expression to this ethic (notes 1–8, 11, 15, 17–18 to pp. 23–25 above). The topos "concerning household management" was used in Bithynia near the date of 1 Peter by Dio Chrysostom (see above p. 28), another fact which suggests its popular use and availability.

Chapter III noted that this topos appears with an exact outline in Aristotle. It consists of three pairs: master and slave, husband and wife, father and children; and Aristotle observed that some persons included the discussion of "the art of getting wealth"(see above p.33–34).The concern for authority and subordination within these three relationships is central. Aristotle argued that authority and subordination are natural conditions.[1] Various kinds of justice are involved in the three relationships (above p. 36). Freedom or democracy on the part of wives or slaves in the household is detrimental both in regard to the purpose of the constitution and the happiness of the state (above pp. 35–36 with n. 10). The ruling of husbands by wives leads to a dissolute and luxurious life in the state, which corrupts it. Any group accused of upsetting proper subordination in the household would be criticized by those charged with maintaining the constitution.

The Peripatetics were concerned with this topos: the author of the Peripatetic *Great Ethics* used the three pairs (above p. 38), and other disciples wrote on the subject.

The Epicurean Philodemus showed an awareness of the Peripatetic topos with its concern for the distinction between domestic and civic managing, the manner of living with a wife, the treatment of slaves, etc. But he rejected the Peripatetic topos "how to live well at home" when he said that one should be concerned only with "how to use and keep one's property" (above p. 40).

The Stoic Areius Didymus summarized Aristotle's ideas on politics and domestic affairs in detail. He related the various constitutions to relationships within the house (above p. 42). The man—not women, children, or slaves—by nature rules the house. Areius noted that the discussion of "household management" includes "fatherhood, the art of marriage, being a master and money-making" (above p. 43), the four parts of the topos outlined by Aristotle. This discussion was still related to "civic affairs."

Cicero also showed awareness of elements of this discussion, as well as of their Platonic-Aristotelian origin.

Chapter IV evaluated the appearance of these topoi in eclectic Stoics, Hellenistic Jews, and Neopythagoreans. The specific literary sources used by these authors are unknown, but these authors continued the Platonic-Aristotelian discussion. The elements of the topos as outlined by Aristotle appear in Ariston, Hecaton, Seneca, and Hierocles, all eclectic Stoics. With respect to the question of the availability of the topos for Jewish and Christian writers, it is important that the Hellenistic Jew Philo used the topos to interpret the Decalogue (above pp. 52–54). Most of the Neopythagorean fragments probably belong in the first centuries B.C. and A.D., and they are dependent on earlier Greek discussions of the "city" and "house." Callicratidas (above pp. 56–57) mentioned various forms of rule within the household, and Bryson developed the Aristotelian outline of the topos at length (see above p. 56, 58).

I conclude that the classical topoi as they appear in Plato and Aristotle were available in the Roman age. They were known and discussed by Middle Platonists, Peripatetics, Stoics, Epicureans, Hellenistic Jews, and Neopythagoreans.

NOTE TO CONCLUSION TO PART I

[1]Crouch, *Colossian Haustafel* 150, says that marriage is a "natural" relationship while slavery is not. Some ancient thinkers discussed this question (see p. 34 above), but Aristotle objected to such a distinction.

PART II

THE APOLOGETIC USE
OF THE SUBORDINATION ETHIC
BY MINORITY RELIGIOUS
COMMUNITIES
IN ROMAN SOCIETY

Chapters II–IV outlined the philosophical discussions of the topos "concerning household management" with its three pairs of dominant and subordinate persons within the larger discussion of the topos "concerning the constitution." It will be argued below that the topos which expresses this hierarchical Greek ethic, with some increased stress on the obedience of . children, became a standard for household behavior in aristocratic segments of Roman society. Many minority religious communities, including Christians, had to relate to this Greek and Roman household ethic. Devotees of the god Dionysus and of the goddess Isis, as well as Jews and Christians, were forced to come to terms with these household customs. The relationship between the Roman government and the Dionysus cult was characterized by severe social-political tension. Similar tension existed between the Romans and devotees of Isis precisely over how wives were to relate to husbands. The way Jewish slaves related to their Roman masters was resented. These social situations set important precedents before the rise of Christianity. The relationships between these Eastern, foreign, minority religious communities and Roman society with respect to household relationships will be surveyed as an aid to understanding the social-political setting for 1 Peter.

Chapter V

Greco-Roman Criticism of Eastern Religions

The cults of Dionysus and Isis assisted women in attaining more freedom in the Greco-Roman world, according to Crouch.[1] However, Greco-Roman society criticized both these cults, particularly their evil effects on women. Further, these criticisms of the Dionysus and Isis cults were made in texts which also criticized Judaism, and similar criticisms were made of all three.[2] Plutarch, *Table Talk* IV.6 671C-672C, presented the view that Dionysus and the God of the Jews were the same; the feast of Tabernacles was like revelry in the Bacchus cult, involving drinking wine and nocturnal festivals. Tacitus, *Histories* V.5, rejected this opinion.

The three cults were mentioned together by Valerius Maximus, *Memorable Deeds and Sayings* I.3. Book I concerns religion, and section 3 concerns the "rejection of foreign religion." The reference to Valerius is important because this was a collection of examples for rhetorical use. The work is dated in the reign of Tiberius but refers to an event which occurred in 139 B.C.[3] Valerius first mentions the senate's rejection of Bacchus mysteries. Second, he says that G. Cornelius Hispallus (Hispanus) banished the Chaldaeans, who were astrologers for pay. Then the abridgement of Julius Paris adds, "He also compelled the Jews, who attempted to contaminate the morals of the Romans with the worship of Jupiter Sabazius, to go back to their own homes."[4] The reference to Jupiter Sabazius is puzzling, for he was not a Semitic but a Phrygian deity, whose rites had some connection with those of the Greek Bacchus.[5] Some interpreters see here an allusion to Yahwe Sabaot, while others see a confusion with the Jewish Sabbath. But whatever the source of the confusion, in light of the texts cited immediately above from Plutarch and Tacitus, we know that some persons associated the Jews with the god Bacchus. Finally, Valerius Maximus adds that Lucius Aemilius Paullus, who was consul when the senate decreed that the temples of Isis and Serapis should be destroyed, took a hatchet himself and broke open the gates of the temple when none of the workmen would carry out the decree (50 B.C.).[6]

Judaism is coupled with the Dionysus and Isis cults in this text; they are all rejected by Romans.

Texts which describe actual banishments or persecutions also couple these cults with Judaism, again in the reign of Tiberius.

> Another debate of the Senate dealt with the proscription of the Egyptian and Jewish rites, and a senatorial edict directed that four thousand descendants of enfranchised slaves, tainted with that superstition and suitable in point of age, were to be shipped to Sardinia and there employed in suppressing brigandage; "if they succumbed to the pestilential climate, it was a cheap loss." The rest had orders to leave Italy, unless they had renounced their impious ceremonial by a given date. (Tacitus, *Annals* II.85. Trans. Moore)

Suetonius, *Tiberius* 35-36, has a very similar passage, probably dependent on the same source used by Tacitus, but Suetonius includes proselytes among those banished.[7] Josephus, *Antiquities* 18.65-80, mentions the same event:

> About this same time, another outrage threw the Jews into an uproar; and simultaneously certain actions of a scandalous nature occurred in connection with the temple of Isis at Rome. I shall first give an account of the daring deed of the followers of Isis and shall then come back to the fate of the Jews. . . . (18.65. Trans. Thackeray)

The Isis temple was destroyed because a priest arranged the seduction of the lady Pauline within its precincts.[8] Josephus then relates (18.81-84) that the Jews' expulsion was caused by a Jewish embezzler who took money from the Jewish proselyte Fulvia, "a woman of high rank." Again, the problem involved proselytism.[9] But the pretexts for the expulsions were stories which involved the moral corruption of Roman ladies or the embezzlement of their money. Such slanders were commonly directed against the Isis cult,[10] but they could also be directed against the Jews.[11] Of course, all slanders which could have been directed against Roman women have been collected by Juvenal.[12] The central problem again was the involvement of Roman ladies with foreign cults, and characteristic slanders resulted.

The fear of women misbehaving with men at nocturnal wine-feasts of some god must be described as general or typical. This is especially clear in Cicero, *Laws* II.35 and 37, where he prohibited "the performance of sacrifices by women at night." This prohibition was a general one, applying to several cults:

> Assuredly we must make most careful provision that the reputation of our women be guarded by the clear light of day, when they are observed by many eyes, and that "initiations into the mysteries of Ceres be performed only with those rites which are in use in Rome." The strictness of our ancestors in matters of this character is shown by the ancient decree of the Senate with respect to the Bacchanalia, and the investigation and punishment conducted by the consuls with the assistance of a specially-enrolled military force. And that we may not perchance seem too severe, I may cite the fact that in the very centre of Greece, by a law enacted by Diagonas of Thebes, all nocturnal rites were abolished for ever; and furthermore that Aristophanes, the wittiest poet of

the Old Comedy, attacks strange gods and the nightly vigils which were part of their worship by representing Sabazius and certain other alien gods as brought to trial and banished from the State. (Trans. Keys)

Judaism, and later Christianity, inherited criticisms which Greeks and Romans originally directed against the Dionysus and the Isis cults. It is important to reach a clear picture of what those criticisms were.

A. Dionysus (Bacchus)

The conflict between the cult of Dionysus and Greek society is clearly expressed as early as Euripides, *Bacchanals*, the most popular play in the Hellenistic world, first produced posthumously (405 B.C.?).[13]

200-Tieresias: 'Tis not for us to reason touching gods. Traditions of our fathers, old as time, we hold: no reasoning shall cast them down. . . .

215-Penthus the king: It chanced that, sojourning without this land, I heard of strange misdeeds in this my town, how from their homes our women have gone forth feigning a Bacchic rapture, and rove o'er wooded hills, in dances honouring Dionysus, this new God—who'er he be. And midst each revel-rout the winebowls stand brimmed: and to lonely nooks, some here, some there, they steal, to work with men the deed of shame, in pretext Maenad priestesses, forsooth, but honouring Aphrodite more than Bacchus. . . .[14]

233-Men say a stranger to the land hath come, a juggling sorcerer from Lydia-land, with essenced hair in golden tresses tossed, wine-flushed, Love's witching graces in his eyes, who with the damsels day and night consorts, making pretence of Evian mysteries. . . .

260-For when in women's feasts the cluster's pride hath part, no good, say I, comes of their revelry.

352-Ye, range through the city, and track down that girl-faced stranger, who upon our wives bringeth strange madness, and defiles our beds.

1325-Cadmus: If any man there be that scorns the Gods, this man's death [Penthus the king's death] let him note, and so believe. (Trans. Way)

Despite these attitudes which held to tradition over against the foreign, barbarian Dionysus, the custom of nightly celebrations in the mountains by female worshipers continued into Roman times.[15] It was especially important at Pergamon, where the king took part in the cult.[16]

These nightly celebrations by women were so offensive to the Romans that the mystery cult was forbidden. The story of this ban is related by Livy (XXXIX.8-19), who describes the "conspiracy" of 186 B.C., which has many parallels to Euripides' play. A nameless Greek (8.3), a priest of secret rites performed at night (8.4), added wine and feasts to attract numbers (8.6). Then there was the mingling of males with females, which was combined with other vices, including murder. A freedwoman, the courtesan Hispala, warned her lover Publius Aebutius not to be initiated, for his virtue, reputation, and life (10.4) would be destroyed amid the beating of cymbals and drums (10.7). Hispala was then forced to relate an account of the mysteries to the consul

Postumius. It had at first been a ritual for women only (13.8), but this was changed by the priestess Paculla Annia, who began initiating men at night.[17] From that time the rites were performed in common, men mingling with women at night (13.10). Their number made them almost a second state (13.14). Panic seized the Senate when this was reported (14.3). They ordered that the priests of the rites be sought out, and they issued a decree against assembling for the Bacchic rites (14.8–9), which were an offense against the gods of the forefathers (15.2). The consul reported to the Senate that there were many thousands of initiates; "a great part of them are women, and they are the source of this mischief" (15.9). They did not yet have strength enough to crush the state, though their objective was control of the state (16.3). The consul then discoursed on the character of foreign, false religion (16.6):

> How often, in the times of our fathers . . . has the task been assigned to the magistrates of forbidding the introduction of foreign cults . . . , of searching out and burning books of prophecies, and of annulling every system of sacrifice except that performed in the Roman way. (16.8. Trans. Sage)

More than seven thousand men and women were involved in this conspiracy (17.6), many of whom were killed or thrown into prison (18.5):

> Convicted women were turned over to their relatives or to those who had authority over them, that they might be punished in private; if there was not a suitable person to exact it, the penalty was inflicted by the state. (18.6)

The consuls were told to suppress all forms of Bacchic worship (18.7), unless the worshipers obtained permission from the city praetor (18.8).

The cult's moral offensiveness is not adequate to explain the ban. Romans imagined revolution brewing, and they reacted to what they considered to be a politically volatile situation with slanders against the cult: ritual murder and obscenities occurred. These same charges were later made against the Jews and Christians.[18]

Schneider thought that the Dionysan cult attracted enslaved Greeks[19] who worshiped in small "house churches."[20] But one must be cautious about assuming that these cultic groups were composed of slaves. Bömer found no evidence that *enslaved* Greeks were attracted to the cult in this period;[21] rather, Dionysus was popular with the upper classes, especially with women.[22] At the conclusion of his 968 page study of slaves' religion in Greece and Rome, Bömer insists that the religion of the slaves was determined by the religion of their masters.[23] As a rule the slaves assumed the cults of their masters.[24] The Romans never accepted a divinity imported by slaves, except perhaps in the case of Christianity, and even in that case, one should not speak of a "slave religion":[25]

> In Rome the slaves enjoyed, from ancient times, greater independence [than in Greece]

in those spheres in which their masters placed them; but "in those spheres" means that they, willingly or unwillingly, gave up the gods of their homeland and worshiped the gods of the Romans. That was so taken for granted that the first and only groups which behaved differently, the Jews and the Christians, caused a colossal sensation (*ein ungeheures Aufsehen erregten*), and these were not composed exclusively of slaves.[26]

The first case in which slaves did not assume the religion of their masters perhaps involved those Jews enslaved by Pompey and brought to Rome.[27] Philo, *Embassy to Gaius* 155, mentions them; they were so intractable as slaves, insisting on observing their "native institutions," that they were emancipated and became citizens. The descendants of these freedmen were expelled from Rome by Tiberius (see above pp. 65–66). The exotic religious rites of slaves were a problem for the Romans, as Tacitus indicates:

> To our ancestors the temper of their slaves was always suspect, even when they were born on the same estate or under the same roof, and drew in affection for their owners with their earliest breath. But now that our households comprise nations—with customs the reverse of our own, with foreign cults or with none, you will never coerce such a medley of humanity except by terror. (*Annals* 14.44. Trans. Moore)

Tacitus is discussing the possibility of a slave killing a master, not slaves, who are adherents of foreign cults, organizing and revolting. Bömer denies that there is evidence to show that foreign cults composed of slaves were a political threat. Radical forms of slave religion, in which the social-political status quo was completely negated, were rare; in fact all the evidence Bömer collects yields only one example.[28] With reference to the Dionysus cult, then, one should not conclude that the Romans feared a revolt of foreign slaves who were adherents of that cult rather than believers in the Roman gods. The main problem was that Roman women joined the cult, and the Romans reacted with certain typical slanders: the cult was revolutionary, and the rites involved murder and sexual immorality.

B. Isis (Antony vs. Octavian)

Again, the adherents of the Isis cult were not predominantly slaves; they had enough money to rebuild the Isis sanctuary following its repeated destruction by the Roman senate.[29] Already in 55 B.C., the nobleman M. Plaetorius Cestinaus, an associate of Crassus, had a coin minted on which he placed the image of Isis.[30] This evidence indicates that the Isis cult was more than a gathering place for prostitutes as the slanders cited earlier (n. 10) would indicate. The later literary romances demand a very high sexual morality from the devotees, but the romance of Lollianus does not omit the phallic aspect of the ritual pattern.[31] Along with moral considerations, there were important political motives which led to Roman opposition to the Isis cult.[32]

Octavian in his struggle with Antony for power in Rome used all means of propaganda, including religion; this was also true of Antony and Cleopatra

VII. As Antony traveled east after the battle at Philippi, he identified himself with the god Dionysus, the bearer of salvation:

> When Antony made his entry into Ephesus, women arrayed like Bacchus, and men and boys like Satyrs and Pans, led the way before him, and the city was full of ivy and thyrsus-wands and harps and pipes and flutes, the people hailing him as Dionysus Giver of Joy and Beneficent. (Plutarch, *Antony* 24.3. Trans. Perrin)

He summoned Cleopatra so that she might answer charges made against her for aiding Cassius (25.1). She came laden with many gifts, money, and ornaments (25.4), "and a rumor spread on every hand that Venus was come to revel with Bacchus for the good of Asia" (26.3). After the victory of Octavian, Dio Cassius observes,

> He [Antony] lived during this time in many respects contrary to the customs of his country (ἔξω τῶν πατρίων), calling himself, for example, the young Dionysus and insisting on being called so by others. . . . (*Roman History* 48.39.2. Trans. Cary. Cp. 50.5.3 and Athenaeus, *Deipnosophists* 4.148bc)

Cleopatra represented herself as the "new Isis" (Plutarch, *Antony* 54.9). This would appear ominous from Rome, for

> by the time of Augustus the cult of Isis had grown to be the dominant faith of the world. It was an international religion. In the service of the Queen of the Whole Universe fellow slaves could band themselves together and feel free, coloured Africans could join with Romans, and women could claim the same power as men. But Isis could allure men of far more exalted rank than slaves. . . .[33]

In conscious opposition to Antony, Octavian celebrated in Rome a private dinner called that of the "twelve gods," at which he himself was made up to represent Apollo (Suetonius, *Augustus* 70.1), which caused a great scandal.[34] According to Dio Cassius, before their battle at Actium, Antony made a speech to his soldiers (*Roman History* 50.16.1–50.22.4), and Octavian made one to his soldiers (50.23.3–50.30.5).[35] Antony claimed that "justice and reverence for the gods" (50.24.1) were on their side. But in his speech, Octavian asserted that Antony

> has now abandoned all his ancestors' habits of life (τὰ πάτρια τοῦ βίου ἤθη),[36] has emulated all alien and barbaric customs, . . . pays no honour to us or to the laws or to his father's gods, but pays homage to that wench as if she were some Isis or Selene, calling her children Helios and Selene, and finally taking for himself the title of Osiris or Dionysus. . . . (50.25.3–4)

> Therefore, let no one count him a Roman, but rather an Egyptian, nor call him Antony, but rather Serapion; let no one think he was ever consul or imperator, but only [Alexandrian] gymnasiarch. (50.27.1)

> His piety toward our gods? But he is at war with them as well as with his country. (50.27.7. Trans. Cary)

So Octavian calls on his soldiers

> to maintain the renown of your forefathers, to preserve your own proud traditions, to take vengeance on those who are in revolt against us, to repel those who insult you, to conquer and rule (ἄρχειν) all mankind, to allow no woman to make herself equal to a man (μηδεμίαν γυναῖκα περιορᾶν μηδενὶ ἀνδρὶ παρισουμένην). (50.28.3)

The speech associates a stress on the "customs of the fathers" with opposition to the Isis cult of Egypt and with the assertion that the "new Isis" reversed the proper relationship between man and woman. In Rome men ruled women, not vice versa. The Romans were offended that Antony seemed "enslaved" to Cleopatra (50.5.1), but Octavian claimed to know the proper way to "rule" and "be ruled" (50.17.5). Similarly, Plutarch (*Antony* 10) accused Mark Antony's first wife Fulvia with preparing him to be dominated by Cleopatra, for Fulvia wished to rule a ruler; she trained Antony to obey women. As early as Octavian, Romans thought that Isis reversed the proper relationships between men and women:

> The Egyptians also made a law, they say, contrary to the general custom of mankind (παρὰ τὸ κοινὸν ἔθος τῶν ἀνθρώπων), permitting men to marry their sisters, this being due to the success attained by Isis in this respect; for she had married her brother Osiris, and upon his death, having taken a vow never to marry another man, she both avenged the murder of her husband and reigned all her days over the land with complete respect for the laws, and in a word, became the cause of more and greater blessings to all men than any other. It is for these reasons, in fact, that it was ordained that the queen should have greater power and honour (μείζονος ἐξουσίας καὶ τιμῆς) than the king and that among private persons the wife should enjoy authority over her husband (παρὰ τοῖς ἰδιώταις κυριεύειν τὴν γυναῖκα τἀνδρός), the husbands agreeing in the marriage contract that they will be obedient in all things to their wives. (Diodorus Siculus, *Library of History* I.27.1–2. Trans. Oldfather)[37]

There is a parallel account of Egyptian customs in Sophocles, *Oedipus at Colonus* 337–358, [38] and a parallel accusation in the Talmud (b.*Sota* 11b).[39] Another parallel is from Herodotus:

> As the Egyptians have a climate peculiar to themselves, and their river is different in its nature from all other rivers, so have they made themselves customs and laws of a kind contrary to those of all other men. Among them, the women buy and sell, the men abide at home and weave; and whereas in weaving all others push the woof upwards, the Egyptians push it downwards. (*Histories* II.35. Trans. Godley)[40]

These descriptions of Egyptian marriage relationships are supported by *Oxyrhynchus Papyrus* 1380 (lines 214–216), where Isis is praised: "You gave the women the same power as the men" (σὺ γυναιξὶν ἴσην δύναμιν τῶν ἀνδρῶν ἐποίησας).[41] The later romance of Achilles Tatius, *Clitophon and Leucippe* (V.14), gives an account of a marriage ceremony in the temple of Isis in Alexandria which is quite different, more Roman. So there was either a diversity within the Isis cult with respect to marriage custom, or perhaps there was a later assimilation of the cult to Roman society. But in some texts the Egyptian Isis cult is viewed as a threat to Roman customs because it interferes with men's rule of women.

Apparently Herodotus was correct that Egyptian women were often the social equals of their husbands. In the Old Kingdom (before 2270 B.C.), the wife had the same rights as the husband although the social roles were not identical.[42] The wife was "mistress of the house." However, moralists exhort the husband not to allow the wife to dominate him, and further not to allow her to obtain the direction of family affairs.[43] Especially during the eighteenth dynasty (1580–1341 B.C.), women enjoyed equality of status. And Pirenne asserts that in the twenty-sixth dynasty (663–525 B.C.) wives obtained absolute equality in marriage, which continued until the arrival of the Ptolemies in Egypt.[44]

The Greek impressions that Egyptian wives ruled their husbands should be compared with Aristotle's negative evaluation of Spartan wives ruling their husbands.[45] On the other hand, the mythical founder of Rome, Romulus, constructed a constitution which regulated the temperance of women, which included obedience to husbands. And the success of Rome, it was thought, resulted from the constitution.[46] Given such ways of thinking, it is not surprising that Dio Cassius would describe Antony as having "abandoned all his ancestors' habits of life," emulating "alien and barbarian customs," one of which was his "enslavement" to a woman. The Isis cult presented a threat to the Roman constitution.

Romans disapproved of Isis devotees. The goddess appeared to the devotee Lucius Apuleius (*Metamorphoses* XI.30) in his sleep to command him to remain faithful despite the slander of persons who resented his religion. The response which this negative attitude toward the Isis cult produced within the cult itself is instructive. Apuleius gave the following report of the words of the Isis priest during the procession (XI.17):

> And calling together their whole assembly, from his high pulpit [he] began to read out of a book, praying for good fortune to the great Prince, the Senate, to the noble order of Chivalry, and generally to all the Roman people, and to all the sailors, and ships such as be under the puissance and jurisdiction of Rome. . . . (Trans. Gaselee)

In this context, the prayer corresponds to a desire to reassure a suspicious Roman society of the loyalty of the cult to the state.[47]

In this social setting, Octavian was considered a great lawgiver for house and state just as Romulus had been.[48] Horace (*Epistle* II.1.1) speaks of Augustus as "gracing her [Rome] with morals and reforming her with laws," then immediately compares him with Romulus. Horace (*Ode* IV.5) speaks of the blessings of Augustus' sway, addressing him as "best guardian of the race of Romulus" and saying,

> Polluted by no stain, the home (*domus*) is pure; custom and law have stamped out the taint of sin; mothers win praise because of children like unto their sires; while Vengeance follows close on guilt. (Trans. Bennett)

Suetonius, *Augustus* 34.1, says,

> He revised existing laws and enacted some new ones, for example, on extravagance, on adultery and chastity, on bribery and on the encouragement of marriage among the various classes of citizens. . . . (Trans. Rolfe)

This he did hoping to establish the "best possible government" (28.2). For re-establishing constitutional government (Dio Cassius, *Roman History* 53.16.6–8), he was given the name "Augustus."[49]

C. Judaism (Josephus, Against Apion)

Roman society also criticized the Jews' practices, just as they had those of the Dionysus and Isis cults. Praise and/or criticism of various cities' and ethnic groups' constitutions was common in Greek rhetoric, and Josephus' response to slander of the Jews follows a rhetorical pattern, as he himself observes (*Against Apion* I.220–221).[50] The Greeks' view of a city's or a people's constitution included the structure of household relationships, so it is no surprise to find outsiders' descriptions of Jews mentioning their practices with respect to marriage and household relationships. Hecataeus of Abdera observed, "As to marriage and the burial of the dead, he [Moses] saw to it that their customs should differ widely from those of other men" (Diodorus Siculus, *Library of History* 40.3.8). Tacitus, *Histories* has a more negative account:

> To establish his influence over this people for all time, Moses introduced new religious practices, quite opposed to those of all other religions. The Jews regard as profane all that we hold sacred; on the other hand, they permit all that we abhor. (V. 4. Trans. Moore)

> Toward every other people they feel only hate and enmity. They sit apart at meals, and they sleep apart, and although as a race, they are prone to lust, they abstain from intercourse with foreign women; yet among themselves nothing is unlawful. (V.5)

The Jews, according to Tacitus, reversed all Roman customs, including those with respect to marriage.[51]

Philo and Josephus responded to such slanders with statements about Jewish marriage such as: "The woman, says the law, is in all things inferior to the man; let her accordingly be submissive" (see p. 54 above). This was apologetic, a defensive response to prior Roman slanders. According to Philo and Josephus, Hellenistic Judaism accepted the household ethic demanded of it by the dominant Greco-Roman society.

D. The Political Status of the Ethic

It fits the historical situation just described that Dionysius of Halicarnassus, who arrived in Rome "at the very time that Augustus Caesar put an end to the civil war" (*Rom. Ant.* I.7.2), [52] criticizes foreign mystery cults (II.19), especially the cults of Dionysus and Cybele. He insists on the subordination of women to their husbands (II.24.3–II.26.1) and the reverence and obedience of children for their parents (II.26.1–II.27.4). He also compares the power of the master over his slaves (II.27.1–2) with the power a father has over his son, so the three pairs of the Aristotelian topos "on household management" are present. His history was designed for upper class Roman readers. [53] Dionysius' views of ancient Roman virtue were taught to his pupil Metilius Rufus, who later became proconsul of Achaea under Augustus and possibly a legate of Galatia. [54] A second writer, Areius Didymus, is even more important. His doxographical *Epitome*, which, as has been seen above (p. 43), contains the Aristotelian elements behind the NT pattern of household submissiveness, was compiled perhaps for the benefit of Augustus, [55] whom he taught and counseled (Suetonius, *Augustus* 89.1; Plutarch, *Antony* 80.1; Dio Cassius, *Roman History* 51.16.4). Areius became imperial procurator in Sicily but declined Augustus' offer to make him the first prefect of Egypt. [56] His son, Nicanor, looked after Augustan interests in Greece. [57] A third writer, Seneca, outlined the household code in *Epistle* 94. At this point the ethic is brought into close contact with early Christianity in a social situation similar to that addressed in 1 Peter. Seneca's brother Gallio was the governor before whose judgment seat Paul was brought (Acts 18:12). [58] In these three writers we see that the kind of ethic found in the NT household codes was important to the Roman aristocracy, that class from which governors for the provinces was drawn. [59] These are the "governors" mentioned in 1 Pet 2:14 who would be judging Christians. Many of them would be antagonistic to new, foreign cults like the Isis cult, which upset household relationships between man and wife (Dio Cassius, *Roman History* 50.28.3; Diodorus Siculus, *Library of History* I.27.1–2) and could be seen as a threat to the Roman constitution.

E. Summary

This chapter has related the abstract philosophical discussions of the constitution discussed in Part I to actual cultic communities in the Roman age. Roman ideals resulted in certain stereotyped criticisms of the Dionysus cult, the Egyptian Isis cult, and Judaism: they produced immorality (especially among Roman women) and sedition. The Roman constitution insisted on proper worship of the state gods, [60] so Romans reacted negatively when Jewish and Christian slaves—the first groups to do so—rejected the worship of their masters' gods, insisting on an exclusive worship of their own God.

The Dionysus cult came into conflict with traditional Greek culture and religion. Later, the nightly rituals were forbidden by the Romans because they reportedly involved sexual immorality, murder, and sedition. However, contemporary research has thrown doubt on the popular image of slaves, united by worship of Bacchus, opposing the upper-class, ruling Romans. Rather, slaves assumed the religion of their masters.

The Isis cult was involved in the political and military contest between Octavian and Antony. As part of his propaganda during that contest, Octavian exhorted his soldiers not to consider Antony a Roman but an Egyptian, for he had abandoned his ancestors' habits of life for barbarian ones. He was no longer pious toward the Roman gods but at war with them, and he no longer "ruled" in a Roman manner but was "enslaved" to Cleopatra. Octavian claimed to know the proper way to "rule" and "be ruled," so exhorted his soldiers "to allow no woman to make herself equal to a man" (above p. 71). In this sentence there was an appeal to an ancient characterization of the Egyptians: they lived by laws "contrary to the general custom of mankind," laws and customs which were the *reverse* of Greek and Roman laws. These upside-down customs included household relationships: husbands submit to wives; husbands stay at home and weave while the wives go out to buy and sell (above p. 71).

The Roman aristocracy valued the ethic outlined in the NT pattern of household submission. Romans who became governors in the provinces would have been interested in maintaining the Roman customs and constitution against foreign customs like those of the Isis cult which might subvert Roman households and the constitution.

Romans employed certain stereotypes when they criticized the Jewish constitution. They criticized the customs which Moses instituted with respect to raising children, marriage, and the burial of the dead. Tacitus said they were the reverse of Roman customs.

In response to these aspersions, Josephus wrote an apologetic encomium on the Jewish nation. Using the same pattern, Dionysius of Halicarnassus wrote an apologetic encomium of Rome in the late first century B.C. The Romans had been slandered, and Dionysius defended them by insisting that the ancient Romans lived according to the four cardinal virtues of prudence, wisdom, courage, and temperance; Romulus legislated temperance, which included wives' chastity and submission to their husbands. Dionysius' use of the topos "concerning household management" in this context (see above pp. 54–55) sheds light on the NT pattern of household submission. The master-slave pair was present in the Dionysian topos only as a comparison and contrast to the father-son pair, but in special circumstances the master-slave reference could be expanded. Dionysius' use of the topos "concerning household management" with its three pairs is a closer parallel to the NT codes than Josephus, *Against Apion* II.199, the parallel commonly cited.

Both Dionysius and Josephus employed the topos in an encomium, and in both authors the topos had an apologetic function.

Josephus treated the temperance of Moses' laws with respect to marriage and the birth and upbringing of children (see above pp. 54–55). This element of the Hellenistic encomium, like all others, was "reversible": it could be used for praise or criticism. Jewish marital and sexual customs had been criticized (see above pp. 54–55, 65–67). Josephus traditionally criticized the Spartan marriage customs but defended Jewish customs: the Jewish woman was properly submissive.

Aristotle had seen a connection between the authority exercised by wives and the corruption of the Spartan constitution (see above pp. 36–37, 72), a connection also made by Dionysius of Halicarnassus with respect to constitutions in general. Cicero, *Republic* I.67, paraphrasing Plato, saw a connection between "democracy" in the house with respect to sons, slaves, and wives and the consequent rejection of the authority of government and the laws; "so finally they are without a master of any kind." Greco-Roman political science often drew an analogy between the house and the city: the rejection of the husband's authority by the wife, or of the master's authority by the slave, or of the father's authority by sons led to anarchy in both home and city, to the rejection of the king's authority, and to the *degeneration* of the constitution from monarchy to democracy.

Josephus asserted not only that Jewish women obey their husbands but also that they accept the authority of the Roman governors and emperor. The Egyptian women, devotees of Isis, ruled their husbands and corrupted the constitution. The female devotees of Dionysus committed treason by attempting to form "a second state" and overthrow Rome. In contrast Josephus asserted that Jewish women obey their husbands and their emperor: they are "temperate" (cp. *Against Apion* II.199–203, 225, 234–235, 273–275). Such ideas explain Josephus' insistence that Moses' law fosters "obedience" (*Against Apion* II.158, 193, 220, 225, 235, 293). Jews were obedient Roman citizens and Jewish customs would not subvert Romulus' constitution.

NOTES TO CHAPTER V

[1]James Crouch, *Colossian Haustafel* 141–144.

[2]Ilse Becher, "Der Isiskult in Rom—Ein Kult der Halbwelt?" *Zeitschrift für ägyptische Sprache* 96 (1970) 85.

[3]See the discussion of the text in Harry Joshua Leon, *The Jews of Ancient Rome* (Philadelphia: Jewish Publication Society of America, 1960) 2–4. Also Willem Cornelis van Unnik, "Die Anklage gegen die Apostel in Philippi (Apostelgeschichte 16,20f.)," *Mullus, Festschrift Theodor Klausner*, ed. A. Stuiber and A. Hermann (Jahrbuch für Antike und Christentum, Ergänzungsband 1; Münster: Aschendorff, 1964) 372–373.

[4]Ed. Kempf, 17,9–11. Trans. Leon, *The Jews* 3.

[5]Leon, *The Jews* 2–4.

[6]See Dieter Dietrich, "Die Ausbreitung der alexandrinischen Mysteriengötter Isis, Osiris, Serapis und Horus in griechisch-römischer Zeit," *Das Altertum* 14 (1968) 201–211 at p. 209.

[7]See the discussion by Leon, *The Jews* 16-20, who notes (19, n. 4) that the chief motive of Tiberius' action against the Jews was religious: he was attempting to check Jewish proselytism, particularly among the nobility. He cites E. Mary Smallwood, "Some Notes on the Jews under Tiberius," *Latomus* 15 (1956) 314-329. See idem, *The Jews under Roman Rule. From Pompey to Diocletian* (Studies in Judaism in Late Antiquity 20; Leiden: E. J. Brill, 1976) 202-207. Cp. Seneca, *Against Superstition*, in Augustine, *The City of God* VI.11: "The custom of that wicked nation getting head through all the world, the vanquished gave laws to the vanquishers."

[8]Reinhold Merkelbach, *Roman und Mysterium in der Antike* (Munich: Beck, 1962) 17 suggests that the background for this text is the *hieros gamos*, a rite in which an initiate is sexually unified with a god or goddess. That this rite existed at all is denied by Günther Freymuth, "Zum Hieros Gamos in den antiken Mysterien," *Museum Helveticum* 21 (1964) 86-95 and by Carl Schneider, *Kulturgeschichte des Hellenismus* (Munich: C. H. Beck, 1969) 2: 870, 871 with n. 1, 885 with n. 1; see also vol. 1 (1967) 685, n. 2. Reginald E. Witt, *Isis in the Graeco-Roman World* (Aspects of Greek and Roman Life; London: Thames and Hudson, 1971), chap. 18: "Xenophon's Isiac Romance," treats Merkelbach's view positively but does not discuss this particular rite. See also Horst R. Moehring, "The Persecution of the Jews and the Adherents of the Isis Cult at Rome A.D. 19," *NovT* 13 (1959) 293-304 and Leon, *The Jews* 16-20. Support for Merkelbach's viewpoint on this question would seem to come from the recent discussion of the romance of Lollianus by Albert Henrichs, "Pagan Ritual and the Alleged Crimes of the Early Christians," *Kyriakon, Festschrift Johannes Quasten*, ed. P. Granfield and J. A. Jungmann (Münster: Aschendorff, 1970) 1:18-35. It is beyond the scope of this investigation to discuss this complicated issue, but the cult adherents' reputation in Roman society, the primary concern here, can be determined without determining the historical relationship between the negative reputation and this particular rite.

[9]See also Dio Cassius, *Roman History* 57.18.5a.

[10]Ovid, *Erotic Poems* I.8.74; II.2.1; *Art of Love* I.75-78; III.393; 635-638. See Becher, "Der Isiskult" 81-90.

[11]Ovid, *Art of Love* I.75-76, as well as Martial, *Epigrams* VII.30.5-8; XI.94; and Tacitus, *History* V.5.

[12]*Satire* VI: He speaks of wine feasts and sexual activity in the mysteries of Bona Dea (314-345) as illustrated by the exploits of Clodius (337-345), then of the wanton Isis (489), of Cybele (511-513), again of Isis (524-541), of an old Jewess (542-547), and Chaldaean astrologers (553-564).

[13]Schneider, *Kulturgeschichte* 2: 801 with n. 2. On the cult see 801-810 and 876-882. On opposition to the cult, Johannes Leipoldt, *Dionysos* (Angelos Beiheft 3; Leipzig: Eduard Pfeiffer, 1931) 16-19. Charles Segal, "The Menace of Dionysus: Sex Roles and Reversals in Euripides' Bacchae," *Arethusa* 11 (1978) 185-202 discusses this god's threat to the *polis*.

[14]In this one speech several of the slanders which later produced Christian martyrs already appear. On Dionysus and women see Walter F. Otto, *Dionysus. Myth and Cult* (Bloomington: Indiana University, 1965) 171-180.

[15]Schneider, *Kulturgeschichte* 2: 880 with n. 2. Friedrich Matz, ΔΙΟΝΥΣΙΑΚΗ ΤΕΛΕΤΗ. *Archaeologische Untersuchungen zum Dionysoskult in hellenistischer und römischer Zeit* (Akademie der Wissenschaften und der Literatur, Abhandlungen der geistes- und sozialwissenschaftliche Klasse; Mainz: F. Steiner, 1964) 7, 43, 69. See Diodorus Siculus, *Library of History* IV.3.2-5.

[16]Schneider, *Kulturgeschichte* 2: 807-808. Matz, ΔΙΟΝΥΣΙΑΚΗ ΤΕΛΕΤΗ 69.

[17]See Arthur Darby Nock, *Conversion: The Old and the New in Religion from Alexander the Great to Augustine of Hippo* (New York: Oxford University, 1965 repr.) 71-74 and 285. The two accounts of the beginnings of these mysteries differ. In the first (XXXIX.8-11) the sexes are mixed from the beginning; but in the second (XXXIX.12-13) the ritual had at first been for women, men being initiated only at a later date, a change introduced by the priestess Paculla Annia. Cp. Martin P. Nilsson, *Geschichte der griechischen Religion* 2 (Munich: C. H. Beck, 1967), 100, 246-247; A. H. McDonald, "Rome and the Italian Confederation (200-186 B.C.),"*JRS* 34 (1944) 11-33, at 26-31.

[18]See Schneider, *Kulturgeschichte* 2: 882, and Martin P. Nilsson, *The Dionysiac Mysteries of the Hellenistic and Roman Age* (Lund: C. W. K. Gleerup, 1957) 15, who adds that Livy's account is embellished by romantic and exaggerated details. The reality of such rites is accepted by Henrichs, "Pagan Ritual."

[19]Schneider, *Kulturgeschichte* 2: 882.

[20]Ibid. See 878 on the Villa Item, where Schneider says a Dionysan house church gathered. See Nilsson, *Dionysiac Mysteries* 145–146 and idem, *Geschichte der griechischen Religion* 2: 359, 363, 365. Cp. Edwin A. Judge, *The Social Pattern of the Christian Groups in the First Century. Some Prolegomena to the Study of the New Testament Ideas of Social Organization* (London: Tyndale, 1960) chap. 3 on Christian house churches.

[21]See esp. Franz Bömer, *Untersuchungen über die Religion der Sklaven in Griechenland und Rom, Dritter Teil: Die wichtigsten Kulte der griechischen Welt* (Akademie der Wissenschaften und der Literatur, Abhandlungen der geistes- und sozialwissenschaftliche Klasse; Mainz: Franz Steiner, 1961) 127, n. 3; 132; 134; 135, n. 5.

[22]Ibid., 118, 121, 128, 129–130 (esp. women), 131.

[23]Franz Bömer, *Untersuchungen über die Religion der Sklaven in Griechenland und Rom, Vierter Teil: Epilegomena* (Akademie der Wissenschaften und der Literatur, Abhandlungen der geistes- und sozialwissenschaftliche Klasse; Mainz: F. Steiner, 1963) 247. Cp. Elene Michajlovna Staerman, *Die Krise der Sklavenhalterordnung im Westen des römischen Reiches* (Berlin: Akademie, 1964) 60–69, esp. 64–65.

[24]Bömer, *Untersuchungen* 4: 248.

[25]Ibid., 258.

[26]Ibid., 259 (my trans.); cp. ibid., 60 and 62 where he cites Philo, *Embassy to Gaius* 155, and secondary literature.

[27]See Leon, *The Jews* 4.

[28]Bömer, *Untersuchungen* 4: 260. The one example he discusses (201–205) does not belong to the Dionysus cult. Joseph Vogt, *Struktur der antiken Sklavenkriege* (Akademie der Wissenschaften und der Literatur, Abhandlungen der geistes- und sozialwissenschaftliche Klasse; Mainz: F. Steiner, 1957) 7 points out that all slave rebellions occurred in the period 140–70 B.C. Among the most radical of these was that in Sicily led by the slave Eunus (related by Diodorus of Sicily, book 34), who at the initial success of the revolt set up a society which was the political and religious image of his Syrian homeland (Vogt 18–21, 31), perhaps inspired by the Maccabees in Palestine. Eunus did not attempt to alter the basic social order. Cp. p. 115, n. 96.

[29]Kurt Latte, *Römische Religionsgeschichte* (Handbuch der Altertumswissenschaft, 5. Abt. T.4; Munich: C. H. Beck, 1960) 282–283. Becher, "Der Isiskult" 86 cites Dio Cassius, *Roman History* 40.47.3. See above p. 66.

[30]Andras Alfoeldi, "Isiskult und Umsturzbewegung im letzten Jahrhundert der römischen Republik," *Schweizer Munzblätter* 6/18 (Dec. 1954) 25–31, esp. 30–31. Alfoeldi's suggestions are evaluated by Ladislav Vidman, *Isis und Serapis bei den Griechen und Römern* (Religionsgeschichtliche Versuche und Vorarbeiten 29; Berlin: Walter de Gruyter, 1970) 101–103.

[31]See Apuleius, *The Golden Ass* XI.6, 15, 19, 20; see also the romances of Xenophon of Ephesus and Achilles Tatius, where a repeated insistence on chastity occurs. See Witt, *Isis* 244, 246. But see Witt, *Isis* 19, n. 39; 85, n. 42 and Henrichs, "Pagan Ritual," on ritual murder and sexual promiscuity. Note Henrichs' (p. 33) recognition of the subjective element in a historian's judgment about whether such rites existed in the second century A.D.

[32]Otto Immisch, "Zum antiken Herrscherkult," *Aus Roms Zeitwende. Von Wesen und Wirken des Augusteischen Geistes* (Leipzig: Dietrich, 1931) 3–36, followed by Ilse Becher, "Oktavians Kampf gegen Antonius und seine Stellung zu den ägyptischen Göttern," *Das Altertum* 11 (1965) 40–47. See also Arthur Darby Nock, "Notes on Ruler-Cult, I–IV," *JHS* 48 (1928) 33. Cp. Mikhail Ivanovich Rostovtzeff, "Augustus," *Mitteilungen des deutschen archaeologischen Instituts*, Römische Abteilung Bd. 38/39 (1923–1924) 281–299. That the Serapis cult was "imperialistic" in the time of the Ptolemies is successfully denied by Peter Marshal Fraser, "Two Studies on the Cult of Serapis in the Hellenistic World," in *Opuscula*

Atheniensia 3 (Skifter Utgivna an Svanska Institutet I Athen, 48, VII; Lund: C. W. K. Gleerup, 1960) 1–54. But the point in the text is that the Romans *accused* the Isis cult of sedition.

[33]R. E. Witt, "Isis-Hellas," *Cambridge Philological Society Proceedings* 12 (Cambridge: The Philological Society, 1966) 62. The date of Isis' dominance is placed as early as 200 B.C. by Dietrich, "Die Ausbreitung" 207. In general see Jonathan Z. Smith, "Native Cults in the Hellenistic Period," *HR* 11 (1971–1972) 236–249.

[34]Immisch, "Zum antiken Herrscherkult" 27–29, 31; Becher, "Oktavians Kampf" 41.

[35]Becher, "Oktavians Kampf" 42 argues that many points in the speech correspond with contemporary accounts, so that it may be taken as representative of the pre-war propaganda. See also Ilse Becher, *Das Bild der Kleopatra in der griechischen und lateinischen Literatur* (Berlin: Akademie, 1966) 24–25, 109 and Immisch, "Zum antiken Herrscherkult" 20.

[36]In general see Hans Rech, *Mos maiorum. Wesen und Wirkung der Tradition in Rom* (Marburg: Handelsdruckerei, 1936).

[37]Chrysippus was criticised for the approval in his *Politeia* of brothers marrying sisters; see Sextus Empiricus, *Outlines of Pyrrhonism* III.246; cp. 201.

[38]C. H. Oldfather in his ed. and trans. of Diodorus in LCL, 1:87, n. 1.

[39]M. Zipser, *Des Flavius Josephus Werk "Über das hohe Alter des jüdischen Volkes gegen Apion" nach hebraischen Originalquellen erläutert* (Vienna: Beck'schen Universitäts-Buchhandlung, 1871) 164.

[40]See Karl Trüdinger, *Studien zur Geschichte der griechisch-römischen Ethnographie* (Basel: Emil Birkhäuser, 1918) 34. In general see Robert Drews, *The Greek Accounts of Eastern History* (Washington, D.C.: Center for Hellenic Studies, 1973) 56–69, and Jonathan Z. Smith, "Adde Parvum Parvo Magnus Acervus Erit," *HR* 11 (1971–1972) 56–90, esp. 72–76.

[41]Becher, "Der Isiskult" 85. Also Claire Préaux, "Le statut de la femme à l'époque hellénistique," *La femme. Recueils de la Société Jean Bodin* 11 (Brussels: Librairie encyclopédique, 1959) 172. The papyrus belongs to the early second century A.D.

[42]Jacques Pirenne, "Le statut de la femme dans l'ancienne Egypte," *La femme. Recueils de la Société Jean Bodin* 11 (Brussels: Librairie encyclopédique, 1959) 65; idem, *Histoire des institutions et du droit privé de l'ancienne Egypte* (Brussels: Édition de la Fondation egyptologique reine Elizabeth, 1934) 2:345–347, 356–359. See Leonard Swidler, *Women in Judaism. The Status of Women in Formative Judaism* (Metuchen: Scarecrow, 1976) 5–7.

[43]Pirenne, "Le statut" 66–67. Swidler overlooks this qualification. See J. B. Pritchard, *Ancient Near Eastern Texts Relating to the Old Testament* (Princeton: Princeton University, 1950) 413, 421.

[44]Pirenne, "Le statut" 72, 75–76.

[45]See above p. 31, n. 37 on Aristotle, *Rhetoric* I.5.6 and above p. 36 on *Pol.* II 1269b 12–1270a 15.

[46]Polybius, *Histories* VI.2.9–10; Dionysius Hal., *Rom. Ant.* II.3.5–6; 24.1–2.

[47]Several NT *Haustafeln* occur in the context of a communal worship service, which suggests that the intent is related to that of the Isis priest's prayer just cited. See Eph 5:19; Col 3:16; 1 Tim 2:1, 8; cp. 1 Pet 2:13. Prayer for Rome is mentioned in 1 Clem. 61; Justin, *1 Apol.* 17.3; Athenagoras, *Embassy* 37; cp. Rom 13:1.

[48]Kenneth Scott, "The Identification of Augustus with Romulus-Quirinus," *Transactions of the American Philological Association* 56 (1925) 82–105, esp. 95–96 with nn. 50–55. See Ovid, *Metamorphoses* 15.832–834; *Poems of Lament* 2.233–234.

[49]Scott, "The Identification of Augustus" 88. See Octavian's speech (Dio Cassius, *Roman History* 53.3.1–10.8), at the conclusion of which a democratic constitution is rejected in favor of a monarchic one (53.11.2 and 4; 53.12.1), the same choice Romulus had made (Dionysius Hal., *Rom. Ant.* II.3–4).

[50]See the article cited above p. 58, n. 11. See M. Stern, "The Jews in Greek and Latin Literature," *The Jewish People in the First Century*, ed. S. Safrai and M. Stern (Compendia Rerum Judaicarum ad Novum Testamentum; Philadelphia: Fortress, 1976) 2:1101–1159.

[51]Crouch, *Colossian Haustafel* 76, 80 refers to texts like the ones just quoted as "reverse-codes."

[52]But Dionysius seems not to have been an admirer of Augustus for he notes that "the authority of the ancient kings was not arbitrary and absolute as it is in our days" (II.12.4). And it is his opinion that the ancient monarchy has been overthrown (I.8.2; V.1.1–2; see also II.6.1–4; 14.3; 19.2).

[53]G. W. Bowersock, *Augustus and the Greek World* (Oxford: Clarendon, 1965) 131.

[54]Ibid., 132.

[55]This is a conjecture by Hermann Diels, *Doxographi graeci* (Berlin and Leipzig: Walter de Gruyter, 1929) 83. See Peter Marshal Fraser, *Ptolemaic Alexandria* 1 (Oxford: Clarendon, 1972) 490–491.

[56]Bowersock, *Augustus* 40.

[57]Ibid., 38.

[58]It is not improbable that Gallio knew the Aristotelian form. This makes it intriguing that Paul (?), after outlining the *Haustafel* in Colossians, is concerned with "outsiders" and how they are to be "answered" (Col 4:5–6). It is not accidental that household codes appear in letters which state that the author is in a Roman prison. See Col 4:10; Eph 6:20; II Tim 1:8, 16–17; 2:9; 4:6, 16–17; Pseudo-Ignatius, *Tarsians* 9; *Antiochians* 1; 7; 9–10; 11:"Be subject (ὑποτάγητε) to Caesar in everything in which subjection implies no [spiritual] danger. Provoke not those that rule over you to wrath, that you may give no occasion against yourselves to those that seek it."

[59]Cp. Wilhelm Capelle, "Griechische Ethik und römischer Imperialismus," *Klio* 25 (1932) 86–113.

[60]Dionysius Hal., *Rom. Ant.* II.18.1–2.

Chapter VI

The Apologetic Function of the Household Code in 1 Peter

The purpose of this chapter is to clarify the function of the domestic code in 1 Peter. This clarification must be set in the context of the material in chapter V which presents aspects of the tension between Roman society and foreign, Eastern religions. These tensions produced stereotyped Roman criticisms of foreign religions, including criticisms of household relationships among the devotees of Isis.

Several texts in 1 Peter should be read in light of this social situation. These Christians had rejected the "futile ways inherited from the fathers" (1:18b). Their conversion from traditional religion to a new, foreign religion evoked slanders from Roman society. 1 Pet 2:11–12 opens a major new section of the letter (see Appendix I), and the household code follows immediately after these introductory verses, which indicate awareness of pagan slanders of Christians. In 2:15 the purpose of the behavior to which the author is exhorting is "to put to silence the ignorance of foolish men." Thus one primary purpose of proper household behavior was to reduce the social-political tension between society and the churches. 1 Pet 3:8–9 is a concluding summary of the household code and also addresses the situation of social tension revealed by the other texts. The first exhortation in 3:8 is to "harmony." Hellenistic moralists valued harmony in the household, which had been disturbed by the conversion of some slaves and wives to a detested foreign religion. In the same summary, the author exhorts the converted Christians not to return evil for the evil which was being done to them, not to revile despite being reviled (3:9). This awareness of pagan slanders is still the major concern immediately after the code; 3:15–16 encourages the Christians to be prepared to make a defense (an apology) to pagan critics so that those reviling the good behavior of the Christians might be put to shame. The apology called for by the author has its closest parallel in the apology of Josephus, *Against Apion* II.147 (see pp. 54–55, 73, 75 above). Josephus' defense of the Jews against similar slanders involved the presentation of Moses' "marriage laws" (II.199)—which demanded the wife's submissiveness—and the "law for slaves" (II.215). Apparently, the moral enthusiasm of some Christians had stimulated them to "meddle in others' household affairs" (4:15). This was also a source of tension with outsiders. Such meddling was naturally resented, and the author of 1 Peter forbids it. The author shows an awareness that these pagan slanders about the Christians' household behavior might be brought to the attention of the governor, who would punish those whose household behavior was insubordinate but who would also praise those who accepted their place in the hierarchical framework of the Roman state (2:14). The code itself reflects the tensions mentioned in these other verses: slaves are "suffering unjustly" (2:19). Some of the Christian wives have "disobedient" (pagan) husbands, and the wives need to be encouraged not to be terrified by the situation (3:6). The following chapter will argue this interpretation of the texts, concentrating on the verses to wives, and will compare the resulting interpretation with previously proposed functions of the household code.

A. A Christian Apology to Greco-Roman Society

1 Pet 1:18b. "Futile ways inherited from your fathers." These Anatolian Christians had rejected the religious traditions of the Romans, and the Romans resented the exclusive attitude of the new, Eastern religion. "Futile ways inherited from your fathers" (1:18b) and "lawless idolatries" (4:3b) were frankly rejected. In 1:18b the author refers to his readers having been redeemed "from your foolish conduct transmitted from your fathers" (ἐκ τῆς ματαίας ὑμῶν ἀναστροφῆς πατροπαραδότου). This is an unusual use of "conduct," an important word for the author which usually signifies the Christian manner of moral conduct (e.g., 1:15; 3:16). Here, however, the word refers to the readers' former pagan behavior. The adjective "transmitted from one's fathers" is used in a letter of King Attalus III (135 B.C.), who stated that his mother at her marriage brought the "*ancestral* god Sabasius" with her from Cappadocia.[1] Diodorus Siculus, *Library of History* 4.8.5, accused the people of not "preserving even the *traditional* piety toward the god" (my emphasis). This "traditional piety" was clearly conformity to and the performance of the cult as it was instituted by the forebears. In these and other texts, the adjective "transmitted from one's fathers" is not an expression of criticism but of recommendation for Greeks and Romans. It is closely associated with "custom." The attitude expressed in 1 Pet 1:18 offended pagans, who frowned on new religious customs or on any rejection of the ancestral tradition.

One of the arguments in Josephus, *Against Apion*, also centered around "hereditary custom."[2] The Egyptian Apion had written an indictment of the Jews including a charge that when Moses was pledged to the customs of his [Egyptian] fathers (πατρίοις ἔθεσι), he changed the cult (II.10). Josephus responded by stating that the fathers of the Jews were not Egyptians (I.269, 317), that the Jews never shared the frivolous and senseless ancestral custom of regarding animals as gods (I.225). On the contrary, Romans should not be surprised at the Jews' allegiance to their ancestral religious laws. They came to Alexandria from another country (II.67) and did not repudiate the faith of their forefathers (I.191). Jewish customs go back to the greatest antiquity (I.1; II.152, 154, 156). So Josephus laid down the principle:

> A wise man's duty is to be scrupulously faithful to the religious laws of his country, and to refrain from the abuse of those of others. (II.144. Trans. Thackeray)[3]

This is demonstrated by the case of Socrates, who was put to death because he stimulated the young men to hold the constitution and laws of their country in contempt; the Athenians did not spare even women, putting Ninus the priestess to death because someone accused her of initiating people into the mysteries of foreign gods, which was forbidden by their law and punished by death (II.264 and 276). Josephus regarded Apion's accusations as "slanders" (I.219, 220, 275, 319; II.4, 30, 49, 290, 295) and "blasphemies" (I.2, 4, 221, 223; II.5, 237).

In *Against Apion*, Josephus could deny that Jews had abandoned their (supposedly Egyptian) traditional worship. But that response was impossible in the case of proselytes who had converted from Greco-Roman paganism to Judaism. Tacitus, *Histories* V.5, shows that the Romans resented the social problems caused by Jewish proselytes:

> For the worst rascals among other peoples, *renouncing their ancestral religions*, always kept sending tribute and contributions to Jerusalem. . . . Those who are converted to their ways follow the same practice [hating other peoples, being immoral, adopting circumcision], and the earliest lesson they receive is to despise the gods, to disown their country, and to regard their parents, children, and brothers as of little account. (My emphasis. Trans. Moore)

Several texts in Philo[4] confirm that Romans resented these converts. He refers to the "incomer" who

> has turned his kinsfolk, who in the ordinary course of things would be his sole confederates, into mortal enemies, by coming as a pilgrim to truth and the honouring of One who alone is worthy of honour, and by leaving the mythical fables and multiplicity of sovereigns, so highly honoured by the parents and grand-parents and ancestors and blood-relations of this immigrant to a better home. (*Special Laws* IV.178. Trans. Colson)

Proselytes were wrenched out of their social milieu.[5]

One rabbinic text shows the same concern for the proselyte. In a beautiful parable, a king takes special care of a wild gazelle which entered his flock of sheep. When asked why, he replies,

> Shall we then not account it as a merit to this one which has left behind the whole of the broad, vast wilderness, the abode of all the beasts, and has come to stay in the

courtyard? In like manner, ought we not to be grateful to the proselyte who has left
behind him his family and his father's house, aye, has left behind his people and all the
other peoples of the world, and has chosen to come to us? (Num. Rab. 8.2. Trans.
Freedman and Simon)[6]

Two prominent women proselytes exemplify this. The first is Ruth, who
told Naomi, "I cannot return to my family and to the idolatrous 'leaven' of my
father's house" (*Ruth Suta* 1.12–18).[7] The second is Asenath,[8] the Egyptian
wife of Joseph. After she fell in love with Joseph, Asenath broke her idols into
fragments and prayed to the God of the Hebrews,

Deliver me, Lord, the desolate, for my family and my mother have denied me, because
I destroyed and broke up their gods, and I am an orphan and desolate, and I have no
other hope save thee, Lord, for you are the father of orphans and champion of the
persecuted and helper of the afflicted. (12.11. Trans. Brooks)

This seems to be a traditional prayer, as it does not fit the context. The
parents' behavior in 20.5–6 contradicts the description of them in the prayer;
they did not reject her.[9] Traditionally, proselytes were "persecuted" and
"afflicted."

The prayer of Asenath is similar to the prayer of Esther.[10] Esther was not
a proselyte, but her situation was similar to Asenath's in that she also had non-
Jewish relatives, in Esther's case her husband (as in 1 Pet 3:1). Esther was
seized with a deathly anxiety and prayed to the God of Israel, "O my Lord,
thou only art our king: help me, who am alone. . . ." (*Additions to Esther*
4:17,1)

There was a prominent tradition in Greek and Roman literature which
dealt with Esther's situation. The woman was expected to accept the religious
customs of her husband.[11] Socrates supposedly said that the wife should
submit to the usages ($\eta\theta\eta$) of the husband, as he submitted to laws of the city
(Stob. IV.23.58). Xenophon, *Concerning Household Management* 7.8, said
that sacrifice and prayer were common to husband and wife in marriage.
There was a succession of Neopythagoreans intensely concerned with laws
and customs. Perictione insisted that a woman venerate the gods by obeying
the laws and sacred institutions of her country (144,5–6 Thesleff). Phintys
(154,6–9 Thesleff) desired that

women should offer frugal sacrifices to the gods, and such as are adapted to her ability;
but she should abstain from the celebration of orgies, and from those sacred rites of the
mother of the gods, which are performed at home. For the common law of the city
ordains that these shall not be performed by women. (Trans. Taylor)

Dionysius Hal. (*Rom. Ant.* II.25.1) stated that Romulus also legislated that "a
woman joined to her husband by a holy marriage should share in all
possessions and sacred rites"; he then specifically stated that this one law
included the assumption that the husbands rule their wives (II.25.4–5). In the
same discussion of the state, Dionysius (II.19) criticized foreign mystery cults,

especially those of Dionysus and Cybele. Likewise, Cicero, *Laws* II.8.19–22, was concerned about the sacrifices of the women and the household slaves: they should worship the gods duly received from their ancestors; they should not be initiated, except into the Greek rites of Ceres according to the custom. One of the most important references is in Plutarch, *Advice to Bride and Groom* 140D. Women were susceptible to Eastern cults, but

> a wife ought not to make friends of her own, but to enjoy her husband's friends in common with him. The gods are the first and most important friends. Therefore it is becoming for a wife to worship and know only the gods that her husband believes in, and to shut the front door tight upon all queer rituals and outlandish superstitions. For with no god do stealthy and secret rites performed by a woman find any favour.[12] (Trans. Babbitt)

This was a severe domestic problem:

> Those who have to go near elephants do not put on bright clothes, nor do those who go near bulls put on red; for the animals are made especially furious by these colours; and tigers, they say, when surrounded by the noise of beaten drums go completely mad and tear themselves to pieces. Since, then, this is also the case with men, that some cannot well endure the sight of scarlet and purple clothes, while others are annoyed by cymbals and drums,[13] what terrible hardship is it for women to refrain from such things, and not disquiet or irritate their husbands, but live with them in constant gentleness? (Ibid., 144 DE)

The situation of the Christian woman in 1 Pet 3:1 could hardly be described more graphically! A husband in this situation would "slander" the cult of Cybele, Dionysus, or Christianity. There must have been psycho-social reasons for a wife deciding to become a member of a foreign, forbidden cult: she thereby insisted that her personality not be swallowed up in that of her husband (or her master). Plutarch's definition of the wife's "gentleness" in this text and the definition of 1 Pet 3:4 differ considerably: for Plutarch it included a rejection of the foreign cult, but for 1 Peter it did not. Plutarch viewed the situation from outside the minority group, 1 Peter from within.[14] In 1 Peter slaves and wives were to remain Christians and to endure suffering (e.g., 1:6; 2:20; 3:17; 4:14, 16). So Christian wives would have been unwilling to conform to the chief demand of the husbands, to give up the foreign cult.[15]

Despite the Greco-Roman attitude, many women became Jewish proselytes.[16] Josephus, *War* II.560–561, asserted that the wives of all the citizens of Damascus had become converts to the Jewish religion. The king's wives brought about the famous conversion of King Izates (*Ant.* XX.34 and 38). The wife of Caesar, Poppaea Sabine, was thought to have been a Jewish Godfearer (*Ant.* XX.8.11; *Life* 3.16). Finally, Acts mentions women proselytes to Judaism (13:15) and converts to Christianity (16:1, 13–14; 17:4, 12).[17]

There are many examples from later Christian history which reveal that conversion caused household problems for slaves and women.

When differences arise in any household between a believer and an unbeliever, an inevitable conflict arises, the unbelievers fighting against the faith, and the faithful refuting their old error and sinful vices. (*Recognitions of Clement* 2:29)[18]

Tertullian, *Apology* 3, says,

Though jealous no longer, the husband expels his wife who is now chaste; the son, now obedient, is disowned by his father who was formerly lenient; the master, once so mild, cannot bear the sight of the slave who is now faithful. (Trans. Glover)

The three pairs in this quotation are the same as those in the household code in Colossians, and the social situation which produced a reference to them is the same as that in 1 Peter. The emperor Julian, *Against the Galileans* 206A, said that Christians were "content if they could delude maidservants and slaves, and through them the women. . . ." It was offensive to the pagan critic Celsus that Christianity was a religion of slaves and the lower classes.[19] He maintained that Christians had

the one possibility to persuade only the simple, proletarian and stupid men, the slaves and women and small children. (in Origen, *Against Celsus* III.44. Trans. Chadwick)

Celsus wondered why the Christian God taught Christians to run away from their masters, from their fathers (VI.53; cp. I.62).

Emperor worship is not mentioned in the texts just quoted, nor is it the problem presupposed by 1 Peter. Rather Christians faced persecution because they worshiped Christ to the exclusion of the Roman gods. They were persecuted "as a Christian" (1 Pet 4:16) and "in the name of Christ" (4:14). The newly Christian slaves and wives refused to worship the gods of their fathers (1:18 and 4:3),[20] and this divided the household. The Christians refused to preserve the religious customs of their ancestors, to perform cultic acts which were central in pagan religion.[21] The result was that Christians were slandered and persecuted.

1 Pet 2:11–12, 15. Pagans glorifying God. 1 Pet 2:11–12 opens a major new section of the letter (see Appendix I). The household code follows immediately after the reference to pagan slanders in these introductory verses, and pagan slanders are still the concern immediately after the code (3:15–16), which suggests that the kind of behavior described in the code has some relation to the slander. Roman society typically suspected foreign, Eastern cults of being associated with sexual immorality, and so Christians are exhorted to "abstain from the passions of the flesh" (2:11) in a context concerned with the opinions of outsiders (cp. 2:15). The description of a Christian woman by Apuleius, *The Golden Ass* IX.14, is instructive:

The baker which bought me was an honest and sober man, but his wife the most pestilent woman in all the world, in so much that he endured with her many miseries and afflictions to his bed and house, so that I myself did secretly pity his estate and bewail his evil fortune: for there was not one single fault that was lacking to her, but all the mischiefs that could be devised had flowed into her heart as into some filthy privy: she was crabbed, cruel, cursed, drunken, obstinate, niggish, covetous in base robberies, riotous in filthy expenses, an enemy to faith and chastity, a despiser of all the gods whom others did honour, one that affirmed that she had instead of our sure religion an only god by herself, whereby inventing empty rites and ceremonies, she deceived all men, but especially her poor husband, delighting in drinking wine, yea early in the morning, and abandoning her body to continual whoredom. (Trans. Gaselee)

If this is a typical reaction to the conversion of a wife to Christianity, exhortations like 1 Pet 2:11 are easy to understand! "Good conduct" and "good deeds" (2:12) were important for the author. 1 Pet 2:14 makes it clear that society and its rulers approved good conduct, in fact, that society *demanded* such conduct, the kind of "submission" described in the code in 1 Peter.

In 1 Pet 2:12 Christians are exhorted ($\pi\alpha\rho\alpha\kappa\alpha\lambda\hat{\omega}$) to good conduct among Gentiles "so that ($\H{\iota}\nu\alpha$) in case they speak against you as wrongdoers ($\kappa\alpha\kappa\sigma\pi\sigma\iota\hat{\omega}\nu$), they may see your good deeds and glorify God on the day of visitation." This clearly supplies the reason for the conduct described in the code which follows.[22] Is the good conduct intended to convert those now slandering the Christians, i.e., how do they "glorify God"? And what or when is the "day of visitation"?

Several commentators[23] understand that pagans watched the Christians' good deeds over a period of time, reflected on them, and converted. An important parallel is Matt 5:16, and Selwyn adds Test. Naphth. 8:4. However, the word "visitation" ($\epsilon\pi\iota\sigma\kappa\sigma\pi\acute{\eta}$), common in the Septuagint, is clearly eschatological in Jer 6:15, 10:15, as is the word "day" in the NT. According to van Unnik, the "day of visitation" refers to Jesus' imminent coming, the Parousia, at which time those now slandering will "glorify God."[24] In 1 Pet 2:12 "the day of visitation" is the equivalent of פקדה יום = the day of judgment (see 1QS 3:14, 18; 4:6, 11, 19, 26, etc.). "Visitation" is also a variant reading in 1 Pet 5:6, and van Unnik suggests that it is the original reading.[25]

Discussing "glorify," van Unnik points especially to 1 Enoch 62–63, which describes the nations at the judgment glorifying God but being condemned (see Rev 11:13). The pagans slandering the Christians will glorify God, in whose service the Christians did their works, in the day of visitation. This interpretation of 2:12 is also most probable because it corresponds to the statement in 2:8 that the pagans are "destined" to be disobedient to the word. Further, it corresponds to Dalton's interpretation of 3:19–20, in which Christ as the new Enoch "proclaims" to the rebellious spirits their own condemnation.[26] The pagans will have to give an account before "the one judging the living and the dead" (4:5). I conclude that there is no reference to the conversion of the pagans in 2:12 but rather to a "doxology of judgment."[27]

A second purpose of the behavior described in the code is clear in 2:15, "by doing good to put to silence the ignorance of foolish men."[28] The purpose was to reduce tension between society and the churches, to stop the slander.

Christians had to conform to the expectations of Hellenistic-Roman society so that society would cease criticizing the new cult. The author of 1 Peter wrote to advise the Christians who were being persecuted about how they might become socially-politically acceptable to their society. The code described the behavior *demanded* by the governor (2:14) even of "aliens." The author was clearly aware, however, that even if his readers conformed socially and politically, their new and different *religious* attitudes might remain unacceptable to society (1:18; 3:13–17; 4:15–16; 5:8).[29]

1 Pet 3:8–9. Christian harmony. 1 Pet 3:8–12 constitutes a summary of the preceding code and stresses harmony in the household. The summary repeats several ideas introduced earlier in the code. First, the exhortation not to return evil for evil (3:9) completes the topos concerning responding to slander with quietness, to be discussed below in the interpretation of 1 Pet 3:4.[30] Second, the same exhortation repeats the instruction to slaves in the code (2.23). Third, the lack of "guile" (3:10d) repeats the exhortation given to slaves (2:22). Fourth, the quotation of Psalm 34 in 1 Pet 3:10–12 stresses "peace" in the household, summarizing the *Haustafel*. In 1 Clement 22 also this OT text is quoted after a household code. Fifth, the exhortation to "unity of spirit" or "harmony" (ὁμόφρονες; 3:8) sums up the exhortation about household relationships. In 1 Peter the harmony sought is primarily domestic harmony between husband, wife, and slaves, not harmony among Christians as in 1 Clement.

The discussion of "harmony" (ὁμόνοια) between husband and wife is an old topos especially important for understanding the household code. Xenophon, *Memorabilia* IV.4.16, said that everywhere in Greece there was a law that the citizen should preserve harmony in obedience to the laws, since the prosperity of the city as of the house depended on such harmony. A fragment of the work *Concerning Harmony* by Antiphon the sophist[31] (5th century B.C.) is concerned chiefly with harmony between husband and wife.

Dio Chrysostom gave four speeches "On Concord" (*Dis.* 38–41).[32] Among his examples of harmony were those of a ship whose sailors must be obedient to the skipper, causing no strife and mutiny (38.14; see 39.6).

> Again, take our households (οἴκων)—although their safety depends not only on the like-mindedness (ὁμοφροσύνη) of master and mistress but also on the obedience of the servants, yet both the bickering of master and mistress and the wickedness of the servants have wrecked many households. . . . The good marriage, what else is it save concord (ὁμόνοια) between man and wife? And the bad marriage, what is it save their discord? Moreover, what benefit are children to parents, when through folly they begin to rebel against them? (38.15–16; see 40.26. Trans. Crosby)

Husbands, wives, and servants are exactly those exhorted in the code in 1 Peter. Dio lists matters which should produce concord between the two cities of Nicomedia and Nicaea:

Besides, you [men of Nicomedia] worship the same gods as they do, and in most cases you conduct your festivals as they do. In fact, you have no quarrel as to your customs (ἐθῶν) either. Yet, though all these things afford no occasion for hostility, but rather for friendship and concord (ὁμόνοια), still we fight. (38:22; see 39.3, 40.28, and esp. 41.10)

This kind of harmony—worshiping the same gods—had been disturbed by the conversion of the slaves and women being addressed in 1 Peter. Hierocles assumes that "harmony" in the house includes both husband and wife being consecrated to the gods (IV.505,5-22 Hense, quoted p. 5 above). The *absolute* harmony typically demanded by a pagan master or husband was *rejected* by the newly converted Christians.

The treatise of the Neopythagorean Perictione in Stobaeus' chapter "On Household Management" (Stob. IV.28.19) is entitled *On the Harmony of a Woman*. It defines a wife's duties in relation to the gods, parents, husband, children, and servants, and it cautions her about luxury and riches. This discussion of her harmony includes the demand that she venerate the gods by "obeying" the laws and sacred institutions of her country (144,5-6 Thesleff). She must conform to her husband's opinion in what pertains to their common life (145,3-5). Those things are to be pleasant and disagreeable to her which are thought so by her husband, unless she is without harmony (145,5-6). From Perictione's viewpoint, the Christian women whose husbands were still pagan would be "without harmony."

Plutarch pictures Philip inquiring about the harmony of the Greeks, but because he himself was at odds with his wife and son, he received the reply:

A glorious thing it is for you Philip to be inquiring about the concord of Athenians . . . while you let your own household (οἰκία) be full of all this quarrelling and dissension. (*How to Tell a Flatterer from a Friend* 70C=179C. Trans. Babbitt)

The orator Gorgias made a speech about concord, but Melanthius said:

This fellow gives us advice about concord, and yet in his own household he has not prevailed upon himself, his wife and maidservant, three persons only, to live in concord. . . . A man therefore ought to have his household well harmonized who is going to harmonize State, Forum and friends. (Plutarch, *Advice to Bride and Groom* 144BC. Trans. Babbitt)

In referring to husband, wife, and slave in the household, this text refers to persons in the same social classes as those addressed in 1 Peter; both Plutarch and 1 Peter think it a duty to live "harmoniously" in such relationships. For Musonius, harmony is an important attribute in a wife (40,26; 90,7 and 16-20 Lutz). "Without harmony of mind and character between husband and wife, what marriage can be good, what partnership advantageous?" (*Or.* XIIIB, *What is the Chief End of Marriage?* 90,13-14 Lutz)

The author's term "harmonious" or "like-minded" in the summary of the code in 1 Peter expresses the purpose of the ethic: slaves and wives converted to Christianity are to maintain harmony in pagan households by remaining submissive to their non-Christian masters and husbands, even if they are harsh.

Tragedy, slander, and suffering resulted nevertheless, for the submission had one qualification which destroyed harmony: the Christian wives and slaves were not submissive in that they refused to worship the gods of their masters and husbands. They rejected the "tradition of the fathers." In this sense Christianity, following Jewish precedent, brought a new understanding of personhood to slaves by teaching that they had a right to choose their own God. A similar right was taken by Christian wives.

1 Pet 3:15. "Be prepared to make a defense." The primary function of the household code in 1 Peter is given by the author's insistence in 3:15 that newly converted slaves and wives be prepared to give a "defense" (ἀπολογία) of their behavior to shame pagan critics. The "defense" referred to concerns "the hope that is in you." Modern persons, misled by contemporary analogies, might think this verse simply calls for rational defense of the kerygma or of the ideas of Christian eschatology, etc. But apologetic in this early period also involved a defense of one's lifestyle, as parallels in Luke-Acts indicate. Paul, "accused for this hope" (Acts 26:7; cp. v. 6), made an apologetic (26:1, 2, 24) speech before King Agrippa. In this apologetic speech, Paul refers to his "manner of life" (26:4) and how he has lived (26:5; cp. vv. 9-11, 19-20). Paul gives two other apologetic speeches as recorded in Acts (see 24:20; 25:11). In one case he claims to have a clear conscience toward God and men (24:16), and in the other case the king was clearly more interested in Paul's actions than in his ideas (25:18-19). Some Christians needed to "apologize" before kings and governors because they had been accused by parents, brothers, kinsmen, and friends (Luke 21:12, 14, 16). In this case, explanation of one's household relationships might well have been involved. Defending one's hope in Roman society meant more than explaining the ideas in the kerygma.

1 Pet 3:15 has its closest parallel in Josephus, *Against Apion* II.147 (see above pp. 54-55, 73, 75-76).The "defense" anticipated in 1 Pet 3:15 would include the ethics of the household code,[33] just as Josephus' "defense" of the Jews involved the presentation of Moses' "constitution" which included "marriage laws" demanding the wife's submissiveness (II.199) and "the law for slaves" (II.215). Josephus' defense is to be understood in relation to Hecataeus' charge that Moses "with respect to marriage . . . saw to it that their customs should differ widely from those of other men" (Diodorus Siculus, *Library of History* 40.3.8) and Tacitus' charge that the Jews engaged in unlawful sexual intercourse (*Histories* V.5). Jews were accused of *reversing* proper relationships: "The Jews regard as profane all that we hold sacred; on the other hand, they permit all that we abhor" (ibid., V.4). They teach proselytes "to despise the gods, to disown their country, and to regard their parents, children, and brothers as of little account" (ibid., V.5). The

Hellenistic Jew Philo did teach proselytes just such behavior (above, p. 83). Epictetus praised Christians for such a reversal of normal social behavior, although he blamed the Epicureans for such antisocial behavior (see above p. 86, n. 18).

In this social-philosophical context, a close parallel to the situation which called forth the domestic code in 1 Peter is found in Julian, *Misopogon*. The basic problem was that the people of Antioch had become Christians and refused to worship the old gods, as had many of the Christians addressed in 1 Peter. This situation prompted the Roman emperor Julian to criticize the city using a "reverse code": they permitted the women to govern themselves, who in turn feared that their children would experience harsh authority; the people of Antioch, i.e. the Christians, began by refusing slavery to the gods, then to the laws, finally to the emperor, the guardian of the laws (355A–357A). Julian used old ideas, as old as Plato (*Rep.* III 701B). The Christians' "atheism" caused Romans to charge the new cult with *reversing* Roman customs, not only with respect to piety, but also with respect to wives, children, and slaves. Although the slave section of the household code was as old as Plato and Aristotle, it was expanded in 1 Peter because the conversion of slaves created an especially intense social problem. Romans were not accustomed to slaves other than Jews who refused to worship the old gods (see p. 69).

Roman reaction to Christian religious customs is reflected in Acts 16:21. After Paul had converted the prominent lady Lydia and cast a demon out of a slave girl (the two classes of persons prominent in the domestic code in 1 Peter), the owners of the formerly-possessed slave girl dragged Paul and Silas before the rulers and charged:

> These men are Jews and they are disturbing our city (πόλιν). They advocate customs (ἔθη) which it is not lawful for us Romans to accept or practice. (Acts 16:20–21)

The "customs" of the city of Rome were described by Dionysius of Halicarnassus, who used the term throughout his description of the Roman constitution.[34]

> And one will see among them, even though their customs are now corrupted (διεφθαρμένων . . . τῶν ἐθῶν), no ecstatic transports, no Corybantic frenzies, no begging under the colour of religion, no bacchanals or secret mysteries, no all-night vigils of men and women together in the temples, nor any other mummery of this kind; but alike in all their words and actions with respect to the gods a reverence is shown such as is seen among neither Greeks nor barbarians. And—the thing which I myself have marvelled at most—notwithstanding the influx into Rome of innumerable nations which are under every necessity of worshiping their ancestral gods according to the customs of their respective countries, yet the city has never officially adopted any of these foreign practices. (II.19.2–3. Trans. Cary. Cp. I.89.4)

Rome did allow some Phrygians to carry Cybele in procession, but no native Roman participated.

So cautious are they about admitting any foreign religious customs (ἔθη) and so great
is their aversion to all pompous display that is wanting in decorum. (II.19.5)

In describing Moses' "constitution," Josephus also used the term
"custom."[35] Both Dionysius and Josephus tended to use the term when there
was a contrast between the customs of two cities or peoples, and this contrast
included customs with respect to the gods. In Josephus this is clear both in
Against Apion II.139, where the Egyptian custom of worshiping the beasts as
gods is ridiculed, and in II.179, where the absence of diversity in Jewish
customs is mentioned, including the absence of contradictory statements
about God.

Seneca (*Ep*. 95.45) mentions Brutus' work *Concerning Duty* with its
precepts to parents, children, and brothers. "Precepts are commonly given as
to how the gods should be worshipped. But let us forbid lamps to be lighted on
the Sabbath, since the gods do not need light, neither do men take pleasure in
soot" (ibid., 95.47). Again, Roman customs of worship excluded foreign
(Jewish) ones; further, "duties" were to be performed toward the gods *and*
parents, children, brothers, etc. As in Hierocles, these religious and social
duties were not separated, as they often are in our secular, Western societies.

Christians were sensitive to outsiders' reactions to their household
customs. Several texts, especially in the Pastorals, reveal this sensitivity:

> Bid the older women likewise to be reverent in behavior . . . , and to train the young
> women to love their husbands and children, to be sensible, chaste, domestic
> (οἰκουργούς), kind, and submissive to their husbands (ὑποτασσομένας τοῖς ἰδίοις
> ἀνδράσιν) in order that the word of God may not be discredited. (Titus 2:3–5; cp.
> 2:8,10)

> So I would have younger widows marry, bear children, rule their households
> (οἰκοδεσποτεῖν), and give the enemy no occasion to revile us. (1 Tim 5:14)

> And thy strife with all, and especially with thy husband, check and restrain as a
> believing woman; lest thy husband, if he be a heathen, be offended by reason of thee
> and blaspheme against God, and thou receive a Woe from God: for, "Woe to them, by
> reason of whom the name of God is blasphemed among the gentiles." (*Didascalia
> Apostolorum* 3 = *Apostolic Constitutions* I.10)[36]

These texts show clearly that the lack of submission of wives to their husbands
would be a source of slander or blasphemy against Christianity. They support
the suggestion that the "apology" anticipated in 1 Pet 3:15 would assure
outsiders that Christians would conform to the kind of behavior in the
household demanded by society, i.e., demanded by masters, husbands, and
governors.

In view of the kind of summary description contained in Heraclitus
Lembus' excerpts of Aristotle's *Constitutions* (above p. 37), it is appropriate
to speak of the domestic code as a brief Christian constitution. That
Christians would outline their constitution to outsiders if asked (1 Pet 3:15)
has its antecedents in Philo, *Apology for the Jews* 7.14, and Josephus, *Against*

Apion II.178, 181.[37] The response in 1 Pet 3:15 differs from the response outlined in the preceding code (2:11-3:12) in that 1 Pet 3:15 assumes a *verbal* response while the code itself involves non-verbal good *conduct* (2:12, 15, 22, 23; 3:1, 9; but cf. 3:6). The constitution, the domestic code, which the Christians would outline to outsiders, just like Josephus' presentation of "Moses'" constitution, has a striking similarity to the relevant sections of the Roman constitution as outlined by Dionysius of Halicarnassus (above pp. 54–55). One purpose of such a presentation of the household code in 1 Peter was acculturation to Roman society.

1 Pet 4:15. Meddling in others' domestic affairs. Christians' ethical concern was one of the sources of the tension with society which resulted in persecution. In 4:15 the author refers to the person who meddles in others' affairs (ἀλλοτριεπίσκοπος).[38] This was an activity commonly practiced by the Cynics. Diogenes came to the Isthmian games "as an observer (ἐπισκοπῶν) of mankind and of men's folly" (Dio Chrysostom, *Dis.* 9.1). The mission of the Cynic is described by Epictetus, *Dis.* III.22.72:

> Where, pray, is this kind [the Cynic], whose duty it is to oversee (ἐπισκοπεῖν) the rest of men; those who have married; those who have had children; who is treating his wife well, and who ill; who quarrels; what household is stable, and what is not; making his rounds like a physician, and feeling pulses?[39] (Trans. Oldfather)

Such an activity naturally met with objections, which Epictetus felt he must overcome. The Cynic, he says, is led by Zeus, so

> that is why the man who is in this frame of mind is neither a busybody (πολυπράγμων) nor a meddler; for he is not meddling in *other people's affairs* when he is *overseeing* the actions of men (οὐ γὰρ τὰ ἀλλότρια πολυπραγμονεῖ, ὅταν τὰ ἀνθρώπινα ἐπισκοπῇ), but these are his proper concern. (III.22.97. My emphasis. Trans. Oldfather)

Zeller noted[40] that precisely the terms in italics above were combined in 1 Pet 4:15, and he suggested that some Christian missionaries had become overly zealous and that society had responded with the objections presupposed by the quotation from Epictetus above. The author of 1 Peter was advising these Christian missionaries to mind their own affairs, not the affairs of others.

The term "busybody" (πολυπράγμων), used by Epictetus, refers to minding others' affairs.[41] According to Plutarch, *On Curiosity* 516E, minding others' domestic affairs was a favorite activity of the busybody:

> Nowadays there are doormen . . . to give warning, so that the stranger might not catch the mistress of the house or the unmarried daughter unawares, or a slave being punished or the maidservants screaming. But it is for these very things that the busybody slips in. (516DE. Trans. Helmbold)

> [The busybody] creeps in, searching out with slanderous intent drunken revels and dances and all-night festivals. (517A)

Such activity led to reviling and abusing each other in the market place
(521E). Such slander typically concerned the wife or the godlessness and
impiety of someone (Lucian, *Slander* 14).[42]

Given the apologetic function of the conduct described in the household
code, i.e., that such behavior is a response to outsiders' criticisms, I suggest
that the "evil speaking" and "minding others' affairs" forbidden to Christians
(2:1 and 4:15) were being practiced also by the pagans toward Christians.
Certain busybodies spoke against (2:12; 3:16), slandered (2:23; 3:9), and
blasphemed (4:4) the Christians' *household* relationships and their impiety,
perhaps even to the governor (2:14; cp. Justin, 2 *Apol.* 2).

*1 Pet 2:14. Governors punish those who do wrong and praise those who
do right.* Submissive behavior was demanded not only by masters and
husbands but was expected by governors. Areius Didymus, Dionysius, and
Seneca most clearly outlined the household code for the Roman imperial age.
They were associated with the Roman aristocracy and with high offices in the
provinces (see pp. 74). The "governors" mentioned in 1 Pet 2:14
demanded such household relationships, for many of them certainly
thought that "the house is like a small city,"[43] that insubordination in
one led to insubordination in the other.

Therefore, van Unnik goes too far in suggesting that "we have to leave
out the whole thought of state action."[44] The possibility of opposition to
Christians by the state did exist. Precisely "statesmen" were concerned with
this ethic (Dionysius Hal., *Rom. Ant.* II.18.1; 24.2). Caesar sent governors to
punish "evildoers"—those slaves and wives who were not submissive to their
masters and husbands—but to "praise those doing good" (1 Pet 2:14).[45]
Elsewhere I have argued that the text in Dionysius of Halicarnassus has the
form of an encomium; Dionysius is *eulogizing* Rome because her constitution
places wives in their properly subordinate role. Similarly, Libanius (*Or.*
XI.154 and 151) in his encomium of Antioch praises the common people
because they show obedience toward their superiors. Josephus in his
encomium of the Jews constantly insists that Moses' laws foster "obedience"
(*Against Apion* II.158, 193, 220, 225, 235, 293). It was common for Hellenistic
rhetoricians and for the governors trained by them to "praise those doing
good" (1 Pet 2:14), to praise those who were properly obedient. The Christians
presented the domestic code as their defense. The examples just given from
Hellenistic rhetoric suggest that the governor's praise which they hoped to
receive might also be given in the form of the Aristotelian topos on the
household. Christians hoped the governor would praise them for being
obedient.

The "defense" is to be given "to anyone who asks" (3:15), so this verse
does not specifically contemplate a legal defense before a governor. But this
exhortation is supported by the reference to Christ which follows. Christ was
"put to death in the flesh" (3:18), an expression which "possibly [puts] some
accent on His judicial trial and condemnation" (cp. 4:6).[46] Further, the author

probably intended a parallel between the Christian who was to give an "account" (λόγον; 3:15) to the pagans and the "account" (λόγον; 4:5) to be given in the future by the pagans "to the one prepared to judge the living and the dead," a phrase which has an unmistakably judicial flavor. I conclude that the code in 1 Peter exhorted Christians to the kind of "good conduct" which a Roman governor would have approved. However, the writer of 1 Peter seems to view the judicial trial of Christians as a possibility, not as a present reality.

Several texts refer to or hint at civil disturbances directed against Christians in Asia Minor before the end of the first century: Rev 6:9, 13:7, 17:6, 20:4; Ignatius, *Magn.* 8; *Rom.* 5.[47] The tension between Roman society and Christians resulted in the latter being persecuted. The author of 1 Peter exhorts (2:11; 5:12) Christians who are in the midst of "suffering" (2:19, 20, 21, 23; 3:14, 17, 18; 4:1, 15, 19; 5:10).[48] The combination of the words "blessed," "be glad," "righteous," "rejoice," and "to be reproached" in both 3:14 and 4:13-14 indicate that the words of Jesus in Matt 5:10-11 are used in 1 Peter to encourage these Christians in their suffering.[49] They are "slandered" (2:23, 3:9) and "spoken against" (2:12, 3:16; cp. Matt 5:11). The author is concerned about those who are "disobedient" to the word (2:8; 3:1, 20; 4:17). Various "trials" (1:6, 4:12) are mentioned.[50] Finally, fear is mentioned (3:6, 14; cp. Isa 8:12). The women (3:6) and the readers (3:14) are exhorted not to be afraid of those who might injure (3:13)[51] or slander (3:16) them, but rather to fear God (2:17-18; cp. 3:14).

There is an old debate about the date and nature of the persecutions referred to in these passages: are they persecutions, as Beare[52] thinks, initiated by the Roman emperor and his governor, or on the contrary, as Selwyn suggests,

> persecutions which are spasmodic and flare up suddenly, promoted now by Jews, now by Gentiles . . . passing through various forms ranging from pure mob-law to the tribunals of Caesar's representatives, issuing in stoning, scourging, imprisonment, sometimes death.[53]

I disagree with Beare. There is no allusion in 1 Peter to state persecution because Christians refused to worship the emperor. Rather, certain slaves and wives converted to Christianity; therefore, persons in Roman society reacted by accusing them of being immoral, perhaps seditious, and certainly insubordinate. The author of 1 Peter directed the Aristotelian household duty code to this tense situation.

B. Let Wives Be Submissive (1 Peter 3:1-6)

I will describe the form of the code in 1 Peter, compare this with the Aristotelian form, and then discuss 1 Pet 3:1-6 in detail.

The code in 1 Peter is not as complete as the form used in Colossians and Ephesians,[54] where three pairs are exhorted: wives and husbands, children and fathers, slaves and masters. 1 Peter follows this pattern only in the case of wives and husbands (3:1-7). Only slaves are exhorted (2:18-25), not masters, and the children-father section is omitted. In the one instance of a pair in 1 Peter, wives and husbands are exhorted with respect to their relationship with each other. Slaves are exhorted about their relationship to their masters. The exhortation to husbands in 1 Peter is so short because it is not concerned with suffering, the social problem which the rest of the code addresses.[55] The primary concern is to instruct Christian slaves and wives about relationships to non-Christian members of their households, pagan masters and husbands. The code in 1 Peter has features not present in the pattern in Colossians and Ephesians. It is introduced by an exhortation to submit "to every human institution" (κτίσει; 2:13),[56] and it is closed by an injunction to "all of you" (3:8-9).

In Colossians the social classes are addressed in the order wives-children-slaves, but in 1 Peter first the slaves, then the wives are addressed. Danker explains this by noting that 1 Pet 2:17 has altered Prov 24:21 in view of Mal 1:14; fear is reserved for God. This does not exclude the son's honor of his father and the slave's fear of his master (Mal 1:6; 1 Pet 2:18). 1 Pet 2:16 refers to "slaves of God," not surprising in view of the stress in Mal 3:17, 18, 24 (4:4) that Israel is God's slave. Danker concludes, "It is perhaps with this in mind that 1 Pet 2:18 begins the 'Haustafel' with directions to slaves."[57]

The codes in Colossians and 1 Peter have several striking differences from the Aristotelian topos. First, the concern for money, for household income, is dropped. Aristotle himself said they sometimes were discussed separately (*Pol.* I 1253b 12-14; also Seneca, *Ep.* 94.1-2). And in the late first century B.C., Philodemus rejected the Aristotelian discussion of "how to live well at home," instead concentrating on how to use and keep one's property (see above p.40). The NT authors take the other option, discussing only household relationships. One reason for this in the case of 1 Peter is that the slaves and wives had little control over household income. Further, for the author of 1 Peter, the relevant sections of the topos concerned precisely "how to live well at home," i.e., how Christian slaves should relate to pagan masters and how Christian wives should relate to their pagan husbands.

Second, Aristotle mentioned masters, husbands, and fathers *before* slaves, wives, or children (*Pol.* I 1253b 6-8; cp. *NE* VIII 1160b 25, 29, 33; *MM* I 1194b 5-29), and he addressed only the male—the master, husband, and father. In the NT, however, the wives are addressed, and this is done before the exhortation to husbands. Slaves are addressed before masters in Colossians (masters are not exhorted in 1 Peter). The NT writers emphasize the subordinate members who were in a difficult social situation.[58] But even this has its antecedent in Dionysius Hal., *Rom. Ant.* II.25.4, precisely in a context where the influx into Rome of strange, Eastern religions was a problem (II.19). Slaves and wives are addressed first by these early Christian moralists because they were the focus of an intense social problem between the church and Roman society. Romans frowned on their wives and slaves being seduced by bizarre foreign cults, and this led the author of 1 Peter to address the household code to those who were the focus of the tension.

Third, the NT writers dropped the discussion of the city, which had been prominent in Aristotle and Areius Didymus. Christians were concerned with the "house."

1 Pet 3:1a. "Wives." In 1 Pet 3:1-6, vv.1-2 are the basic exhortation, vv. 3-4 have a topos on adornment, and vv. 5-6 give an example. Schroeder[59] observes that within the domestic codes in the NT, exhortations to each social group generally have four parts: (a) address, (b) exhortation, (c) connecting word, (d) rationale; for example in 1 Pet 3:1, (a) wives,[60] (b) be submissive to your own husbands, (c) so that (d) some, though they are disobedient . . . , may be won. The direct, collective address of various classes is the rule in Colossians, Ephesians, and 1 Peter, although not in 1 Tim 2:8-15, 6:1-10, or Titus 2:1-10.[61] An address is also common in Stoic sources and occurs in contexts in which a list of duties is given (e.g., Epictetus, *Dis.* III.7.21). But in Stoic sources, the man is addressed and told how to relate to his wife. Neither the woman nor the child is exhorted, and Epictetus, at least, never refers to slaves in such contexts, though he himself was a former slave.[62] Marcus Aurelius Antonius, *Meditations* V.31, and ps.-Plutarch, *The Education of Children* 7E, speak of slaves but not of how they are to act.[63] Even ps.-Phocylides only mentions slaves and children; however, he does exhort the wife to love her husband (*Maxims* 195) and not to betray him (177).

In Platonic and Neopythagorean literature there is a tradition of ethical exhortation to wives. Timaeus presents Pythagoras as a teacher of married women, instructing them in proper behavior.[64] Iamblichus, *Life of Pythagoras* 54-57, amplifies Pythagoras' speech to wives. Callicratidas (*On the Happiness of Households* 105,20-22 Thesleff) gives some reflections which are closely related to 1 Pet 3:1. Perictione (*On the Harmony of a Woman* 142,17-145,26 Thesleff) discusses duties of women, as does Phintys (*Concerning the Temperance of a Woman* 151,18-154,11 Thesleff). The third chapter in Bryson, *Concerning Household Management*, gives a full list of duties of a wife, especially stressing that she must be submissive to her husband. The letter of Theano to Nicostrata (115,24-116,17 Thesleff) is concerned with proper conduct of the wife toward the husband. Similar material is found in Plutarch, *Advice to Bride and Groom* 138B-146A, as well as in Porphyry, *To Marcella*.

1 Pet 3:1a. "Be submissive." The participle in the exhortation has imperative force, an unusual construction in Greek. David Daube[65] explains that three-fourths of the Tannaitic laws are so formulated, and Schroeder[66] adds the early example of IQS 1:18ff. The participle never attained the full strength of an imperative but rather had the character of describing what should be. Imperatives occur in the duty lists in Epictetus, the most interesting being *Dis.* III.21.5 and *Manual* 30, which call on persons in a natural relationship to "endure revilings." However, these imperatives are not participles.

Goppelt notes the following contrast: the Stoic duty list occurs in the diatribe, but the NT domestic code is given as the apodictic law of God.[67] Hellenistic Judaism used the imperative in duty lists more commonly than the Stoics; for example, ps.-Phocylides gives commands and prohibitions to man and wife with the imperative (*Maxims* 176, 179, 180, 195, etc.) and the subjunctive with μή (175, 177, etc.). Philo, *Decalogue* 165–167, does not use the imperative, but he describes the ethic as a command drawn from the fourth commandment. Goppelt concludes that the formulation of the domestic code as apodictic imperative is due to the OT and Jewish style, which is confirmed, he thinks, by the use of the imperative participle.[68] This change in style is a basic change in the meaning of the ethic.[69] The Stoic wise man developed himself through these relationships in a manner that corresponded with reason while the Christian obeyed the apodictic commands of God.

"Be submissive" might be viewed as the superscript of the whole code (2:13, 18; 3:1, 5; cp. 5:5). The root is used 31 times in the Septuagint, the strongest idea being that all things are subject to God. Even Antiochus finally admitted that "it is right to be subject to God" (2 Macc 9:12). David submitted only to God (Ps 61:2, 6 [62:1, 5]). The term is also used in reference to submission to a human ruler: Judas defeated Antiochus, who then submitted to him (2 Macc 13:23). All Israel obeyed Solomon and the leaders submitted to him (1 Chr 29:23–24). God "subdued" all things under man (Ps 8:7 [6]), a text cited four times in the NT (1 Cor 15:27–28, Phil 3:21, 1 Pet 3:22, Heb 2:8). However, the verb never describes the relation of wife-husband, slave-master, or children-father in the Septuagint.

Epictetus subordinates everything else to one's own moral choice (*Dis.* II.10.1). The experience of desiring something not under one's own control makes one neither faithful nor free, and even leads a person to "subordinate" himself to others (I.4.19), a very negative result for Epictetus. The following passages are close to 1 Peter:

> The good and excellent man must, therefore, inquire into all these things, before he subordinates (ὑποτέταχεν) his own will to his who administers the universe, precisely as good citizens submit to the law of the state (τῷ νόμῳ τῆς πόλεως). (I.12.7. Trans. Oldfather)

One ought to be submissive to the laws of God, not those of Masurius and Cassius (IV.3.12; cp. IV.24.65). Epictetus, the self-sufficient Stoic, is cautious about submitting to another man, even the governor of the city, while 1 Pet 2:13–14 demands exactly such submission.

There are two texts which stress that the woman should "submit" to her husband.[70] Alexander told his mother, "It is proper for the wife to be submissive to her own husband" (πρέπον γάρ ἐστι γυναικὶ τῷ ἰδίῳ ἀνδρὶ ὑποτάσσεσθαι), despite the fact that Philip had just wronged her (ps.-Callisthenes, *A Narrative, Remarkable and Really Marvelous, of the Lord of the World, Alexander the King* I.22.19–20, from the first century B.C.). And Plutarch, *Advice to Bride and Groom* 142E (late first century A.D.), affirms:

So is it with women also; if they subordinate themselves to their husbands (ὑποτάττουσαι μὲν γὰρ ἑαυτὰς τοῖς ἀνδράσιν), they are commended, but if they want to have control (κρατεῖν), they cut a sorrier figure than the subjects of their control. And control ought to be exercised by the man over the woman, not as the owner has control of a piece of property, but, as the soul controls the body, by entering into her feelings and being knit to her through goodwill. (Trans. Babbitt)

The culture demanded this relationship between husband and wife; this hierarchical relationship was not a Christian creation.[71] (See Appendix V.)

1 Pet 3:1b. Those disobedient to the word. This reference to pagan husbands should be understood against the social background in which a wife was expected to accept the customs and religious rites of her husband. One may assume that on some occasions this disobedience to the word was more than passive disbelief. Some husbands were almost certainly among those actively disobedient, those slandering the Christians.[72] Both the verb (Acts 19:9) and the participle (Rom 15:31; Acts 14:2) are used elsewhere to describe the activity of those who actively opposed the preaching (see Luke 21:16).

1 Pet 3:1c. "Without a word." The woman is to remain "without a word" (ἄνευ λόγου). When Aristotle discussed the virtues appropriate to husbands and wives and the subordination of the latter, he noted that the poet said of the women, "Silence gives grace to woman" (*Pol.* I 1260a 31). By being silent, the wife would appear *virtuous* to her husband. The behavior of the Christian wife in 1 Pet 3:1 was very different from that of Xanthippe (Plutarch, *How to Profit by One's Enemies* 90E). According to Plutarch,

Pheidias made the Aphrodite of the Eleans with one foot on a tortoise, to typify for womankind keeping at home and keeping silence. For a woman ought to do her talking either to her husband or through her husband, and she should not feel aggrieved if, like the flute-player, she makes a more impressive sound through a tongue not her own. (*Advice to Bride and Groom* 142D; cp. 138D. Trans. Babbitt)[73]

There is a play on the term "word" (λόγος) in 1 Pet 3:1. The wives are to remain silent, "without a word," so that the husbands "disobedient to the word" may be converted. By being silent, perhaps not verbalizing *the* word (the gospel) to resistant husbands, the wives would appear *virtuous* to them (again see Aristotle, *Pol.* I 1260a 20–33). This virtue might attract the husbands to Christ.

1 Pet 3:1c. "By the behavior of their wives . . . they may be won." Through a wife who was submissive, quiet, and chaste, the disobedient husband might "be gained," i.e., converted.[74] The idea of conversion by one's behavior is also found in Musonius, *Must One Obey One's Parents under All Circumstances? (Or.* XVI). The question discussed is whether a son should obey a father who insists that his son should not study philosophy. Musonius gives an example of a son who refused to obey the immoral command of a father, then asks, "Should we say that he was disobedient (ἀπειθές) or that he was showing purity of character?" (83,8 Hense; 102,10–11 Lutz). Certainly disobedience is a term of reproach (λοιδορία; 83,10 Hense; 102,12 Lutz), but

refusing to do what one ought not do merits praise rather than blame (οὐκ
ὄνειδος, ἀλλ᾿ ἔπαινος; 83,11 Hense; 102,13 Lutz), whether one's father or the
archon or even the tyrant orders something wrong.

> Now if your father, knowing nothing about the subject, should forbid you who had
> learned and comprehended what philosophy is to study philosophy, would you be
> bound to heed him, or would you not rather be obligated to teach him better
> (μεταδιδακτέον), since he is giving bad advice? That seems to me to be the answer.
> Perhaps by using reason alone (λόγῳ μόνῳ) one might persuade his father to adopt
> the attitude he ought in regard to philosophy if the father's disposition is not too
> obstinate. If, however, he should not be persuaded by argument (μὴ πείθοιτο τῷ
> λόγῳ) and would not yield, yet even then the conduct (ἀλλὰ τά γε ἔργα) of his son
> will win him over if his son is truly putting his philosophy into practice. For as a
> student of philosophy he will certainly be . . . most well-behaved (κοσμιώτατος) and
> gentle (πρᾳότατος). . . . He will control his tongue . . . and he will stand fast in the
> face of danger. (85,15–86,8 Hense; 104,9–21 Lutz).

> Your father forbids you to study philosophy. . . . If you obey your father, you will
> follow the will of a man; if you choose the philosopher's life, the will of God. (86,19 and
> 87,8–10 Hense; 104,30 and 104,37–106,1 Lutz)

Gentleness and control of the tongue characterize the conduct which might
convert the father.

Outsiders also observe (ἐποπτεύσαντες; 1 Pet 3:2; cp. 2:12) the good
conduct, although the response expected in 3:1 is different from that in 2:12.
Much of the conduct urged in the letter was directed not to fellow Christians
but to those outsiders.

In one passage in Epictetus, the term "conduct" (ἀναστροφή) refers to
"proper relations" with associates (Dis. I.22.13). According to another
passage in Epictetus, Socrates, who was offered acquittal if he would cease
holding philosophical discussions with the young, replied,

> You make yourselves ridiculous by thinking that, if your general had stationed me at
> any post, I ought to hold and maintain it and choose rather to die ten thousand times
> than to desert it, but if God has stationed us in some place and in some manner of life
> (ἀναστροφῇ) we ought to desert that. (I.9.24. Trans. Oldfather)

For Epictetus, God (nature) calls human beings to live in certain relationships.

The word "conduct" became a familiar term in Jewish catechetical
teaching, e.g. Tobit 4:14, "Be disciplined in all your conduct" (cp. Aristeas
252). Christian catechetical instruction took over this word to denote the kind
of conduct it inculcated (Didache 3.9, Barnabas 19.6; both are parts of the
"two ways" document). Some texts associate conduct with a corresponding
reputation. Eleazar maintained excellent conduct (καλλίστης ἀναστροφῆς;
2 Macc 6:23) from childhood to old age and became a martyr, an example of
one who refused to go over to an alien religion. Paul expected that his readers
would have heard of his "conduct when in the Jewish religion" (ἀναστροφήν
ποτε ἐν τῷ Ἰουδαϊσμῷ; Gal 1:13).

There is a tremendous stress placed upon doing good in 1 Peter (2:15,20; 3:6, 17; see 2:14; 4:19; 3:11, 13). Such good *conduct* ("without a word") is an apologetic response to the slanderers of Christians. The "chaste conduct" of the wives (3:2) should be related to the observation in 2:14 that the governor praises those who "do good." Given the omnipresent suspicion in Roman society that foreign cults were sexually immoral, the author cautioned Christians about "fleshly lusts" in the introduction to the code (2:11, cp. 2:16). Those speaking against the Christians as evildoers (2:12) would have used the common charge of immorality. And the *state* punished such immorality in the case of the Bacchanalia.

1 Pet 3:3–4. Not outward adorning but a gentle and quiet spirit. 1 Pet 3:3–4 stresses that proper conduct is not manifested in the external wearing of clothes but in a meek and quiet spirit (cp. the parallel in 1 Tim 2:9–11). This is a typical contrast. The Neopythagorean Phintys, *On the Temperance of a Woman*, insisted that a woman's garments should be white and simple; she should not decorate herself with gold and emeralds, for they are very expensive and exhibit pride and arrogance. She should adorn herself through modesty rather than through art (κοσμὲν δὲ μᾶλλον αὐτὰν αἰσχύνᾳ; 153,15–28 Thesleff). Another Neopythagorean, Perictione (*On the Harmony of a Woman* 143,10–14 Thesleff), legislated that the woman must be moderate with respect to nutriment, clothes, bathing, anointing, dressing the hair, and in wearing gold and jewels, for sumptuous things dispose women to be guilty of every crime and to be unjust to their husband's bed. For the beauty produced by prudence (κάλλος γὰρ τὸ ἐκ φρονήσιως) and not by these things pleases women who are well born (143,26–28 Thesleff). Musonius had typical ideas on extravagance with respect to food, clothing, shelter, and furnishings in the house (cp. *Or.* XVIIIA–XX). For example:

> . . . the best lawgivers—and I think first of all Lycurgus, who drove extravagance (πολυτέλειαν) out of Sparta and substituted frugality, who preferred a life of deprivation as a means of producing courage to a life of excess, and who did away with luxury as a corrupting influence and considered the will to bear hardships the salvation of the state. (XX,112,10–16 Hense; 126,4–8 Lutz)

In *Or.* III, *That Women Too Should Study Philosophy*, he said,

> In the first place, a woman must be a good housekeeper. . . . But above all a woman must be chaste and self-controlled; she must, I mean, be pure in respect of unlawful love, exercise restraint in other pleasures, not be a slave to desire, not be contentious, not lavish in expense (πολυτελῆ), not extravagant in dress. (10,2–4 and 11–14 Hense; 40,10–11 and 17–20 Lutz)[75]

The austere dress recommended in 1 Pet 3:3–4 would be a great contrast with the practices in the cult of Artemis of Ephesus or with the cult of Isis. Xenophon of Ephesus, *Anthia and Habrocomas* I.11.2–6, describes a procession at a feast of Artemis in elaborate detail, in which "every maiden

was adorned as for her lover" (4). Xenophon describes how beautiful they
were, noting their braided hair and purple chiton, which made them erotically
attractive (5–6). Among the elements so offensive to husbands according to
Plutarch, *Advice to Bride and Groom* 144DE, were precisely such bright
clothes in the cult. Also in the cult of Isis, the braiding of hair was especially
important. Apuleius, *The Golden Ass* II.8–9, concludes, "If her hair be not
curiously set forth, she cannot seem fair."[76]

I find no polemic against these cults in the text of 1 Pet 3:3–4. Rather in
1 Peter the common contrast between the external adornment of a woman
and her inner character is used, and an eschatological context is added. The
"decoration of gold" disparaged in 3:3 takes on added meaning in light of 1:7,
where there is a similar contrast: Christians' faith is "more precious" than
"gold which is perishing." In 3:4 the adjective "very precious" (πολυτελές)
does not modify "gold," as it would normally, but the "gentle and quiet spirit."
This "spirit" is "imperishable" (3:4), an eschatological contrast.

Quietness as a Response to Slander. The phrase "meek and quiet spirit"
(πραέως καὶ ἡσυχίου πνεύματος; 3:4,. cp. 3:16) further supports the
suggestion that the husbands who were "disobedient to the word" were among
those slandering the Christians. A topos dealt with this situation: slander was
to be met with quietness (see above pp. 99–100 on Musonius, *Or.* XVI). In
Musonius, *Will the Philosopher Prosecute Anyone for Personal Injury?* (*Or.*
X), the verb "to slander" (λοιδορεῖν) is used six times and "to suffer"
(πάσχειν) twice. The ones who are slandered and suffer "will easily and
silently (πράως καὶ ἡσύχως) bear what has happened" (54,10 Hense; 78,10
Lutz).

Examples were often used to illustrate quiet response to slander. In *Or.*
X, Musonius notes that Socrates was ridiculed by Aristophanes but was not
angry (54,11–13 Hense; 78,12–14 Lutz). Phocion's wife was reviled, but when
the repentant slanderer asked his forgiveness, Phocion replied, "But my wife
has suffered nothing at your hands . . ." (55,7–8 Hense; 78, 20–21 Lutz). In
fact, many others might be mentioned who "very meekly" (πάνυ πράως) bore
their wrong (55,14 Hense; 78,26 Lutz). In this action they were correct, "for to
scheme how to bite back the biter and to return evil for evil (ἀντιποιήσει
κακῶς τὸν ὑπάρξαντα) is the act not of a human being but of a wild beast
which is incapable of reasoning . . ." (55,15–56,3 Hense; 78,26–29 Lutz).

This same topos was used by Plutarch, *How to Profit by One's Enemies*:

Silence cannot under any circumstances be called to an accounting . . . and in the
midst of reviling (λοιδορίαις) it is dignified and Socratic, or rather Heraclean, if it be
true that Heracles "Not so much as to a fly gave heed to words of hatred." Indeed there
is nothing more dignified and noble than to maintain a calm demeanour (ἡσυχία)
when an enemy reviles (λοιδοροῦντος) one, "passing by a man's scoffs. . . ." But far
more important is the practice. If you once acquire the habit of bearing an enemy's
abuse in silence, you will very easily bear up under a wife's attack when she rails (κακῶς
λεγούσης) at you. (90D. Trans. Babbitt)

An example follows: Socrates bore with Xanthippe, who was irascible and acrimonious. So one should "even forego taking vengeance on an enemy when he offers a good opportunity." (90F)

> But in case a man shows compassion for an enemy in affliction . . . , I say that whosoever does not feel affection for such a man because of his kindliness, or does not commend (ἐπαινεῖ) his goodness, "hath a black heart forged . . . from steel." (90F)[77]

There is a relevant story in b. Šabb. 31a and 'Abot R. Nat., chap. 15.[78] Two defiant heathen came before Shammai in succession with offers to convert but were rejected with scorn; when they came before Hillel, he convinced them with learned answers that they should be more submissive. A third heathen came to Shammai with the request that he be converted in order to become high priest and was shoved away; on applying to Hillel, he received a learned response and came to his senses.

> Thereupon the proselyte went to Shammai and reproached him for not explaining the situation to him, and exclaimed to Hillel: "O gentle Hillel, blessings rest on thy head! for thou broughtest me nigh under the wings of the Shekinah!"

A conclusion was added to the story only in b. Šabb. The three converts ultimately met and declared, "Shammai's irascibility almost drove us from the world; Hillel's gentleness brought us nigh under the wings of the Shekinah."[79]

The last story as well as Musonius XVI (discussed above, pp. 99–100) suggest that gentleness helped in conversion. It was this "conduct" through which the husbands might "be gained" (1 Pet 3:1). The above texts support (although they do not necessitate) the suggestion that such conduct was necessary because the "disobedient" husbands were among those "slandering" the Christians. The wife was to respond with quietness. 1 Pet 3:9 in the summary of the code further supports the suggestion. When a wife reacted to her own husband's slander with quietness, only he with a heart forged from steel would fail to praise her goodness (Plutarch, *How to Profit by One's Enemies* 90F). This is precisely the argument of 1 Pet 2:15; 3:13, 16.

A theological rationale is added to this common topos: such a spirit is "precious before God" (3:4). The slaves' suffering is also "pleasing to God" (2:20). Those suffering according to the will of God are to commit their souls to a faithful creator in doing good (4:19).

1 Pet 3:5–6. "As Sarah obeyed Abraham." It was customary to add an example of quiet conduct in response to slander (Musonius, *Will the Philosopher Prosecute Anyone for Personal Injury?* X; Plutarch, *How to Profit by One's Enemies* 90F; Philo, *On Dreams* II.89–90; *On Creation* 84–85; *Every Good Man is Free* 108). In 1 Peter Sarah is an example of this "adorning" (3:3 and 5) with a quiet spirit and of submission to her husband (3:5).

Gen 18:12, "calling him lord," and Ps 34:15b, "seek peace." Sarah obeyed Abraham, calling him "lord" in Gen 18:12.[80] This text has an interesting

history of interpretation. In *Sifre* to Num 6:26, 42 (12b), it is used to interpret
the important blessing in Num 6:26.

> ". . . and give you peace." By your entering peace, by your leaving peace, peace with
> every man. R. Hananja, the captain of the priests, [shortly before 70] said, "'and give
> you peace' in your house. . . ."[81] Great is peace,[82] for (on account of it, God) changed
> the remark of Sarah. For it says, "for I am old." (Gen 18:13)

The meaning of the last part of the quotation is clarified by the later form of
the tradition[83] in *Midrash Rabbah* to Lev 9:9 (111b):

> Bar Kappara said three things: Bar Kappara said: Great is peace, for the Scriptures
> reported in the Torah a prevarication which was used in order to maintain peace
> between Abraham and Sarah. This is proved by what is written, "And Sarah laughed
> within herself, saying: . . . and my master is old" (Gen 18:12); but [when He repeated
> this] to Abraham, He said: [Sarah said]: "And I am old" (Gen 18:13).

Bacher noted[84] that this saying came from the school of Ishmael, which means
that it probably came either from Ishmael himself (c. 135 A.D.) or from one of
his two students, Josiah and Jonathan. Bar Kappara (c. 220 A.D.) was known
to have passed on traditions from this school, specifically from Jonathan.[85]
Such interpretations were often paraenetic.[86] One of the anonymous
traditions (the fourth out of the twenty) which follows in *Sifre Num.* is
attributed to Ishmael in *Midrash Rabbah* to Lev 9:9:

> R. Ishmael taught: Great is peace, for even of the Great Name, written though it be in
> sanctity, did the Holy One, blessed be He, say that it may be blotted out in water (Num
> 5:23) for the purpose of making peace between husband and wife.[87]

Gen 18:12-13 was used to stress the importance of peace between husband
and wife by the middle of the second century A.D. The use of Gen 18:12 in 1 Pet
3:6 does not exhibit the wit of the rabbis, but the same text in 1 Peter stresses
the hierarchical, peaceful relationships in the household.

Even if the citation of Gen 18:12 in 1 Pet 3:6 reflects a rabbinic
interpretation of that text, the method of exegesis differs! Or better, the
method of interpretation in 1 Peter comes closer to Rabbi Akiba's in ignoring
the context than it does to Rabbi Ishmael's insistence on retaining the
meaning of the context. Unlike Ishmael's interpretation, where it remains
clear that Sarah insulted Abraham, the interpretation in 1 Pet 3:6 picks out
one word, "lord," and concludes that Sarah is a pattern for "obedience."

Both the summarizing exhortation to "harmony" (1 Pet 3:8) and the
concluding citation of Psalm 34 correspond to the author's interpretation of
Gen 18:12. An important exhortation in Psalm 34 is "seek peace" (Ps 34:15b;
1 Pet 3:11b). This same phrase is cited in Heb 12:14, an exhortation also
addressed to a persecution situation.[88] Strack-Billerbeck[89] cite *m. 'Abot* 1.12
(Hillel) and *'Abot R. Nat.* 12 (R. Simeon b. Eleazar, c. 190 A.D.), which show a
similar stress on the phrase.

I conclude that both prooftexts were used by the author of 1 Peter to stress the importance of Christians seeking peace and harmony in their household relationships and with society, an interpretation which corresponds to the function of the code as a whole (cp. 2:15–16).

Sarah was also the mother of the women proselytes,[90] and winning converts was the purpose of the women's submission given in 1 Pet 3:1. In fact, Sarah assisted Abraham in advancing from the inferior creeds of Chaldea to the vision and knowledge of God. Philo allegorizes Sarah's gift of Hagar to Abraham (Gen 16:3); this means that Abraham first had to do preliminary studies: grammar, geometry, and music, as recommended by Sarah, before he could progress to philosophy and the study of the highest virtue (*Preliminary Studies* 71–82, 88). Sarah helped Abraham in his progress toward philosophy, which "teaches us the control of the belly and the parts below it, and control also of the tongue" (ibid., 80), which is close to the task of the wives addressed in 1 Peter. Philo also contrasts the wife of Potiphar with Sarah, the former being an example of vice, the latter of paramount virtue (*Allegorical Interpretation* III.236–245). Abraham is persuaded by Sarah when she gives him paraenesis (ibid., 244). Sarah recommends that Abraham take up preliminary studies and sojourn in the schools until he can apply himself to virtue (ibid.).

"In all that Sarah saith to thee listen to her voice" (Gen. xxi.12). . . . For if we choose to hearken to all that virtue recommends, we shall be happy. (ibid., 245)

By obeying their husbands, that is, by being virtuous women as that was understood in the Greek world, the wives addressed in 1 Peter hoped to lead their husbands to virtue and to God.[91]

1 Pet 3:6c. "Let nothing terrify you." Sarah is an example of fearlessness (3:6; Philo, *Abraham* 205–207; *Special Laws* II.54–55). Some philosophers taught that the wife must fear the husband (Xenophon, *Concerning Household Management* 7.25; ps.-Aristotle, *Concerning Household Management* III.144.2). Asenath's fear came close to that insisted on by Xenophon. 1 Pet 3:6 teaches that wives must fear God (cp. 2:17; 3:2?) and not be terrified of those in house or city who oppose their faith (cp. 3:14).

The goal of the wife's behavior as stated in 3:1 is missionary: the author of 1 Peter hoped that the wives' conduct would convert their husbands. But the last phrase in the pericope, encouraging the wives not to be terrified, shows that the purpose of the conduct is also apologetic. The exhortations in this pericope address the same situation as the rest of the letter: Christians may be or perhaps already are being persecuted. They are to conduct themselves toward outsiders so that they will be praised, even by the governor (2:14). If that fails (3:13–14), they are not to be afraid (3:6 and 14) but to deliver themselves to the faithful creator (4:19) whose judgment of the world has already begun.[92]

C. Other Proposed Functions of the Household Code

1. Paraenesis (Dibelius and Weidinger)

Some modern interpreters of the NT codes have argued that these texts are general ethical exhortations not addressed to any specific situation. However, even Dibelius conceded that the occurrence of the codes in some letters and variations among the codes indicate where such advice was needed in early Christianity.[93] The argument that the ethic of the household code served as an apologetic to Roman society is quite different from the function suggested by Dibelius. He maintained that because the imminent hope of the parousia had faded, the church acculturated to Roman society. However, in 1 Peter there is still hope for the imminent coming of the glory of the Lord (4:13; cp. 1:6, 13, 17; 4:5, 7). In fact, there is a close connection between the present persecution and the approaching final judgment (4:17–19).[94] So the fading of a futurist eschatology could not have been the motive for the adoption of the code in 1 Peter. Furthermore, the stimulus for the adoption of this ethic in 1 Peter did not come from within the church; rather, it came from society, which demanded that all members of society accept Roman social-political customs and "slandered" Christians who did not seem to conform. The church as a "defense" stressed that part of the ethic which it was being accused of violating. The code in 1 Peter is paraenetic: the author of the letter is exhorting the readers to a common kind of conduct. But the traditional Greek ethic is intended to have a specific—apologetic—function in a problematic situation in certain provinces of Asia Minor in the last third of the first century A.D.

2. Social Repression (Schroeder and Crouch on Gal 3:28 and 1 Cor 7)

Some scholars have argued that the household codes functioned to repress social unrest on the part of wives and slaves within the church, an unrest stimulated by Gal 3:28. I agree that social tensions did motivate the author of 1 Peter to address the domestic code to Christians, but the code was not a response to unrest stemming from *within* the church caused by the baptismal formula in Gal 3:28.[95] The motivation for the slanders from society mentioned in 1 Peter was not that Christian slaves were politically revolutionary or that they were demanding their freedom from their masters, but simply that they had become Christians and refused to worship the traditional gods. There was a lack of unrest on the part of slaves in the time of the Caesars; there were no more slave revolts. The three revolts had been limited to 136–71 B.C. They were all in the time of mass-enslavement by the Romans, and all occurred on Italian or Sicilian soil.[96] The Dionysus and Isis cults do not provide parallels of revolutionary slave religion. Neither attracted primarily slaves who were then, because of their foreign religion, feared as a social group by the Romans (see chap. IV above). In fact, the movement in Christianity was sometimes in the other direction: some sold themselves into slavery "and provided food for others with the price they received for themselves" (1 Clem. 55:2; see 1 Cor 13:3).[97] Even this was not so horrible as it seems, for after selling oneself and subsequently being freed, one attained Roman citizenship.[98]

Crouch makes several similar observations, but then in view of 1 Cor 7:20–24, he reverses himself and concludes,

> In any case, it is inconceivable that Paul would have chosen illustrations which were meaningless for his Corinthian readers. Circumcision was a live issue. . . . It is a safe assumption that the desire of Christian slaves to obtain their freedom, though not as crucial for Paul, was just as real a problem.[99]

So, he says, 1 Corinthians 7 exhorts the slave to "abandon his concern for freedom"[100] and to fulfill his commitment to Christ in the social situation of slavery. He agrees with Schroeder[101] that formulas like Gal 3:28 created unrest on the part of many Christian slaves by fostering a misunderstanding of the gospel; slaves thought that such a theological formula nullified all obligations to a master.

Gal 3:28 was so understood in Corinth that the *women* there attempted to modify their role in society.[102] However, it is improbable that the Corinthian *slaves* understood the formula to suggest a modification of their role. Bartchy[103] points out that Gal 3:28 appears in altered form in 1 Cor 12:13, without the clause "There is neither male nor female," which he explains by suggesting that Paul dropped this out precisely because it was a problem. He did not want to see it socially realized by the Corinthian women. The formula in Gal 3:28 was understood differently by different parties: Paul insisted on a social realization of the clause "There is neither Jew nor Greek," but he insisted, on the contrary, that male and female maintain their distinctive social roles. The Corinthians had no interest in maintaining the Jew-Greek distinction, but in contrast to Paul, some of them were interested in modifying the male-female roles.

The Corinthians seem to have ignored the master-slave clause in the formula. Bartchy suggests that Paul was able to use circumcision-uncircumcision and free-slave as illustrations in 1 Cor 7:17–24 because these were *not* problems in Corinth. He used them to clarify what was a problem, the male-female role distinction.[104] If Gal 3:28 was not understood by the Corinthian slaves as modifying their social role, the assumption that this baptismal formula stimulated such "unrest" among slaves that it formed the background against which the household code must be understood is without a foundation. There is no indication whatever in 1 Peter itself that slaves' demand for freedom was the central problem. Nor is there any indication in 1 Peter that wives were attempting to expand their social roles toward more equality with men (contrast 1 Cor 7:3–4; 11:2–16; 12:13; 14:33b–36). But there are specific references in 1 Peter which indicate that conversion from traditional to new, foreign religious beliefs and practices caused severe problems (1:18; 2:12; 3:1, 13–17; 4:3–4, 16).

3. Mission (Selwyn and Schroeder)

Several scholars suggest that 1 Pet 2:12 gives a missionary purpose to the whole household code.[105] In the preceding discussion of this verse (pp. 87–88) I agreed with van Unnik that 2:12 does not refer to the conversion of pagans observing Christian conduct but rather to a "doxology of judgment."[106]

The following observations are also pertinent. Given Bömer's conclusions after studying the religion of slaves in the Roman empire (see p. 68–69), I doubt that the author of 1 Peter expected the conduct of slaves to convert some masters.[107] Christ, not as a missionary but as a martyr, is the model for the slaves (2:21; 3:18; 4:1). However Sarah, who brought Abraham to a vision of God (see p. 105), is the model for the wives' missionary conduct (3:1, 6). This difference supports the conclusion that only 3:1–6 exhorts to conduct which is intended to convert those observing such behavior.

It is also relevant to the debate that the conduct described in the household code is intended to be apologetic (3:15). The problem whether apologetic speeches and literature themselves have missionary intent has the following elements:

1) Jewish apologetic (Josephus, *Against Apion*) utilized the form of an encomium (see the research cited p. 58, n. 11). Hellenistic encomia did not have a missionary function; for example, Aristides in his encomium of Athens (*Or.* 1) was not inviting members of his audience to apply for Athenian citizenship.

2) Bernays[108] understood Philo in his *Apology for the Jews* to be recommending that Gentiles follow the Mosaic laws. Bernays was successfully contradicted by Wendland,[109] who denied that Philo's *Apology* was missionary.

3) However, second-century Christian apologetic was missionary.[110]

The apologetic response suggested by the author in 1 Pet 3:15 must be located at some stage in the development (1) from Hellenistic encomia (2) to first- and early second-century Hellenistic-Jewish apologetic (3) to second-century Christian apologetic. While the behavior of the wives in 1 Pet 3:1 was expected to convert their husbands, the behavior outlined in the domestic code as a whole had a function similar to the apologies written by the Hellenistic Jews Philo and Josephus, apologies which did not have a missionary intent. The author of 1 Peter exhorted these Christians to live in family relationships which Greco-Roman culture had defined as normal and proper. The author hoped that this would cause Roman masters, husbands, and governors to cease criticizing and even to praise persons who had rejected the traditional gods for faith in Christ.

D. *Summary and Conclusion*

Close attention to the text of the household duty code in 1 Peter in its Greco-Roman context enables further specification of the socio-religious situation in which the code functioned. The general situation was similar to the tensions described in chap. V: Greco-Roman society suspected and criticized foreign religions. Many of the Christians addressed by the author had rejected traditional religion (1:18b), and the author exhorted Christians to the kind of behavior that would silence the negative reactions which such conversions generated (2:11-12, 15). The stress on "harmony" in the conclusion of the code (3:8) reveals that the author was especially concerned about divided households: many masters and husbands were still pagans while some slaves and wives had converted to Christianity. In these divided houses, the harmony demanded by the Hellenistic moralists had been disturbed, which was judged to be a negative reflection on the new religion. The author exhorts his readers to make a "defense" (3:15) by reassuring the masters and husbands, perhaps even the governor, that they are obedient slaves and wives, just as the culture expected them to be. Christians are not to exacerbate the situation by meddling in others' domestic affairs (4:15). The readers are warned that governors punish insubordinate persons but are reassured that the authorities praise those who accept their role in the socio-political system (2:14).

The household duty code addressed by the author to this situation is adapted from the Aristotelian topos "concerning household management." He modified the form by addressing the persons in those roles where tension was focused: slaves and wives. As was traditional in certain strands of Platonic and Neopythagorean literature, the author exhorted wives to be submissive. He silently passed over the Greco-Roman expectation that such submission would include worship of the gods of the husband and master. Some of the husbands had not converted, and given the cultural assumptions of that society, they were probably among those persons slandering the converts. The author exhorted the women to submissive, gentle, quiet, chaste behavior, which might gain the husbands for Christ. They were to take Sarah for their model, who was submissive to Abraham, in whose house God had made "peace," and who led Abraham to a higher vision of God. Whatever domestic, social, or political developments might occur, the wives were not to be terrified (3:6).

As Dibelius suggested, the code is paraenetic; it is addressed to Christians, not outsiders. But it was not adopted because eschatological hopes had faded and Christians felt more at home in society. Rather, the code has an apologetic function in the historical context; the paraenesis is given in light of outside criticism. Persons in Roman society were alienated and threatened by some of their slaves and wives who had converted to the new, despised religion, so they were accusing the converts of impiety, immorality, and insubordination. As a defense, the author of 1 Peter encouraged the slaves and wives to play the social roles which Aristotle had outlined; this, he hoped, would shame those who were reviling their good behavior (3:16, 2:12). The conduct of the slaves was not expected to convert masters. However, the author hoped that the wives would convert their husbands by laudable behavior.

NOTES TO CHAPTER VI

[1]My emphasis. Cited by Willem Cornelis van Unnik, "The Critique of Paganism in 1 Peter 1:18," *Neotestamentica et Semitica. Studies in Honour of Matthew Black*, ed. E. Earle Ellis (Edinburgh: T. and T. Clark, 1969) 129–142, at pp. 132–133.

[2]Πάτριος; I.191, 225, 269, 317; II.10, 29–30, 47, 67, 182, 264, 267, 269, 281.

[3]G. E. M. de Ste. Croix, "Why Were the Early Christians Persecuted?" in M. I. Finley, ed., *Studies in Ancient Society* (Past and Present Series; London: Routledge and Kegan Paul, 1974) 239–240 points out that Christians would not even accept this principle.

[4]For the importance of these texts, see Abraham J. Malherbe, "Hellenistic Moralists and the New Testament," in *Aufstieg und Niedergang der römischen Welt*, ed. Hildegard Temporini and Wolfgang Haase, II. 26 (Berlin: Walter de Gruyter, forthcoming). Also above p. 66, n. 7. See van Unnik, "The Critique."

[5]See Philo, *On Dreams* II.273; *Special Laws* I.51 and 317; *On the Virtues* 102–103; *On Rewards and Punishments* 16–17; *Abraham* 17–26.

[6]See Bernhard Jacob Bamberger, *Proselytism in the Talmudic Period* (Cincinnati: Hebrew Union College, 1939) 155–156, n. 29 for other references. The social alienation which resulted from proselytism may have been the source for the often-repeated (e.g., *b. Sanh.* 58a beg. by R. Meir) dictum: "The convert is like a child newly born." Bamberger, *Proselytism* 63, 86, 142.

[7]Ibid., 196.

[8]Ibid., 180–181. See Victor Aptowitzer, "Asenath, the Wife of Joseph," *HUCA* 1 (1924) 239–306; M. Philonenko, ed. and trans., *Joseph et Aseneth* (Leiden: W. J. Brill, 1968). The discussions about its Jewish or Christian origin and its precise date are not crucial for the present purpose. There is an English translation by E. W. Brooks, *Joseph and Asenath* (London: Society for Promoting Christian Knowledge, 1918).

[9]In the conflicts which followed Asenath's conversion and marriage, both Levi (23:9 and 29:3) and Asenath herself (28:4 and 14) twice insist that one does not return evil for evil. Cp. 1 Pet 2:23; 3:9 and the two-ways document: Didache 1 and Barnabas 19.

[10]Aptowitzer, "Asenath" 274–276.

[11]See above pp. 66–69. E. Best, *1 Peter* (New Century Bible; London: Oliphants, 1971) 116–117, 124 stresses this situation as a social problem.

[12]A text cited by W. Schrage, "Zur Ethik der neutestamentlichen Haustafeln," *NTS* 21 (1975) 12.

[13]F. C. Babbitt, the ed. in LCL, here notes: "an indication that the wife was interested in some foreign religion like the worship of Cybele." Cp. Livy, *History* 39.10.7 of the Dionysus cult.

[14] Many women followed the religions of Isis and Cybele. See Franz Cumont, *The Oriental Religions in Roman Paganism* (Chicago: Open Court, 1911) 44 with n. 40; Ludwig Friedländer, *Roman Life and Manners under the Early Empire* (New York: Barnes and Noble, 1968) 1: 255–261.

[15]A striking text reflects a woman's view from *within* the Isis cult: Achilles Tatius, *Clitophon and Leucippe* VI.21–22. Leucippe, a free woman of Ephesus who had been enslaved and had undergone many tragic misadventures, defiantly addressed her lecherous master Thersander: "Feast your eyes with a new sight; one woman contends against all manner of tortures, and overcomes all her trials. . . . Tell me, pray, have you no fear of your own patroness Artemis, that you would ravish a virgin in the virgin's city? . . . I am defenseless and alone and a woman; but one shield I have, and that is my free soul, which cannot be subdued by the cutting of the lash, or the piercing of the sword or the burning of the fire. That is a possession I will never surrender; no, not I: and burn as you will, you will find that there is no fire hot enough to consume it!" (Trans. Gaselee) Achilles Tatius' literary romance, associated with the cult of Isis, called women and slaves to a high morality in the social situation where a master demanded rights over the body of his female slave. See H. Gülzow, *Christentum und Sklaverei in den ersten drei Jahrhunderten* (Bonn: R. Habelt, 1969) 112–113.

[16]See H. J. Leon, *The Jews* 256. According to George Foot Moore, *Judaism* 1 (New York: Schocken, 1971) 326, women were in the large majority among proselytes, but he is incorrect in stating that they "had only their fathers or husbands to deal with." Sherman E. Johnson, "Asia Minor and Early Christianity," *Christianity, Judaism and Other Greco-Roman Cults, Studies for Morton Smith at Sixty*, ed. Jacob Neusner (Leiden: E. J. Brill, 1975) 2:77–145 notes (98) that "women are very prominent in the Jewish inscriptions [in Sardis]." Johnson only briefly treats 1 Peter (see 93, 106, 108, 114–117).

[17]Wives' participation in a despised cult, the problem in 1 Pet 3:1 from the pagan husband's viewpoint, was used later as an "orthodox" accusation against the heretics (2 Tim 3:6–7).

[18]Trans. Smith, ANF VIII, 105. See Adolf von Harnack, *The Mission and Expansion of Christianity in the First Three Centuries* 1 (New York: Harper, 1961, orig. pub. 1902) 393–398, who says, "How deeply conversion must have driven its wedge into domestic life!" (393) See Eusebius, *On the Theophany* IV.12; Justin Martyr, 2 *Apol.* 2; Epictetus, *Dis.* IV.7.5–6 on the "customs" of the "Galileans." Contrast Epictetus III.7.20–21 (cited p. 54 above).

[19]See Carl Andresen, *Logos und Nomos: Die Polemik des Kelsos wider das Christentum* (Berlin: Walter de Gruyter, 1955) 174.

[20]On persecution "for the name" see de Ste. Croix, "Why" 213–216. He thinks such persecution began "either in 64 or at sometime between 64 and 112" (p. 216).

[21]Ibid., 240. See Cicero, *On the Nature of the Gods* 3.5–9; *Divination* 2.148; *Laws* 2.18–22.

[22]See the important discussion of 2:12 by W. C. van Unnik, "The Teaching of Good Works in 1 Peter," *NTS* 1 (1954–1955) 103–106.

[23]For example Edward G. Selwyn, *First Epistle* 171 on 2:12; W. J. Dalton, *Christ's Proclamation to the Spirits. A Study of 1 Peter 3:18–4:6* (An Bib 23; Rome: Pontifical Biblical Institute, 1965) 106–107. Also Leonhard Goppelt, "Prinzipien neutestamentlicher Sozialethik nach dem 1.Petrusbrief," *Neues Testament und Geschichte*, Festschrift Oscar Cullmann, ed. H. Baltensweiler und B. Reicke (Tübingen: Mohr, 1972) 285–296, esp. 287–288.

[24]van Unnik, "The Teaching of Good Works" 105. See L. Ramsey Michaels, "Eschatology in I Peter iii.17," *NTS* 3 (1966–1967) 397–398, although his further conclusion that the distinction between "doing good" and "doing evil" in 1 Peter has no reference to good and bad citizenship in the Roman state is incorrect. Prof. Wayne Meeks suggests the comparison of the "doxology of judgement," e.g., Joshua 7:19. See Gerhard von Rad, *Old Testament Theology* 1 (New York: Harper and Row, 1962) 357–359 and Odil Hannes Steck, *Israel und das gewaltsame Geschick der Propheten* (Neukirchen: Neukirchener, 1967) 123, n. 5; also 125 with n. 2, 137–162, 196–199. Prof. Meeks also pointed out to me that *yom pequdah* clearly is the equivalent of "day of visitation." See Hermann W. Beyer, "ἐπισκοπή," *TDNT* 2 (Grand Rapids: Eerdmans, 1964) 606–607.

[25]W. C. van Unnik, "The Teaching of Good Works" 103–104.

[26]Dalton, *Christ's Proclamation* 112, 165, 176.

[27]The strongest consideration pointing toward conversion is that the husbands in 3:1–2 are "observing" (ἐποπτεύσαντες) the chaste conduct of their wives, which conduct leads to the husbands' conversion. Similarly the "Gentiles" in 2:12 are observing (ἐποπτεύοντες) the good works of Christians, then "glorify God." However, van Unnik, "The Teaching of Good Works" 103, points out that the phrase "in the day of visitation" (2:12) makes the two texts different, not parallel. So 3:1–2 is the only reference in the letter to a missionary intent of "good conduct," and this is a traditional reference to wives converting their husbands (cp. 1 Cor 7:16; Josephus, *Ant.* XX.34 and 38). See the long catalogue of Christian women in Adolf von Harnack, *Mission* 2:64–84.

[28]Cp. Eduard Lohse, "Paraenese und Kerygma im 1.Petrusbrief," *ZNW* 45 (1954) 74.

[29]According to 1 Pet 4:18 the pagans are "impious"; it is easy to suspect that pagans were accusing these Asian Christians of "impiety."

[30]On not returning evil for evil, see Musonius, *Or.* X,78,26–28 Lutz; Plutarch, *How to Profit by One's Enemies* 90F; *Joseph and Asenath* 23:9; 28:4, 14; 29:3.

[31]H. Diels, ed. and trans., *Die Fragmenta der Vorsokratiker* 2 (Berlin: Weidmann, 1954) 356–360 (87 [80] B 44a–49). See the sketch in Kathleen Freeman, *The Pre-Socratic Philosophers. A Companion to Diels, Fragmenta der Vorsokratiker* (2nd ed.; Cambridge: Harvard University, 1959) 399–402.

[32]C. P. Jones, *The Roman World of Dio Chrysostom* (Cambridge: Harvard University, 1978) chap. 10: "On Concord." Cp. Aristides, *Or.* 42, *Concerning Harmony in Cities* and *Or.* 44, *To the Rhodians Concerning Harmony.* The latter oration discusses harmony in the house between husband and wife (vol. I, p. 827,1–5, ed. Dindorfii). In the house, fathers rule children and masters rule slaves (ibid., 834,17–18).

[33]On the close connections between 3:13–17 and the *Haustafel* (2:11–3:12), see Appendix I, esp. pp. 125–126.

[34]E.g., *Rom. Ant.* II.1.1; 9.2; 10.3; 13.4; 17.1; 19.2, 4, 5; 21.1, 3.

[35]See *Against Apion* I.166, 272, 317; II.10, 139, 142, 155, 164, 179, 269, 282. Willem Cornelis van Unnik, "Die Anklage gegen die Apostel in Philippi (Apostelgeschichte 16, 20f.)," in A. Stuiber and A. Hermann, eds., *Mullus*, Festschrift Theodor Klausner (JAC, Ergänzungsband 1; Münster: Aschendorff, 1964) 370–371 cites texts in Josephus, *Antiquities*, and denies (p. 367) that "customs" in Acts or Josephus includes a reference to "new gods," an incorrect conclusion.

[36]Cited by W. C. van Unnik, "Die Rücksicht auf die Reaktion der Nicht-Christen," *Judentum, Urchristentum, Kirche*, Festschrift Joachim Jeremias, ed. W. Eltester (Berlin: Alfred Töpelmann, 1960) 226. Trans. R. H. Connolly, *Didascalia Apostolorum* (Oxford: Clarendon, 1929) 26–28.

[37]There may be a parallel to 1 Pet 3:15 in Col 4:6, a verse just following the *Haustafel* in that letter. The verse refers to conduct directed toward outsiders, then refers to proper speech, "that you may know how you ought to answer (ἀποκρίνεσθαι) every one." Some interpreters treat this verse as if it suggests missionary activity, but van Unnik, "Die Rücksicht" 228 points out that the verb "to answer" suggests a defense rather than mission preaching. Zeller's suggestion that this kind of ethic may have had an apologetic function in Stoicism was noticed above (p. 18, n. 87); see also p. 80, n. 58 above on ps.-Ignatius.

[38]See Eduard Zeller, "Über eine Berührung des jüngeren Cynismus mit dem Christentum," *Sitzungsberichte der königlichen preussischen Akademie der Wissenschaften zu Berlin* 23 (1893) 129–132. Zeller depends on the earlier work of Eduard Norden, "Beiträge zur Geschichte der griechischen Philosophie," *Jahrbuch für classische Philologie*, Supplementband 19 (1893) 365–460. See 373–385 on Antisthenes, κύρος ἢ κατάσκοποι (Diog. Laert. VI.18).

[39]Norden, "Beiträge" 379.

[40]Zeller, "Über eine Berührung" 132.

[41]See Victor Ehrenberg, "Polypragmosyne: A Study in Greek Politics," *JHS* 67 (1947) 46–67. Being a busybody is often contrasted to quietness (ἡσυχία). See also Gustav Grossmann, *Politische Schlagwörter aus der Zeit des peloponneisischen Krieges* (Zürich: Dissertations-druckerei Leemann, 1950) 126–130.

[42]"Slander" is often associated with "envy" in this work of Lucian. See Ernst Milobenski, *Der Neid in der griechischen Philosophie* (Wiesbaden: O. Harrassowitz, 1964) 44, n. 83. This association may explain the appearance of "envy" in the vice list of 1 Pet 2:1. Envy there is not directed from the lower classes to the upper class, despite such texts as Euripides, *Suppliants* 238–243; Dio Chrysostom, *Dis.* 38.43; Dionysius Hal., *Rom. Ant.* II.9.1. Sp. p. 17, n. 72.

[43]Areius Didymus, II.148,8 Wachsmuth (quoted p. 42 above).

[44]van Unnik, "The Teaching of Good Works" 102.

[45]On citizens being "praised" by the governor, see August Strobel, "Zum Verständnis von Röm. 13," *ZNW* 47 (1956) 80–83. The following statements are based on the research cited p. 58, n. 11.

[46]Dalton, *Christ's Proclamation* 125–126.

[47]H. Last, "Christenverfolgung II (juristisch)," *RAC* 2 (1954) 1212. On the date of 1 Peter see Appendix III.

[48]Lohse, "Paraenese" 73–85.

[49]See Ernest Best, "I Peter and the Gospel Tradition," *NTS* 16 (1969-1970) 95-113. Wolfgang Nauck, "Freude im Leiden," *ZNW* 46 (1955) 68-80 showed that the tradition of "rejoicing in suffering" arose during the Maccabean conflicts (see, e.g., syr. Baruch 48:48-50; 52:5-7; 54:16-18). Note the consequences of "accusations" directed toward Christians "suffering" in Heb 10:32-34.

[50]"Trials" in Asia are also referred to in Rev 3:10 and Acts 20:19 (see the prayers in Luke 11:4; 22:40). Nauck, "Freude" 77-78, cites Judith 8:25-27 and Wisdom 3:4-6, which mention trials by fire.

[51]Cp. Acts 12:1; 14:2; 18:10.

[52]Francis W. Beare, *First Epistle of Peter* 13-15, 162, who dates 1 Peter at about the same time as Pliny's letter to Trajan (*Ep.* X.96), i.e., A.D. 111-112.

[53]Edward Gordon Selwyn, "The Persecutions in I Peter," *Bulletin of the Studiorum Novi Testamenti Societas* Nos. 1/3 (Cambridge: Cambridge University, 1963) 44. See also de Ste. Croix, "Why" 240 and W. C. van Unnik, "Christianity according to I Peter," *Exp Tim* 68 (1956) 80.

[54]Cp. the insightful comparison of the various NT codes by J. Paul Sampley, *"And the two shall become one flesh." A Study of Traditions in Ephesians 5:21-33* (SNTSMS 16; Cambridge: Cambridge University, 1971) 17-27. I do not need to repeat his discussion here. Whether 1 Pet 5:5 originally belonged after 3:7 is discussed by J. H. Elliott, "Ministry and Church Order in the NT: A Traditio-Historical Analysis (I Pt. 5, 1-5 and plls.)," *CBQ* 32 (1970) 366-391, esp. 371, 388-389. Note the development in ps.-Ignatius, *Tarsians* 8-9; *Antiochians* 8-10; *Hero* 4-5, tr. A. Roberts and J. Donaldson, ANF 1:108, 111, 114.

[55]Lohse, "Paraenese" 74. Now see also Leonhard Goppelt, *Erste Petrusbrief* 56-64, 165, 214-215.

[56]See Horst Goldstein, "Die politischen Paränesen in 1 Petr 2 und Röm 13," *Bib Leb* 15 (1974) 88-104, esp. 92, 96, 101.

[57]F. W. Danker, "I Peter 1,24-3,17—A Consolatory Pericope," *ZNW* 58 (1967) 99.

[58]Pace Schrage, "Zur Ethik" 5, n. 4.

[59]David Schroeder, *Haustafeln* 92.

[60]The absence of the article is exceptional in the form.

[61]Sampley, *"and the two shall become one flesh"* 19-20.

[62]Conversely, in the NT codes the important Stoic terms πατρίς, πολίτης, and ἀδελφός are missing.

[63]Gülzow, *Christentum und Sklaverei* 68-73 notes the uniqueness of the direct address to slaves in the Christian *Haustafeln*, which he explains in the case of 1 Peter by the social situation: Christian slaves are addressed whose masters are pagan. But the Neopythagoreans Zaleucus (228,13-14 Thesleff) and Eccelus (78,10-11 Thesleff) are also concerned about slaves' behavior. So the ethical exhortation to women is not novel, whereas the address to slaves is unusual and requires the assumption of a major change in attitudes. But see the earlier statements of Philo (above p. 54).

[64]K. von Fritz, *Pythagorean Politics in Southern Italy: An Analysis of the Sources* (New York: Columbia University, 1940) 65-66 traces the source of Iamblichus, *Life of Pythagoras* 37, 42, 54, 56, and 71 to Timaeus (c. 356-260 B.C.). It is incorrect that "among Pythagoreans women enjoyed equal rights with men," pace Markus Barth, *Ephesians. Translation and Commentary on Chapters 4-6* (Garden City: Doubleday, 1974) 657. See above pp. 56-58.

[65]David Daube, "Appended Note. Participle and Imperative in I Peter," in Selwyn, *First Epistle of St. Peter* 467-488. For one view of this term see A. F. J. Klijn, "Die Ethik des neuen Testaments. Eine Umschau," *Nederlands Theologisch Tijdschrift* 24 (1969-1970) 241-249.

[66]Schroeder, *Haustafeln* 103.

[67]Goppelt, *Erste Petrusbrief* 171.

[68]Ibid., 172.

[69]Ibid.

[70]Gerhard Delling, "τάσσω," *TDNT* 8 (1972) 40. Also Erhard Kamlah, "ὑποτάσσεσθαι in

den neutestamentlichen Haustafeln," in O. Böcher and K. Haacker, eds., *Verborum Veritas*, Festschrift G. Stählin (Wuppertal: Theologischer Verlag Brockhaus, 1970) 237–243, esp. 239.

[71]Against Karl Heinrich Rengstorf, "Die neutestamentliche Mahnungen an die Frau sich dem Manne unterzuordnen," in W. Foerster, ed., *Verbum Dei Manet in Aeternum*, Festschrift Otto Schmitz (Wittenberg: Luther, 1955) 131–145. Also idem, *Mann und Frau im Urchristentum* (Arbeitsgemeinschaft für Forschung des Landes Nordrhein-Westfalen, Abhandlungen Geisteswissenschaften 12; Cologne: Westdeutscher,1954) 25–46.

[72]Goppelt, *Erste Petrusbrief* 58 speaks of aggression against the Christians from fellow citizens, relatives, and acquaintances..

[73]Cp. Plutarch, *Lycurgus and Numa* 3.5; Philo, *Special Laws* III. 169–177, esp. 172, 174.

[74]David Daube, "κερδαίνω as a Missionary Term," *HTR* 40 (1947) 109–120.

[75]Cp. Plutarch, *Numa* 3.6; *Advice to Bride and Groom* 141E, 145EF. Melissa to Cleareta (116,7–13 Thesleff) asserts that a woman's adornment is to follow the will of her husband (116,12–13).

[76]This is said about the goddess; see XI.17. See Plutarch, *Isis and Osiris* 357AB; Athenaeus, *Deipnosophists* XII 525ef, 531d; Dionysius Hal., *Rom. Ant.* II.22.2; Augustine, *City of God* VI.10.

[77]See Philo, *On Dreams* II.78; *Moses* I.285.

[78]*'Abot R. Nat.* a, chap. 15, ed. Schechter, p. 61. Trans. J. Goldin, *Aboth Rabbi Nathan* (New Haven: Yale University, 1955) 80–81. Also *'Abot R. Nat.* b, chap. 29, ed. Schechter, p. 61.

[79]See Bamberger, *Proselytism* 223–225.

[80]See Hermann Strack and Paul Billerbeck, *Kommentar zum neuen Testament aus Talmud und Midrasch* (5 vols.; 5th ed.; Munich: C. H. Beck, 1969) 3:764. In some texts, instead of Sarah obeying Abraham, the opposite occurs: Abraham "obeys" Sarah in taking Hagar as a wife (*Jubilees* 17:6; Philo, *Cherubim* 9; *Preliminary Studies* 68; *Allegorical Interpretation* III.244–245).

[81]Wilhelm Bacher, *Die Agada der Tannaiten* 1 (Strassburg: K. J. Trubner, 1903, 1965) 51.

[82]Karl Georg Kuhn, trans. and commentary, *Der tannaitische Midrasch Sifre zu Numeri* (Rabbinische Texte; Stuttgart: W. Kohlhammer, 1959) 131, n. 27 points out that the following section brings twenty sayings on peace, all of which are introduced with the formula "Great is peace." They are ordered 3+7+7+3. The one quoted in the text is the first of the series. My English translation in the text above is based on Kuhn's German translation.

[83]Parallels are listed by Wilhelm Bacher, *Die Agada der Tannaiten* 2 (Strassburg: K. J. Trubner, 1890, 1965) 338, n. 4 and by Strack-Billerbeck, *Kommentar* 1:217 on Matt 5:9; cp. p. 635.

[84]Bacher, *Agada* 2:335.

[85]Ibid., 335, n. 3; cp. 507 and 503.

[86]Ibid., 336.

[87]This teaching is followed by a story concerning R. Meir (c. 150 A.D.): a husband is offended because his wife habitually goes to hear a preacher in the synagogue on the Sabbath, but Meir is able to effect "peace between husband and wife." Cp. 1 Pet 3.

[88]Cited by Kuhn, *Tannaitische Midrasch* 131, n. 22 along with Rom 12:18 in reference to the saying of R. Hananja, the captain of the priests, quoted above.

[89]Strack-Billerbeck, *Kommentar* 1:217.

[90]The texts are given by Louis Ginzberg, *Legends of the Jews* 1 (Philadelphia: The Jewish Publication Society of America, 1913) 203, n. 42 and include the early ones in *'Abot R. Nat.* 12, 53 and *Sifre Deut.* 32.

[91]Sarah=Virtue produces better conditions in households, city, and country (Philo, *On the Change of Names* 149).

[92]Tentatively, I suggest that the exhortation to husbands in 1 Pet 3:7 has elements which should be read in light of pagan criticism of Christian women. The author accepts the cultural assumptions that men are more intelligent (they live "according to knowledge") and that women are "weaker." Nevertheless, unlike the pagan critics, Christian husbands are to "bestow honor" on

their Christian wives because they are "joint (equal) heirs of the grace of life." Cp. ps.-Ignatius, *Hero* 4: "Be not ashamed of servants. . . . Do not hold women in abomination. . . "

⁹³W. Schrage, "Zur Ethik" 4, n. 1. Schrage accepts (3, n. 2) Dibelius' distinction between "usuelle" and "aktuelle Paraenese," the former of which is not formulated for particular congregations or concrete situations. Schrage rejects the extreme of making the codes into a uniform early Christian catechism. Rather the codes combine tradition with some concern for the situation, convention with flexibility (4). For Zeller's suggestion that such an ethic had an apologetic function in Stoicism see p. 18, n. 87.

⁹⁴Edward Gordon Selwyn, "Eschatology in I Peter," in W. D. Davies and D. Daube, eds., *The Background of the New Testament and its Eschatology, In Honour of C. H. Dodd* (Cambridge: Cambridge University, 1956) 299. But when he says "Eschatology is for the most part eschatology fulfilled" (ibid.), the "realized eschatology" is stressed too much.

⁹⁵See Karl Weidinger, *Haustafeln* 7; Schroeder, *Haustafeln* 89–91; Crouch, *Colossian Haustafel* 122–131, 140–145. For a discussion of 1 Cor 7:29–31, Gal 3:27–28, and 1 Pet 2:13–3:7, see S. Schulz, "Evangelium und Welt. Hauptprobleme einer Ethik des neuen Testaments," in H. D. Betz and L. Schottroff, eds., *Neues Testament und christliche Existenz*, Festschrift H. Braun (Tübingen: Mohr, 1973) 483–501. For Jewish parallels to Gal 3:28 see M. Boucher, "Some Unexplored Parallels to I Cor. 11,11–12 and Gal. 3,28: The NT on the Role of Women," *CBQ* 31 (1969) 50–58.

⁹⁶See Carl Schneider, *Kulturgeschichte des Hellenismus* (Munich: C. H. Beck, 1969) 2:167–168, 177; E. Meyer, "Die Sklaverei im Altertum," *Kleine Schriften* 1 (Halle: M. Niemeyer, 1910) 210–212. See Gülzow, *Christentum und Sklaverei* 104–105; see also p. 78, n. 28 above. Aristonicus appealed to slaves in Asia Minor in 133 B.C.; see Samuel Dickey, "Some Economic and Social Conditions of Asia Minor Affecting the Expansion of Christianity," in S. J. Case, ed., *Studies in Early Christianity* (New York: Century, 1928) 393–416, esp. 396–399. He cites Strabo, *Geography* 14.1.38 (646); Diodorus Siculus, *Library of History* 34.2.26; Plutarch, *Tiberius Gracchus* 8 and 20.

⁹⁷See Gülzow, *Christentum und Sklaverei* 77–82.

⁹⁸Ibid., 83 with n. 3. See pp. 66, 69 above.

⁹⁹Crouch, *Colossian Haustafel* 124.

¹⁰⁰Ibid., 126.

¹⁰¹Ibid. See Schroeder, *Haustafeln* 89. See also Goppelt, *Erste Petrusbrief* 41, 176.

¹⁰²See esp. Wayne A. Meeks, "The Image of the Androgyne: Some Uses of a Symbol in Earliest Christianity," *HR* 13 (1974) 165–208, esp. 180–183, 199–203.

¹⁰³S. Scott Bartchy, ΜΑΛΛΟΝ ΧΡΗΣΑΙ. *First-Century Slavery and I Corinthians 7:21* (SBLDS 11; Missoula: Scholars Press, 1973) 129–130. See also David L. Balch, "Backgrounds of I Cor. 7: Sayings of the Lord in Q; Moses as an Ascetic ΘΕΙΟΣ ΑΝΗΡ in II Cor. 3," *NTS* 18 (1972) 351–364.

¹⁰⁴In his review, Peter Stuhlmacher, *TLZ* 101 (1976) 838, agreed with this position. On whether slaves had any choice concerning their freedom, see the theory in ps.-Aristotle, *Concerning Household Management* I.5.6, 1344b 15–17.

¹⁰⁵Selwyn, *First Epistle of St. Peter* 171 on 2:12; Schroeder, *Haustafeln* 138, 157–158. Also Goppelt, "Prinzipien" 285–296, esp. 287–288. But Goppelt in his later commentary, *Erste Petrusbrief* 161, notes van Unnik's opposing interpretation and calls the verse "ambivalent."

¹⁰⁶For Elliott's suggestion that 1 Pet 2:9d and 5d give the following household code a missionary intent, see Appendix II.

¹⁰⁷A typical process may be described by Julian, *Against the Galileans* 206A, who accuses Christians of converting slaves, "and through them the women."

¹⁰⁸Jacob Bernays, "Philon's Hypothetika und die Verwuenschung des Buzyges in Athen," *Gesammelte Abhandlungen*, ed. H. Usener (Berlin: Wilhelm Hertz, 1885) 1:272.

¹⁰⁹Paul Wendland, "Die Therapeuten und die philonische Schrift vom beschaulichen Leben," *Jahrbücher für classische Philologie*, Supplementband 22 (1896) 714–715. P. W. van der Horst, "Pseudo-Phocylides and the New Testament," *ZNW* 69 (1978) 187–202, at 197: "The

context of this material in Philo and Josephus is apologetic, not missionary." See p. 18, n. 95 above.

[110]Abraham J. Malherbe, "The Apologetic Theology of the Preaching of Peter," *Restoration Quarterly* 13 (1970) 205–223. Jean Danielou, *Gospel Message and Hellenistic Culture* (Philadelphia: Westminster, 1973) 7–15.

Final Summary and Conclusions

In Part I classical topoi about "ruling" in the city and house were outlined. As early as Plato, *Republic* and *Laws*, the topos "concerning the constitution" included the assertion that some persons were superior, others inferior, so that the former should "rule" and the latter should "be ruled." The pairs which later appeared in NT household codes were already present. This topos was common in Plato's time, and it remained a concern in the Roman Empire as can be seen in the Middle Platonists, Stobaeus, and Dio Chrysostom.

The topos "concerning household management," which was related to the broader discussion "concerning the constitution" because "houses" make up "cities," was given an exact outline by Aristotle. It involved three pairs of relationships—master and slaves, husband and wife, father and children—as well as a concern for household income. There was an extensive discussion of the kind of rule—monarchic (or tyrannic), aristocratic, or democratic—proper to each of these three relationships. Improper rule, e.g., a woman ruling her husband, would corrupt the constitution of the state, as happened in the case of the Spartans. These Aristotelian political ideas were preserved by the Peripatetics. They were outlined in detail by the Stoic Areius Didymus in a popular handbook perhaps intended for Augustus Caesar. They were discussed at length, and rejected, by the Epicurean Philodemus. Elements of the topos were known to the Roman Cicero and to the Hellenistic Jew Philo. The pervasive influence of such Platonic-Aristotelian political ideas may be seen in the fact that Philo used them to interpret the Old Testament Decalogue!

The Aristotelian outline of the topos also appeared in the eclectic Stoics Ariston, Hecaton, Seneca, and Hierocles. Except in the case of Seneca, it remains uncertain whether these Stoics were directly dependent on Aristotle.

The Neopythagoreans, to be dated in the first centuries B.C. and A.D., were also dependent on these classical Greek topoi. Callicratidas discussed the proper relationship between husband and wife at length, and Bryson developed the four-part Aristotelian outline of the topos.

Chap. V moved from such abstract philosophical discussion to social reality in the Roman world. Romans made certain stereotyped criticisms of new, foreign cults. Their rites involved immorality (especially corrupting women), murder, and sedition. Romans were accustomed to slaves who were willing to worship the Roman gods and were very disturbed by Jewish slaves—and later Christian ones—who were unwilling to conform to that practice. The Egyptian Isis cult was criticized because it was thought to reverse the proper household relationship between husbands and wives. These were stereotyped criticisms, and Romans seem to have used them indiscriminately. A new religion would face many of the same slanders which had earlier been directed against other foreign, Eastern religions. Judaism and Christianity inherited slanders which Greeks and Romans originally directed against the Dionysus and Isis cults. In Roman culture it was inevitable that Judaism and Christianity would be charged with sedition, with murder, and with practicing rites which corrupted the morality of Roman women. The old conception that the Isis cult advocated household relationships which were the reverse of Greco-Roman ones was used by Octavian in his propaganda against Antony and Cleopatra. Christianity as a new, foreign religion from the East also faced the criticism that it upset proper household management, a criticism which was voiced by persons concerned with maintaining the constitution of the Roman state (cp. pp. 71–72).

Faced with these and other slanders of the Jewish constitution, in the late first century A.D. Josephus wrote an apologetic encomium on the Jewish nation, *Against Apion*. The rhetorical form of an encomium was outlined by Menander of Laodicea (see p. 58, n. 11). The same form had been used a century earlier than Josephus by Dionysius of Halicarnassus in his praise of Rome (*Rom. Ant.* II.24.1–6; 25.4–5; 26.1; 27.1–2). These authors discussed the public constitution, including consideration of "temperance," which involved the wives' chastity and submission to their husbands and the proper training of children. In his encomium, Dionysius used the topos "concerning household management" with its three pairs of household relationships. Although Josephus did not use pairs, his encomium did include consideration of marriage laws, the birth and upbringing of children, and the law for slaves (*Against Apion* II.199, 206, 216). Jewish marital customs had been criticized, so Josephus defended them when he said that the Jewish woman was properly submissive. The Jewish "house" in a Roman "city" was properly "ruled." Jews were "obedient," and their customs would not subvert the Roman constitution. Philo, *Apology for the Jews*, probably had apologetic interests similar to those of Josephus.

Appendix I argues that 1 Pet 3:13–17, with its concern for the possibility of suffering and the need to give a "defense," is closely related to the household code (2:11–3:12). The concern for those who were "speaking against" the Christians is present in the introduction to the code and in the pericope which follows it (2:12; 3:16), a fact which suggests that the conduct recommended in the code is a response to such outside slanders and a part of the "defense" to outsiders anticipated in 3:15.

The "persecutions" assumed by the letter have their source in these criticisms from society, not in the demand that Christians worship the emperor. Both in the topos "concerning the constitution" and in the Stoic discussions of "duties," religious and social customs were inseparable. Whenever Judaism or Christianity made proselytes and changed the new converts' religious habits, they were accused of corrupting and reversing Roman social and household customs. These religious conversions were the source of the slanders about the insubordination of Christian slaves and wives. The mere use of the household code does not require the assumption that there was active social-political unrest on the part of Christian slaves or wives, an unrest supposedly stimulated by a desire to realize Gal 3:28 socially. Religious insubordination called forth slanders about social insubordination, as in Julian, *Misopogon.*

The author of 1 Peter exhorted the recipients of his letter to the behavior outlined in the code with the intention of encouraging conduct which would contradict the Roman slanders. Such behavior would have been demanded not only by pagan masters and husbands but also by the aristocratic Roman "governors" mentioned in 1 Pet 2:14. Christians were instructed to give "a defense to anyone who asks"; in this context Christians would outline their constitution, the household code, to outsiders, even to the governor concerned with maintaining the Roman constitution. Christians claimed that their customs would not subvert the Roman constitution despite the fact that Christian slaves and wives refused to worship Roman gods. The governor's "praise of those doing good" (2:14) might also take the form of the Aristotelian code. The topos "concerning household management" was used in Hellenistic encomia to praise a city or a people for being obedient, as in Dionysius of Halicarnassus' encomium of Rome. Libanius praised the common people of Antioch because they showed obedience toward their superiors (*Or.* XI.154). The code constituted both part of the Christians' "defense" and part of the "praise" they hoped for from the governor. This ethic encouraged Christians, as a new, Eastern religious community, to acculturate to Roman society.

1 Peter stresses a futurist eschatology in which the "disobedient" pagans are expected to perish while giving a "doxology of judgment" (2:12). This eschatology is found both in the verses introducing the code (2:11–12) and in those verses following the code which give theological support to the ethic (3:18–4:6). The summary of the code (3:8–9) stresses that in the short time before Jesus' coming, Christians should be harmonious in their household relationships with pagans.

The code in 1 Peter does not have three pairs, as does the code in Col 3:18–4:1. There is only one pair (wives-husbands) who are exhorted about their relationship to each other. Slaves are exhorted at length, but not masters; and the children-father pair disappears. Crouch's assumption that "the other Christian Haustafeln . . . are further developments of the Colossian Haustafel"[1] is problematic. The exhortations to slaves in 1 Peter and Colossians show few parallels.[2] The exhortation to wives in 1 Pet 3:1 is closer to Titus 2:5 than to Col 3:18;[3] but 1 Pet 3:1 has just as close a parallel in ps.-Callisthenes, although the infinitive, not the participle, is used (above p. 98). Placing a particular code in a "Christian Haustafel tradition"[4] seems more complex than Crouch suggests. There is no compelling reason to posit a literary dependence of the author of 1 Peter on the earlier Christian code in Colossians.

It seems *a priori* probable that the Jewish-Christian author of 1 Peter became aware of this ethic and its apologetic possibilities through Hellenistic Judaism rather than through pagan sources. However, that assumption is difficult to demonstrate. 1 Peter does not verbally reproduce sentences from Philo; Philo, *Apology* 7.14, is not concerned with "submission." Nor are the parallels in Josephus, *Against Apion*, so verbally similar that the dependence of 1 Peter on that treatise or its source could be posited. Pressure for the adoption of this ethic came from Greco-Roman society, which impressed its concerns directly on the author. I will only observe that a similar ethic is found in other Christian documents, in Hellenistic Judaism, and in pagan authors. The ultimate origin of the ethic is to be found in Greek political thought, but I cannot draw firm conclusions about the immediate source of the code in 1 Peter.

Schroeder and Crouch assert that the order of the exhortations found in Colossians—wives, children, slaves—is rarely found in pagan texts. Crouch[5] finds this order only in Seneca, *Ep*. 94 (Ariston), and ps.-Plutarch, *The Education of Children* 7E. It is argued above (p. 44, n. 51) that ps.-Plutarch used Chrysippus as a source. Chrysippus debated Ariston about 250 B.C., and this debate may have included disagreement about whether to include the Aristotelian concern for the domestic role of women, children, and slaves. It may not be accidental that Seneca, *Ep*. 94 (Ariston), and ps.-Plutarch, *The Education of Children* 7E (Chrysippus), list duties toward women, children, and slaves in the same order as the list in Colossians. Aristotle uses this order in *NE* V 1134b 17, discussing justice toward wife, children, and slaves. The same order appears in Areius Didymus (II.149,6–8 Wachsmuth), in Philo, *The Posterity and Exile of Cain* 181, and in Dionysius of Halicarnassus, *Rom. Ant*. II.24.4; 25.4; 26.1 and 3; 27.1. Areius Didymus lived somewhat earlier than Philo, and both men were from Alexandria, so again the common order might not be accidental. Women and marriage were traditionally treated first in these discussions (Plato, *Laws* IV 721A; Aristotle, *Pol*. I 1252a 24–35; ps.-Aristotle, *Concerning Household Management* I 1343b 7; Philodemus, *Concerning Household Management* 28,7–30,1). However, Dionysius' discussion gives a more important clue why the exhortations to wives were so prominent in the NT codes. His discussion includes a concern for the suppression of foreign, Eastern cults, which typically attracted numerous women converts. This was precisely the social context of the author of 1 Peter 3, although, of course, he did not mention wives first. The author of 1 Peter may have mentioned slaves first because of his reflections on Malachi, as Danker suggests.[6]

In 1 Pet 3:1 the author continued a Platonic-Neopythagorean tradition of instruction to wives. The common Greco-Roman demand that wives be submissive to their own husbands was addressed to Christian wives. The exhortation in 1 Pet 3:1 differed from the pagan conception of submission because the wife was encouraged to maintain her own religion, so not to conform completely to the customs of her husband. The intent of the ethic was to convert the husband through the wife's submissive, silent, chaste conduct. As Schroeder suggested, the motive for the wife's conduct was missionary. Sarah was an example of such submissive, harmonious conduct. She called Abraham "lord" (Gen. 18:12) and led him to a knowledge of God.

The final phrase in the pericope, that the wife should not fear any terror (3:6c), indicates that the ethic being taught to the wives was not only missionary but also apologetic. The verses addressed to wives were meant for Christian women who were suffering because they lived in households which were only partially Christian, households in which Romans perceived a lack of orderly submission and harmony.

NOTES TO SUMMARY AND CONCLUSIONS

[1]James Crouch, *Colossian Haustafel* 35.
[2]See Edward G. Selwyn, *First Epistle of St. Peter* Table XII on p. 430.
[3]Ibid., Table XIII on p. 432.
[4]Crouch, *Colossian Haustafel* 34–35.
[5]Ibid., 72. See David Schroeder, *Haustafeln* 41–43 and Appendix II.
[6]See above p. 96, n. 57.

Appendix I

The Structure of 1 Peter

The most successful attempt to analyze the plan of 1 Peter is that by Dalton.[1] He uses the methods developed by Vaganay[2] in his work on the structure of Hebrews as well as those used by Lyonnet[3] in his study of Romans. The six types of indications which reveal the literary structure of Hebrews are: prior announcement of the theme, inclusion, link words, repetition of key words, change from statement to exhortation or vice versa, and symmetrical disposition of the matter. "Inclusion" occurs when a word is used at the beginning and at the end of a literary unit, thus binding the unit together. The term "link word" describes the function of a word or phrase which is set at the end of one section, then taken up again at the beginning of the next. The "repetition of a key word" often indicates the homogeneous nature of a literary unit. Symmetry, such as a chiasm, can tie a unit together. Dalton adds a seventh criterion of literary structure: the use of quotations from the OT. There are many ways in which this can be done, but the author of 1 Peter most often ends the development of a thought with a biblical citation, bringing the thought to an impressive climax.[4]

A.   1 Peter 1:1–2; 1:3–2:10

The epistle is addressed to the "chosen" and ends with a greeting from her (the church) who is "likewise chosen" (1:1, 5:13), thus bracketing the whole letter by an inclusion.[5] Dalton (pp. 76–77) gives two other significant examples of inclusion: "*For a little while* you may have *to suffer* . . . may redound to praise and *glory* and honour at the revelation *of Jesus Christ*" (1:6–7) together with "And after you have *suffered a little while*, the God of all grace who had called you to his eternal *glory in Christ* . . ." (5:10).[6] Second, "In this you *rejoice*, though . . . you may have to suffer various *trials* so that the genuineness of your faith, more precious than gold which . . . is *tested by fire*, may redound to praise . . . *at the revelation of Jesus Christ*" (1:6–7) together with "Do not be surprised at the *fiery ordeal* which is taking place for your *trial* . . . that you may *rejoice* and be glad *at the revelation of his glory*" (4:12–13). These two examples of inclusion reach across the division suggested by Preisker and Cross;[7] they become an indication of the literary unity of the whole.

Dalton (pp. 76–79) also makes the fundamental observation that, as in Romans and Hebrews, the opening address (1 Pet 1:1–2) is expanded to announce some of the chief themes to be treated in the first chapter. God the "Father" is mentioned again only in the first chapter (1:17). The Spirit is mentioned only four times in the work (1:2, 11, 12; 4:14; but cp. 2:5, 3:18, 4:6), with three of these in the opening section. "Jesus" occurs eight times in the whole letter (never after 4:11); half of these occurrences are in the first thirteen verses. Sanctification, obedience, and the sprinkling of blood, aspects of salvation mentioned in the opening address, all appear in the second part of the chapter (1:13–25). There is an exhortation to holy living "as children of obedience" (1:14; cp. 1:2, 22), which is followed and supported by a citation of Lev 19:2, "You shall be holy, for I am holy" (1:16; cp. 1:2, 22). If they call God "Father," they will conduct themselves with fear during their time of exile (1:17; cp. 1:1 and 2:11), not according to the local traditions of their former "fathers," but as persons ransomed by the "blood" (1:19; cp. 1:2) of Christ.

So the address is an announcement of the chief themes of the first chapter, which is then a literary unit, ending with an appropriate climaxing citation from Scripture (1:24–25a). The chief idea in the citation concerns the word of God which was preached to them (1:25),[8] the content of which is defined by 1:3 and 21: God gave glory to Jesus Christ, whom he raised from the dead. The addressees have been "born anew" by this "incorruptible," "living" word (1:23–25); taken with the reference to an "incorruptible," "living" hope (1:3–4), this is an inclusion. Chap. 1 is therefore a unit, which is confirmed by the fact that chap. 2 begins with a new exhortation ("Therefore put away . . ."). Finally, 1:22–24 summarizes the preceding: love (1:8, 22), soul (1:9, 22), glory (1:7, 11, 21, 24), corruptible (1:18, 23), living (1:3, 23), to be reborn (1:3, 23), obedience (1:2, 14, 22). Noting the repetition of these terms and the inclusions which Dalton has pointed out, I share Dalton's (p. 79) conclusion: 1:3–25 is not a consciously planned exposition of certain themes, but the terms "God the Father," "Jesus Christ," "Spirit," "sanctification," "blood of Jesus Christ," "obedience," and "foreknowledge" must have been turning in the mind of the writer as he continued, after the address, with the first chapter. This indicates that the epistolary address and the opening section of the epistle are a literary unity,[9] an argument against the partition required by the hypothesis of a baptismal homily.[10]

2:1 begins the next division of the letter. Dalton regards two terms as link words: "rebirth" (1:23; 2:2) and "hypocrisy" (1:22; 2:1). The description of the Christian rebirth is followed by traditional catechesis:[11] one must "put off" certain vices. Then this imperative is followed by an indicative. This indicative section (2:4–10) takes up the themes of the church's election (2:4, 6, 9; cp. 1:1, 15) and holiness (2:5, 9; cp. 1:2, 15, 16), which serve as the basis of the previous exhortation.[12] "Faith" as a theme is also picked up again (2:6, 7; cp. 1:7, 8, 9).

The pericope concludes (2:9-10) on the themes of election and mercy, themes which introduced the letter (1:1, 3).[13] It should be noticed that the Scripture citations in 2:4-10 summarize earlier themes. Further, there is an emphatic break at 2:11, which returns to exhortation, again addressing the recipients ("beloved"), referring again to them as "aliens" (cp. 1:1). From this perspective, 1:1 to 2:10 is a literary unit containing smaller units.

B.   1 Peter 2:11-4:11

Determining the transition points of the household code which follows is relatively easy, although determining its relation to the context and its function in the letter as a whole is somewhat more difficult. As just mentioned, a major new section begins at 2:11; there is the address, the change from statement to exhortation, and the repeated reference to "aliens." The section can almost be divided by simple reference to the exhortation to "submit" (2:13, 18; 3:1), which would however ignore the exhortation to husbands (3:7 [cp. the adverb "likewise" in 3:1 and 7, which is repeated in 5:5]) and the final summation (3:8-9) climaxed by a long Scripture quotation (3:10-12).[14]

The concern for "slander" is announced in the slave section of the code, and the same concern is evident in the summary (2:23, 3:9).[15] Dalton (p. 81), however, sees the repetition of the commendation of Christian "love of the brethren" in 3:8 (cp. 1:22) and concludes that this is the natural climax of this hortatory section. He then determines that one of the two major divisions in the whole letter lies between 3:12 and 13, so that 2:11-3:12 ("Obligations of the Christian Life") and 3:13-5:11 ("The Christian and Persecution") form two separate units. This is based on a misunderstanding not only of the small unit 3:13-17 but also of the household code (2:11-3:12). The code does conclude at 3:12, but it is intimately tied to the pericope which follows. In fact, as I have tried to demonstrate above, the behavior recommended in the household code prepares the Christian to give an "account" to critics, as mentioned in 3:15. Michaels sees the similarity between 2:12 and 3:16 and concludes: "The conduct required of Christian believers is the same in both passages ('good conduct,' 'good works,' 'good conscience'). . . ."[16]

The "repetition of key words" in 3:13-17, words announced and stressed by repetition in the code, indicates this intimate tie. The theme of "suffering" (see esp. the verb πάσχω)[17] is one of six repeated ideas. This theme is announced early in the letter (1:6, 11), but it receives stress when the author begins exhorting slaves (2:19, 20, 21, 23). This interest is continued into the pericope following the household code (3:14, 17) and into 3:18-4:6, which Dalton (pp. 81, 82, and passim) well describes as the doctrinal ground for Christian confidence in persecution. Here again, the author's exhortation in the household code is corroborated and supported by a subsequent indicative. It is thus a mistake to reserve the description "The Christian and Persecution" for 3:13-5:11 when suffering has such an important place in the preceding *Haustafel*.

"Doing good" and "doing evil" are the second and third key words tying the code to the succeeding pericope.[18] The theme of "doing good" is introduced by the author in 2:14, the verse dealing with the "governor." It is the governor who exacts vengeance on the "one doing evil" but who gives praise to the "one doing good." Christians should do good in order to silence the ignorance of foolish men (2:15), so that they will not be harmed as Christians (3:13), and so that those threatening them will be ashamed (3:16). It is important that the quote of Ps 34:12–16 (33:13–17 LXX) in 1 Pet 3:10–12 is not only a summary of the preceding household code but is also a link to what follows. The Psalmist's phrases "let him do good" (quoted 3:11) and "doing evil" (quoted 3:12) are reflected in 3:13, 16, 17.

There is a concern for those "speaking against" the addressees which is found in the introduction to the household code (2:12) and is present in the pericope following it (3:16).

A fifth cluster of words concerns justice or righteousness.[19] This concern is introduced in the section exhorting slaves, where the assumption is made that they will at times be treated "unjustly" (2:19).[20] They are offered the example of Christ, who delivered himself to the one (God) who judges[21] "justly" (2:23) and who died that we might live to "righteousness" (2:24). This concern is taken up in the summarizing Psalm quotation (3:12), which in turn is picked up in 3:14 and 18. It is clear that God's just judgment (2:23; 3:12 [his judging "impartially" is mentioned in 1:17]) is in contrast to the present situation, where Christians are harmed because of their "righteousness" (3:14). The "account" ($\lambda\acute{o}\gamma o\varsigma$, 3:15) which Christians must now give pagans will soon be followed by the "account" ($\lambda\acute{o}\gamma o\varsigma$, 4:5) which pagans will give to the judging God. Again, a concern for "justice" and "judgment" in the code is continued into the immediately succeeding context.

Sixth, there is the concern for the "will" of God.[22] It is the will of God that Christians do good to silence ignorant men (2:15). It is better to suffer for doing right, if that is God's will, than for doing wrong (3:17). Through these six concerns, the household code is closely related to the exhortations in 3:13–17.

As Dalton notes (p. 81), at 3:18 a new development begins, with 3:17 playing a double role. 3:17 recalls the ideas of "good," "suffering," and "doing evil" found in 3:12–14, thus by inclusion binding 3:13–17 into a unity; but the term "suffer" also forms a link to 3:18.[23] 3:18 begins a statement about the activity of Christ, an indicative which justifies the exhortation of the preceding passage; Christ's suffering, resurrection, and "proclamation" somehow provide grounds for the confidence of the Christian in persecution. This unit has a natural conclusion at 4:6, indicated by the inclusion flesh-spirit (3:18; 4:6). But this unit has two parts, indicated by the change from declaration to exhortation at 4:1. Generally, they indicate the doctrinal ground for confidence: Christ's victory over evil (3:18–22) and the application of that victory to the life of the baptized (4:1–6).

There seem to be few terminological links between this section and 4:7–11. The pericope must be simply an additional exhortation in view of the coming parousia and judgment (cp. 4:5 and 7).

C. 1 Peter 4:12–5:11; 5:12–14

A major break appears at 4:12; the doxology of 4:11 is followed by a renewed address ("beloved"; cp. 2:11) and a new, earnest exhortation. However, the evaluations of this break have been extremely diverse. Beare,[24] for example, says,

> It must be observed, however, that while the ever-present possibility of being called to suffer for righteousness' sake comes into view in several different passages, it is only in the section from 4:12 to the end that the writer speaks in specific terms of a persecution which is actually raging. In the remainder of the book, the problem of suffering is not the central theme, but is raised and dealt with only in relation to a general exposition of the nature of the Christian life. The long section from 1:3 to 4:11 is not epistolary in form or in content; it contains not a single local or personal reference, and not a line to suggest that the people to whom it is addressed are undergoing persecution. This section is complete in itself, and has all the appearance of a separate composition. It has an easy and natural beginning in a comprehensive exordium (1:3–12), and it is rounded off with a concluding paragraph of succinct general exhortations (4:7–11), sealed by a doxology. . . . It is not a letter but a sermon, and its theme is the nature and significance of the Christian life.

I consider such a theory insupportable. The mere frequence of reference to the theme of suffering in 1:3–4:11 (see n. 17) indicates that this is not "a general exposition of the nature of the Christian life." Given the inclusions pointed out by Dalton between 1:6–8 and 4:12–13, as well as between 1:6–7 and 5:10, it is improbable that there was a fundamental change in the political situation, and so in the author's description of Christians' suffering, between the writing of 1:3–4:11 and 4:12–5:11. Further, the use of the optative in 3:14, 17 does not mean that suffering is there regarded as a mere possibility. The force of the optative there

> conveys rather the delicate and affectionate attitude of the writer, who wishes to spare the feeling of his readers rather than frighten them with too blunt a reference to the painful trial of persecution.[25]

Beare,[26] arguing for the contrary view, that there is a difference in the political situations assumed in 1:3–4:11 and 4:12–5:11, stresses 4:17; "terror" which "can only be regarded as the beginning of the Judgment of God" is beginning with his own household and will come upon those who do not obey the gospel. However, there is a similar contrast in the supposedly earlier section of the letter: Christians are to be prepared to give a defense (3:15), and the pagans will give an account to the judging God (4:5) at the end, which is at hand (4:7).

4:12–19 seems rather to be a renewed, earnest exhortation, using themes announced earlier and stressing that sufferings are not an abnormal experience for Christians.[27] Thirty-five significant terms which are employed in 1:1–4:11 are taken up again in 4:12–5:11,[28] but an equal number of significant terms do not appear again after 4:13.[29] Several terms appear for the first time after 4:12, but this does not prove a separate origin for 4:12–5:11.[30] While the meaning of this evidence is debatable, it leaves me with the impression of a strong continuity between 4:12–5:11 and that which precedes. Nothing decisively new is introduced, though themes dealt with earlier are given a new twist.

After the exhortation of 4:12–19 with its reference to the end at hand, there is an exhortation along traditional lines[31] to the older and younger men of the community, an exhortation crowned by a citation from Prov 3:34 (1 Pet 5:5; cp. James 4:6). The reference to the "humble" is taken up again at the beginning of the last exhortation of the epistle (Dalton, p. 82), which is addressed to all (5:6). The Sermon on the Mount is reflected again (5:7; see Matt 6:25). The last words before the doxology (5:10) recall three of the chief themes of the letter: suffered, called, glory.[32] The mention of these three themes forms an inclusion with 1:6–7, which suitably closes the letter.

The outline which results from this analysis follows.

D.   An Outline of 1 Peter

1:1–2. Address and greetings (including the announcement of several themes).

I.   1:3–2:10. The Father's election, through the sacrifice offered by the Son, revealed by the Spirit, of a holy, believing, suffering, rejoicing, hoping, worshiping people, unto future grace and salvation which are shortly to appear in glory at the revelation of Jesus Christ.

A.   1:3–25. The word of Jesus' suffering and resurrection preached to the recipients; their resultant new birth, suffering, faith, obedience, and hope.

1.   1:3–12. The new birth accomplished by the Father through Jesus' resurrection; his suffering and that of those believing in him; this suffering and glory previously revealed by the Spirit and preached to them.

2.   1:13–25. Exhortation to obedience and holiness, in view of this new birth through the word.

B.   2:1–10. Moral and spiritual life of the faithful.

1.   2:1–3. Exhortation to put away evil.

2.   2:4–10. The worship offered by the elect, holy, believing people-priests, and the ordained stumbling of the disobedient.

II.   2:11–4:11. Interim ethics of submission to the pagan governors, masters, and husbands (who, if Christians, must treat their wives as fellow heirs of the future grace); these superiors may judge unjustly, but Christ after suffering proclaimed the destruction of the disobedient, who will soon be judged by God. Those with the charisma are to preach.

A. 2:11–3:12. The household duty code.
    1. 2:11–12. Introductory exhortation to aliens to behave so that their conduct will not be slandered by the resident nations, who will eventually praise the aliens' sovereign.
    2. 2:13–17. Exhortation to submit to human governors, who are supposed to praise good conduct.
    3. 2:18–25. Slaves are to submit even to hard, unjust masters, following Christ's example.
    4. 3:1–6. Wives are to submit to husbands, even if they are disobedient to the word, so that they may be gained.
    5. 3:7. Husbands are to treat their wives as persons who are also inheriting the future grace.
    6. 3:8–12. Summary, and climaxing quotation of Psalm 34.
B. 3:13–17. Pagan society's judgment of righteous Christians, who are to be able to give a defense for their behavior, but who may have to suffer because of their good conduct in Christ.
C. 3:18–4:6. Christ also suffered, but then in the Spirit he proclaimed their damnation to the disobedient spirits. As a few were saved in Noah's day, so Christians are saved through baptism, and they are to conduct themselves in view of the impending judgment of God.
D. 4:7–11. Final exhortation in view of the near end: love each other, pray, and those with the charisma are to preach the word.

III. 4:12–5:11. Renewed exhortation.
A. 4:12–19. Christian joy and trust in the midst of persecution, which is the beginning of God's judgment.
B. 5:1–5. Exhortation to older and younger men; exhortation to all to put on humility toward one another.
C. 5:6–11. Assurance that God cares and exhortation to remain firm in faith against the devil, who as a lion seeks to devour them.
5:12–14. Personal note and closing greetings.

NOTES TO APPENDIX I

[1]William J. Dalton, *Christ's Proclamation* 72–86. Cp. J. N. D. Kelly, *A Commentary on the Epistles of Peter and Jude* (HNTC; New York: Harper and Row, 1969) viii: "The single study which has helped me most is W. J. Dalton's brilliant monograph." Also W. J. Dalton, "Interpretation and Tradition: An Example from I Peter," *Gregorianum* 49 (1968) 11–37; Max-Alain Chevallier, "I Pierre 1/1 à 2/10. Structure littéraire et conséquences exégétiques," RHPR 51 (1971) 129–142. Now see L. Goppelt, *Erste Petrusbrief* 42–45, whose analysis of the structure of the letter corresponds to that proposed below.

[2]Léon Vaganay, "Le plan de l'Épître aux Hébreux," *Memorial Lagrange* (Paris: J. Gabalda, 1940) 269–277.

[3]Stanislas Lyonnet, "Note sur le plan de l'epître aux Romains," *RSR* 39–40 (1951–1952) 301–316.

[4]Dalton, *Christ's Proclamation* 76. Cp. John Hall Elliott, *The Elect and the Holy. An Exegetical Examination of I Peter 2:4-10 and the Phrase βασίλειον ἱεράτευμα* (NovTSup 12; Leiden: E. J. Brill, 1966) 205, n. 5: "Bornemann's conclusion that I P is thus best understood as a baptismal homily based on the text of Ps 33 fails to comprehend Peter's use of OT material. OT citations and allusions made by the author are never the objects of his exegesis. The point of departure is never an OT text but the situation of his addressees, i.e., the reality of their new life through Christ. . . . Ps 33:6 has not been used as text but as illustration for the text proper—rebirth through the word." Cp. ibid., 216, n. 1: "It is interesting to note that the citation from Ps 33[34]:14-17 in I P 3:10-12 served much the same summarizing and climaxing purpose as did the pericope introduced also by a thought from Ps 33 in 2:4."

[5]Election is a central theme only in the first two chapters: 1:1, 15; 2:4, 6, 9 (twice), 21; 3:9; 5:10, 13. Cp. τίθημι in 2:6, 8.

[6]Dalton's emphasis. The two terms translated by the English "suffer" are not the same verbs; however they are used as synonyms in 2:19.

[7]Hans Windisch, *Die katholischen Briefe*, revised by H. Preisker (HNT; Tübingen: Mohr, 1951) 156-162; Frank L. Cross, *I Peter. A Paschal Liturgy* 36-41.

[8]1:25 thus refers back to 1:12. Chevallier, "I Pierre 1/1 à 2/10" 130 also sees a reference forward to 2:9.

[9]Cross, *I Peter* 36-40, dependent on the earlier work of Preisker, describes 1 Pet 1:3-4:11 as a baptismal liturgy. Perdelwitz and Beare went only so far as to call this same section of 1 Peter a baptismal homily. See above pp. 11-12. All four authors separate the epistolary address (1:1-2) from the rest of the first chapter, which, as Dalton has shown, is a fundamental error.

[10]See esp. Chevallier, "I Pierre 1/1 à 2/10" 138-139, 141.

[11]See Edward G. Selwyn, *First Epistle of St. Peter* 393-400 for some theories about this relationship.

[12]See Elliott, *The Elect and the Holy* 214-216, who observes: "In contrast to 2:1f. the mood [in 2:4-6] is indicative throughout. Analogous to 1:18-21, 1:23-25, and 3:18-22, this section explicates and substantiates foregoing exhortation" (p. 216).

[13]Chevallier, "I Pierre 1/1 à 2/10" 130 stresses that the references to God's "mercy" at the beginning and the end of the unit 1:3 to 2:10 form an inclusion.

[14]It may be that Ps 34 was originally associated with the *Haustafel* material because of the phrase "pursue peace" (quoted 1 Pet 3:11b). That precisely this phrase could be stressed may be seen in Heb 12:14 (where it is also cited in a persecution context). For a sketch of the contemporary interpretation of the phrase see Strack-Billerbeck, *Kommentar* 1:217 (three citations), and 1 Clem. 22, following household ethics.

[15]λοιδορέω, 2:23. ἀντιλοιδορέω, 2:23. λοιδορία, 3:9. Cp. 1 Tim 5:14.

[16]J. Ramsey Michaels, "Eschatology in I Peter iii.17," *NTS* 13 (1966-1967) 397.

[17]πάσχω, 2:19, 20, 21, 23; 3:14, 17, 18; 4:1, 15, 19; 5:10. πάθημα, 1:11; 4:13; 5:1, 9. λυπέω, 1:6. λυπή, 2:19. See the discussion oι the variant readings ἀπέθανεν and ἔπαθεν in 3:18 by Dalton, *Christ's Proclamation* 119-121.

[18]ἀγαθοποιέω, 2:15, 20; 3:6, 17. ἀγαθοποιία, 4:19. ἀγαθοποιός, 2:14. Cp. ἀγαθός, 3:11, 13, 16, 21. Then κακία, 2:1, 16. κακός, 3:9, 10, 11, 12. κακοποιέω, 3:17. κακοποιός, 2:12, 14; 4:15.

[19]ἀδίκως, 2:19. ἄδικος, 3:18. δικαίως, 2:23. δίκαιος, 3:12, 18; 4:18. δικαιοσύνη, 2:24; 3:14.

[20]Contrast Aristotle's attitude on the impossibility of slaves being treated unjustly.

[21]κρίνω, 1:17; 2:23; 4:5, 6. κρίμα, 4:17.

[22]θέλημα, 2:15; 3:17; 4:2, 19. θέλω, 3:17.

[23]The reading ἔπαθεν is to be preferred in 3:18. See n. 17.

[24]Francis W. Beare, *First Epistle of Peter* 6.

[25]Dalton, *Christ's Proclamation* 68. See T. C. G. Thornton, "I Peter, a Paschal Liturgy?" *JTS* 12 (1961) 26; Frederick W. Danker, "I Peter 1,24-2,17—A Consolatory Pericope," *ZNW* 58 (1967) 100, n. 38.

[26]Beare, *First Epistle of Peter* 7-8.

[27]W. C. van Unnik, "Christianity according to I Peter," *Exp Tim* 68 (1956) 80.

²⁸Some of the important terms are in Dalton's two inclusions, mentioned p. 123 above, and in my nn. 5, 15-22.

²⁹Some of the most interesting, found in neither verbal nor nominal form after 4:13, are: Ἰησοῦς, παροικία, ἀναστροφή, φόβος, κύριος, καταλαλία, λυπή, ὑπομένω, λοιδορέω, βλασφημέω.

³⁰The ones which are most striking to me are: κοινωνέω, ὀνειδίζω, Χριστιανός, πρεσβύτερος, μάρτυς, λέων. The first term (4:13) is not a big development beyond the constant association of Christ's and the Christian's suffering apparent at every point in the letter where suffering is mentioned. The second and possibly the third terms are a reflection of Matt 5:11-12, which had already been reflected in 1 Pet 1:6 and 3:14. The term "presbyter" appears with the *Haustafel* in the Pastorals (though not in Col-Eph), so it is not unusual here; to some extent, these thoughts on church order are anticipated in 2:25 and 4:10-11. The term "lion" appears with the word "apology" in 2 Tim 4:16-17, a fact which might be crucial in interpreting 1 Pet 3:15, assuming that 1 Pet 5:8 belongs to the same letter.

³¹See Selwyn, *First Epistle of St. Peter* 436.

³²"Glory" is mentioned in 1:1, 7, 8, 11, 21, 24; 2:12; 4:11, 13, 14, 16; 5:1-5. It is usually contrasted with suffering, but not in 2:12; 5:4.

Appendix II

Elliott's Interpretation of 1 Pet 2:9d and 5d

Elliott[1] has suggested that 1 Pet 2:9d governs the interpretation of the code which follows. This suggestion makes it necessary to review elements of his interpretation. Elliott interprets God's election of the Anatolian Christians as a royal priesthood (or kingdom, body of priests) who are to "proclaim the mighty deeds of Him Who called you out of darkness into His marvelous light" (2:9d) to mean that they are "to preach" the mighty deeds of God[2] to the world, to outsiders, so they might glorify God (2:12), i.e., be converted by this missionary witness.[3] He supports this by noting that 2:9 reflects not only Exod 19:6 but also Isa 43:20-21. (". . . I have formed this people for myself and they shall proclaim my praises [λαόν μου, ὅν περιεποιησάμην τὰς ἀρετάς μου διηγεῖσθαι].")[4] He notices that 1 Pet 2:9 has replaced the Septuagint διηγεῖσθαι with ἐξαγγείλητε, which is synonymous but more emphatic, meaning "to proclaim (widely, publicly)."[5] He also suggests that the author of 1 Peter understood this reference to Isa 43:21b in the light of 42:6-9, where the terms "called," "light," "darkness," and "praises" or "virtues" occur.[6] The reference to 42:6 is crucial for Elliott, I suspect, because there it is clear that the message is directed to "the nations,"[7] whereas this is not clear in 43:21.

Further, Elliott understands 1 Pet 2:5d ("to offer through Jesus Christ spiritual sacrifices acceptable to God") as parallel to 2:9d.[8] As the translation quoted indicates, Elliott thinks the prepositional phrase "through Jesus Christ" qualifies the verb "to offer" rather than the adjective "acceptable" (despite the word order in Greek which places "through Jesus Christ" at the end of the sentence). "Acceptable" belongs with the phrase "to God";[9] this adjective does not qualify the "spiritual sacrifices." The phrase "to God" does not belong to the verb ("to offer to God") but to the adjective ("acceptable to God").[10] "To offer spiritual sacrifices" in 2:5d points to a community of persons charged with a priestly task.[11] For Elliott this does not refer to hymns of praise, so a parallel should not be drawn to Heb 13:15; rather, "spiritual sacrifices" refer to a holy life,[12] so the important parallel is Rom 12:1.[13] The two important terms "conduct" (ἀναστροφή) and "doing good" (ἀγαθοποιία) suggest what "spiritual sacrifices" entail: the goal of a holy life is the glorification of God which further implies a pronounced missionary impulse. Doing good has the purpose of winning the unbeliever for the greater glory of God.[14] "In view of the missionary and witness connotations of 2:5, 9 one might speak of a 'ministry' of the total community to the world. Proclamation, preaching, is the implication of verse 9."[15] This is the "purpose and task" of the elected people.[16]

Certain aspects of Elliott's interpretation are unconvincing. In contexts where ἐξαγγέλλω refers to "proclaiming" the praises, deeds, righteousness, or works of God, the proclaiming is always *to God* in worship (Ps 9:15–16[13–14]; 55:9 [56:8]; 70[71]:15; 72[73]:28; 78[79]:13; 106[107]:22; probably 118[119]:13, 26; Sir 18:4; Philo, *Noah's Work as a Planter* 128).[17] In the first, second, third, and fifth references, this worship occurs in the context of persecution, and the fifth reference (Ps 106:22) includes the observation that those worshiping have been "brought out of darkness" (106:14; cp. v. 10). However, this does not imply mission preaching, either in Psalm 106 or in 1 Peter. In fact, there is no Septuagint text where this verb is used to refer to mission preaching.

It is, of course, true that when an Old Testament text is cited, it is sometimes possible to assume that part of the unquoted context must be known to understand the purpose of the reference. But I doubt whether it is legitimate to take the three words from Isa 43:21b quoted in 1 Pet 2:9d, interpret them by verses which are more than a chapter distant (Isa 42:6–9), and then understand those distant verses as supplying the basic meaning of 1 Pet 2:4–10.

In fact, those who have been "called out of darkness" in 1 Pet 2:9 are the Christian recipients of the letter. It is more natural to understand the phrase "that you may declare the wonderful deeds of him . . ." to refer to the Christians' praise of God in worship for his having elected them, as the following evidence indicates: First, the pattern of (1) election and (2) the resulting praise of God in worship is found in Isa 42:6 and 8, which Elliott argues is in the mind of the author of 1 Pet 2:9 (see n. 6 above). Second, Exod 19:6, quoted in 1 Pet 2:9, is interpreted in Rev 1:6 and 5:10. There Exod 19:6 is cited to mean that Christ made Christians a kingdom, priests *to God* (ἱερεῖς τῷ θεῷ) his father (1:6). Christ made them *to God* a kingdom and priests (5:10). Despite the differences which Elliott points out[18] between 1 Pet 2:9 and Rev 1:6, 5:10, in both books the task of the (active body of) *priests* is directed to God, not outward to the world. Third, 1 Pet 4:10–11 exhorts those with the charisma to speak as the oracles of God. Certain persons have the gift and duty to preach; others do not. Elliott interprets this preaching in worship as an exclusively inner-directed preaching, while the active body of priests referred to in 2:9 has an outer-directed mission to all that is non-church.[19] Although it is not a Petrine text, 1 Cor 14:23–25 shows that the distinction Elliott makes is invalid. Whenever missionary evangelizing is referred to in the letter (1 Pet 1:12, 25; cp. 4:6),[20] the aorist is used and the reference is to the past evangelization of those presently Christians. There is no reference in the letter to the "task" of all Christians doing missionary preaching.

Elements of Elliott's interpretation of 2:5d are also questionable. He argues that "acceptable" belongs with the phrase "to God" and does not qualify "spiritual sacrifices." The word order makes it probable that "acceptable" qualifies "spiritual sacrifices."[21]

The appeal to Rom 12:1 as a parallel overlooks the fact that the verb in Romans is not ἀναφέρω as it is in 1 Pet 2:5d and Heb 13:15. This verb is very commonly used with "God" or "Lord" in the dative case[22] (though the dative is not necessarily expressed), just as in 1 Peter, so that it is forced when Elliott separates the two in 1 Pet 2:5. It is natural in Greek to follow the verb "to offer" with an accusative describing what is offered, which is then followed by the dative telling to whom it is offered (e.g. 1 Sam 18:27; 1 Chr 29:21; 2 Chr 8:12; 23:18; Isa 18:7; Heb 13:15), just as in 1 Peter. 2 Macc 10:7 is a parallel:

Therefore bearing ivy-wreathed wands and beautiful branches and also fronds of palm, they offered hymns of thanksgiving to him who had given success to the purifying of his own holy place (ὕμνους ἀνέφερον τῷ εὐοδώσαντι καθαρισθῆναι τὸν ἑαυτοῦ τόπον).

So I agree with Elliott[23] that there is a correspondence between these two phrases in 2:5d and 9d, but that correspondence does not lie in an "orientation outward to the world," in the implied task of missionary preaching by word and life.[24] I conclude that whether the sacrifices are those of Christian life or worship (probably the latter), they are offered to God, not to the world.

Finally, Elliott's interpretation ignores what *is* said about the pagans in 1 Pet 2:4-10. They have "rejected" the Lord (2:4-7), and as they do "not believe" (2:7), they "stumble because they disobey the word, as they were destined to do (ἐτέθησαν)" (2:8; cp. 1 Thess 5:9). For the author of 1 Peter, election is not only to salvation.

If Dalton is correct in interpreting the difficult pericope 3:18-22, there, too, the Christian attitude to the pagans is not missionary. One basic reality in the letter is persecution, in which the survival of the Christian communities is at stake, and there is a negative expectation concerning the pagans' eschatological fate.[25] The function of 3:18-22 is to give the doctrinal basis for the confidence of the Christian readers in the face of this persecution.[26] What advantage has the suffering Christian over his pagan persecutor? Specifically, in 3:19 the risen Lord is presented as a new Enoch (cp. esp. 1 Enoch 12:4, 13:3, 15:2), proclaiming his triumph and their damnation to the rebellious spirits who "formerly did not obey" (3:19-20; cp. 2:8).[27] Just as Christ was victorious, so the Christian will be victorious over the disobedient world.[28] As pagans now judge Christians (3:15-16), so Christ will soon judge the pagans (4:5).

Christ, the new Enoch, has won, by His passion and resurrection, the definitive victory over these angelic powers of evil. The unbelieving world, allied with and instigated by these powers, shares their defeat and condemnation, a condemnation to be ratified at the last judgment. The Christian, in closest solidarity with Christ, can face with confidence the brutal and unbelieving world, because he knows that its power is illusory. . . . In the great final judgment, which has already begun, the faith of the Christian sets him amongst the saved, while the unbelieving world, including the magistrates who interrogate him, in solidarity with the spirits of unbelief, is doomed to condemnation.[29]

I have referred to 3:18–22 in order to point out that Elliott's failure to give proper weight to the negative expectation with respect to the "disobedient" in 2:4–10 is not a minor matter; it results in a dislocation of the emphasis of that passage and the letter as a whole. On the one hand, the author does hope for a positive response from the state in 2:14 (contrast 5:8, 13), and there is some missionary optimism in 3:1. On the other hand, the church in 1 Peter is a small group[30] in a disobedient world which the author expects to perish soon. In this ambiguous situation, he expects all those elected to praise God; he does not expect all to become missionaries.

Even if Elliott's exegesis of 2:9d were accepted, there is a consideration which requires the conclusion that 2:9d does not theologically introduce the household code. Paul characteristically states the theological indicative first; then out of this he develops an imperative. This is not the case in 1 Peter. The reverse occurs: paraenesis is given first, then an indicative pericope follows which "explicates and substantiates foregoing exhortation."[31] So 2:9d does not introduce the domestic code; it closes the preceding section.

I conclude that the "good conduct" described in the code is not given a missionary thrust by 1 Pet 2:5d and 9d.[32] The function of the code is to be determined from other texts.

NOTES TO APPENDIX II

[1]John Hall Elliott, *The Elect and the Holy. An Exegetical Examination of I Peter 2:4–10 and the Phrase βασίλειον ἱεράτευμα* (NovTSup 12; Leiden: E. J. Brill, 1966). See the reviews in *TZ* 23 (1967) 445–446 (Grob); *CTM* 38 (1967) 329–332 (Danker); *TQ* 147 (1967) 476–477 (Schelkle); *Int* 22 (1968) 103–105 (Schweizer).

[2]Elliott, *The Elect and the Holy* 42.

[3]Ibid., 179–180; also 74–75, 183–185, 192, 195–198, 221, 224. See W. Brandt, "Wandel als Zeugnis nach dem I.Petrusbrief," *Verbum Dei Manet in Aeternum*, Festschrift Otto Schmitz (Wittenberg: Luther, 1955) 10–25. Also Johannes Blauw, *The Missionary Nature of the Church in the New Testament. A Survey of the Biblical Theology of Mission* (New York: McGraw-Hill, 1962) 126–136.

[4]Elliott, *The Elect and the Holy* 39.

[5]Ibid., 41–42. The missionary activity of Hellenistic Judaism, which Elliott (pp. 73–75) assumes as the context for the translation of the Septuagint, is debatable. See Abraham J. Malherbe, "The Apologetic Theology of the *Preaching of Peter*," *Restoration Quarterly* 13 (1970) 210, n. 26.

[6]Elliott, *The Elect and the Holy* 41 with n. 3. However, God's election (Isa 42:6) means that his glory, his praise, should not be given to another, to a graven image (42:8). If Elliott were correct that Isa 42:6–9 was in the mind of the author of 1 Pet 2:9, Isa 42:8 suggests that the "proclamation" of 43:21 would be directed to Yahweh, not outward to the world.

[7]However, Harry M. Orlinsky, *The So-called "Servant of the Lord" and "Suffering Servant" in Second Isaiah* (VTSup 14; Leiden: E. J. Brill, 1967) 75–77 (cp. 157–158) strongly argues that Isa 42:6 did not originally refer to missionary activity.

[8]Elliott, *The Elect and the Holy* 148.

[9]Ibid., 161 with n. 1.

[10]Ibid., 161, n. 3.

[11]Ibid., 167.

[12]Ibid., 167, 174–176.

[13]Ibid., 176. "'Sacrifices' refers not to a cultic act of worship but to a way of life" (ibid., 209).

[14]Ibid., 183; see pp. 179–183, 197. For a different interpretation of the purpose of doing good, see above pp. 87–88, 94–95.

[15]Ibid., 192.

[16]Ibid., 196, 221.

[17]The Philo reference is in a context (93–138) interpreting Lev 19:23–25; the section begins discussing proselytes and then (94 and 100) the καθήκοντα are referred to.

[18]Ibid., 107–120, 170, 197, 223, n. 7.

[19]Ibid., 192–195, 224.

[20]W. J. Dalton, *Christ's Proclamation* 257–263 affirms that 1 Pet 4:6 refers to the preaching of the gospel on earth to those Christians who have died in the meantime (cp. 1 Thess 4:13, 15–18), who thus would not be alive at the Parousia. If Dalton is correct, the statement in the text would be true of all three references to "evangelizing."

[21]Danker, *CTM* 38 (1967) 329 suggests that the accent on acceptable sacrifices here is a contrast to the sacrifices God refuses to accept in Mal 1:10. See Danker, "I Peter 1,24–2,17—A Consolatory Pericope," *ZNW* 58 (1967) 93–102 at 96 with n. 13. See Ernest Best, "Spiritual Sacrifice. General Priesthood in the NT," *Int* 14 (1960) 273–299 and idem, "I Peter II 4–10—A Reconsideration," *NovT* 11 (1969) 270–293, at 287–288.

[22]The Hatch-Redpath concordance gives many examples. Joseph Blinzler, "IEPATEYMA. Zur Exegese von I Petr. 2,5 u. 9," in *Episcopus. Festschrift für Michael Kardinal von Faulhaber* (Regensburg: Gregorius, 1949) 49–65 also argues (p. 51) that the dative "to God" is related to the verb "to offer."

[23]Elliott, *The Elect and the Holy* 148, 184.

[24]Cp. Best, "I Peter II 4–10" 287–288. Blinzler, "IEPATEYMA" 56 notes that the specific acts which constitute the sacrifice remain unspecified. Elliott, *The Elect and the Holy* 173 denies that Rom 15:16 is a parallel to 1 Pet 2:5 and 9; the Gentile converts are not the sacrifice offered to God.

[25]Dalton, *Christ's Proclamation* 108.

[26]Ibid., 103.

[27]Ibid., 112, 165, 176.

[28]Ibid., 196–200.

[29]Ibid., 200. Cp. E. Lohse, "Paraenese und Kerygma im 1.Petrusbrief," *ZNW* 45 (1954) 87.

[30]The recipients of the letter find it meaningful that "few" were saved in Noah's day. See E. F. F. Bishop, "Oligoi in 1 Peter 3:20," *CBQ* 13 (1951) 44–45.

[31]This is said with reference to 1 Pet 2:4–10 by Elliott, *The Elect and the Holy* 16. Cp. Lohse, "Paraenese" 86.

[32]On whether the household code as a whole functioned in the Christian mission, see p. 108 above.

Appendix III

The Date of 1 Peter

Recently scholars have tended to place 1 Peter in the middle of the second half of the first century. Elliott suggests that it was written "perhaps between A.D. 70 and 90,"[1] while Goppelt places it slightly earlier ("zwischen 65 und 80").[2] Elliot is correct that those who explain the references to suffering in the letter by the imperial persecution theory have not refuted the "more likely explanation of the situation, viz., the hostility, harassment, and ostracism of a local, social, and 'unofficial' nature."[3] The philosophical, ethical, and apologetic material collected in this study adds further weight to Elliott's conclusion because the source of this unofficial hostility is clearer. The socio-political tensions reflected in 1 Peter are best explained by the conversion of some persons in Greco-Roman culture to a despised religion and the predictable reaction of their domestic superiors to such conversions. This general cultural situation, not the persecutions of either Domitian or Trajan, stimulated the writing of 1 Peter, so the letter is not datable to the reign of either emperor.

The philosophical and apologetic material reviewed above does not make it possible to be more precise than Goppelt is about the date. The Aristotelian form "concerning household management" was available over several centuries: to Areius Didymus in the first century B.C., to Seneca in the first century A.D., and to Dio Chrysostom in the early second century A.D. And the form was used apologetically by Dionysius of Halicarnassus in the first century B.C. and by Josephus in the early second century A.D.

The form of the household code as outlined by Aristotle included a master-slave section; this makes it significant that the author of 1 Peter omitted an exhortation to masters. It might be argued that there were no masters in the congregation to address, which would distance 1 Peter from Pliny, *Ep.* X.96. He mentions Christians who were "Roman citizens" and affirms that "many of every age, every rank, and even both sexes, are brought into danger." However, the argument that there were no masters to address would not be convincing. The educated author may have had slaves, but he focused his attention on those who were the center of social tension with

Greco-Roman culture, those in religiously divided households whose "harmony" had been disturbed. The household was not divided in cases where the master was Christian, so the author did not direct his exhortations to that relationship. Lohse[4] has argued similarly that "the exhortation to husbands was so short precisely because it was unrelated to the theme of suffering."

Otherwise Goppelt's discussion of the date is persuasive. He makes the following points: It was not until after Nero that Christians viewed Rome as "Babylon" (1 Pet 5:13).[5] However, unlike some slightly later canonical works, the problem of the delay of the Parousia nowhere appears in 1 Peter.[6] The organization of the churches under presbyters indicates a time before Domitian.[7] Civil disturbances directed against Christians in the time of Paul were local, but in the time of this later letter, they occur "throughout the world" (1 Pet 5:9).[8] With other scholars, Goppelt notes Pliny's reference to Christians in Asia Minor who had given up their faith twenty years before his time, so about 90 A.D. (Pliny, *Ep.* X.96,6).[9] Other texts also refer to civil disturbances in Asia Minor before the end of the first century (Rev 6:9, 13:7, 17:6, 20:4; Ignatius, *Magn.* 8; *Rom.* 5).[10] Unlike the later book of Revelation, in 1 Peter the conflict between Christianity and the state does not yet center around the cult of the emperor. The persecutions also seem earlier than those reflected in Hebrews and Luke.[11] Heb 10:32-39 and 12:4 accept persecution as usual, but it is still a surprise in 1 Pet 4:12. The terminology which describes persecution "for the name" is more developed in Luke than in 1 Peter (cp. Luke 21:12 with 1 Pet 5:13; see also Acts 5:41).[12] These considerations convincingly place 1 Peter in the years 65-90 A.D.

NOTES TO APPENDIX III

[1]John H. Elliott, "The Rehabilitation of an Exegetical Step-Child: 1 Peter in Recent Research," *JBL* 95 (1976) 243-254 at 254.

[2]Leonhard Goppelt, *Erste Petrusbrief* 64, 65.

[3]Elliott, "Rehabilitation" 252. See Goppelt, *Erste Petrusbrief* 62-63.

[4]E. Lohse, "Paraenese und Kerygma im 1.Petrusbrief," *ZNW* 45 (1954) 74.

[5]Goppelt, *Erste Petrusbrief* 43, 62, 63.

[6]Ibid., 64.

[7]Ibid., 44, 65.

[8]Ibid., 60.

[9]Ibid., 63.

[10]H. Last, "Christenverfolgung II (juristisch)," *RAC* 2 (1954) 1212.

[11]Goppelt, *Erste Petrusbrief* 63, n. 122.

[12]Ibid., 63. Gerhard Krodel, "The First Letter of Peter," in G. Krodel (ed.), *Hebrews, James, 1 and 2 Peter, Jude, Revelation* (Proclamation Commentaries; Philadelphia: Fortress, 1977) 53-59 strongly states the arguments for pseudonymity.

The Political, Legal, and Economic Status of Women in the Roman World[1]

Women made some political gains in the first centuries B.C. and A.D., and their legal and economic responsibilities increased significantly. The first women's demonstration in history occurred in 195 B.C. when women gathered to oppose the Oppian law (Livy 34.2–8). For twenty years during the war with Hannibal, this law had limited the amount of gold each woman could possess, and it prohibited other luxuries of dress and transportation. Cato argued against repeal of the Oppian law; but even Lucius Valerius' speech, which Livy represents as winning the appeal of the law, assumed the Aristotelian view of the unequal relationship between the sexes (Livy 34.2–4 and 34.5–7).[2]

Q. Lutatius Catulus pronounced the first funeral oration in honor of a woman, his elderly mother, in 102 B.C. In 68 B.C. Julius Caesar delivered the first funeral oration for a young woman, his aunt Julia, whom he said was descended from the gods. When Augustus' sister Octavia died, she was honored by two such orations. The purpose of such speeches, however, was to honor the male relatives of the deceased women.[3]

Among the most important paradigms for the political lives of Roman women were the three wives of Mark Antony.[4] Fulvia's image was negative: she entered spheres reserved for men and ruled Antony. Octavia was devoted to her country, bore Antony two children, and loved her husband. Cleopatra's image as the foreign "wife" was discussed in chap. V. Unlike Cleopatra, Roman women, such as Livia and Agrippina the younger, remained the power behind the throne.[5] Although Roman women had more freedom than Greek women and could be Roman citizens, they were not allowed either to vote or to hold political office.[6] Compared to Roman men, Roman women were not liberated in the political sphere.

Women did acquire economic power, and that was one of the reasons for their enhanced legal status. This legal development took place in areas newly Hellenized, e.g. Egypt, not in the old Greek cities.[7] Women could protect their own interests in Hellenistic Egypt. The legal power of the father over his daughter, for example, was judicially limited: if she wished, she could remain married despite her father's wishes to the contrary.

In Rome, the power of the *pater familias* remained legally in force until Diocletian (285–305), but in reality the father's power declined dramatically. By the late Republic, guardianship over women was a burden for men but only a slight disadvantage to women.[8] By the second century A.D., both the power of the *pater familias* and relationship through the male line (*agnatio*), two of the foundations of the Roman patriarchal family, had been made ineffectual.[9] Part of Augustus' legislation decreed that a freeborn woman who bore three children and a freedwoman who bore four children were exempt from tutelage (*jus liberorum*).[10] Slightly later, Claudius abolished automatic guardianship of male relatives over women.

The power of the *pater familias* exceeded that of a woman's husband unless the father decided to transfer power (*manus*) to the husband.[11] One vital feature of *manus* marriage for the bride concerned domestic religion: the girl worshiped at her husband's hearth, not her father's; her husband's ancestors became hers.[12] However, marriage without *manus*, free marriage, became the rule in Cicero's time, so the wife and her possessions were more independent of the husband's control.[13] The wife could choose to return, with her property, to her father.[14]

Laws which regulated the succession to property underwent considerable change.[15] According to the early XII tablets, daughters and sons shared equally in the estate of a father who died intestate. A daughter under her father's power would share in her father's estate, but a wife under her husband's power would share in her husband's estate just as if she were his daughter. Although until Hadrian Roman women could make wills only with difficulty, they found means to bequeath and receive wealth; by the late Republic, they were controlling vast properties.[16] Finally in 178 A.D., mothers were allowed to inherit from children and children from mothers intestate (*Senatusconsultum Orfitianum*). The second century A.D. was a period of significant change: a woman became legally a member of the family of her husband and children, not of the family of her father.

Given this social-legal status, certain women chose to join foreign cults (as discussed in chap. V) which brought them into legal difficulties, whether married or not. They faced criminal trials before the provincial governor. Roman law concerned with private property was an impressive achievement; but in contrast, Roman criminal and public law was most unsatisfactory.[17] Crimes of the common man (and woman) had to be dealt with as an exceptional measure (*extra ordinem*) even in Rome; the magistrate had very wide discretion, especially in criminal trials, both in setting penalties and in deciding which cases to hear. Imperial instructions to provincial governors bade them to take care of "bad men."[18] They were to keep their provinces settled and orderly. There was no specific *law* which made Christianity itself illegal before 249 A.D.[19] A magistrate's power to martyr a Christian was less formal than a law. The principle is expressed in passages of Cicero's *Laws*:

Commands shall be just, and the citizens shall obey them dutifully and without protest. Upon the disobedient or guilty citizen the magistrate shall use compulsion by means of fines, imprisonment, or stripes. . . . (3.6. Trans. Keyes)

[Praetors] shall be subject to no one; the safety of the people shall be their highest law. (3.8)[20]

NOTES TO APPENDIX IV

[1]For bibliography see Sarah B. Pomeroy, "Selected Bibliography on Women in Antiquity," *Arethusa* 6 (1973) 125–157, esp. 144–147; Susan Treggiari, "Roman Social History: Recent Interpretations," *Histoire sociale. Social History* 8 (1975) 149–164, esp. 159–162; Wolfgang Kunkel, *An Introduction to Roman Legal and Constitutional History* (Oxford: Clarendon, 1973) 192–228; A. Oepke, "Ehe I," *RAC* 4 (1959) 650–666; G. Delling, "Eheleben," "Ehescheidung," *RAC* 4 (1959) 691–719; K. Thraede, "Frau," *RAC* 8 (1972) 197–269. On the period before Augustus see Barbara Förtsch, *Die politische Rolle der Frau in der römischen Republik* (Würzburger Studien zur Altertumswissenschaft 5; Stuttgart: W. Kohlhammer, 1935) and Claudine Herrmann, *Le rôle judiciare et politique des femmes sous la République romaine* (Collection Latomus LXVII; Brussels: Latomus, 1964).

[2]J. P. V. D. Balsdon, *Roman Women. Their History and Habits* (Westport: Greenwood, 1962) 33–36. Sarah B. Pomeroy, *Goddesses, Whores, Wives and Slaves. Women in Classical Antiquity* (New York: Schocken, 1975) 180. K. Thraede, "Ärger mit der Freiheit. Die Bedeutung von Frauen in Theorie und Praxis der alten Kirche," in G. Scharffenorth, ed., *"Freunde in Christus werden . . ." Die Beziehung von Mann und Frau als Frage an Theologie und Kirche* (Berlin: Burckhardthaus, 1977) 82–84 notes that the historicity of the Lex Oppia has been doubted. The speeches in Livy, Thraede says, represent arguments from as many angles as possible both for and against the liberation of women; these arguments were current during the time of the late Republic. This makes it significant that even Lucius Valerius assumes that wives are "weak" and that their husbands exercise a control over them which can approach "feminine slavery" (esp. 34.7.7–15).

[3]Balsdon, *Roman Women* 46–47; Pomeroy, *Goddesses* 182–183.

[4]Balsdon, *Roman Women* 49–50; Pomeroy, *Goddesses* 185; Thraede, "Frau" 213.

[5]Linda W. Rutland, "Women as Makers of Kings in Tacitus' *Annals*," *Classical World* 72 (1978) 15–29.

[6]Förtsch, *Die politische Rolle* 1–8; Pomeroy, *Goddesses* x, 188; Treggiari, "Roman Social History" 161; Ludwig Friedländer, *Roman Life and Manners under the Early Empire* (New York: Barnes and Noble, 1968) 1: 250–251.

[7]Claire Préaux, "Le statut de la femme à l'époque hellénistique, principalement en Egypte," *La femme. Recueils de la Société Jean Bodin* 11 (Brussels: Librairie encyclopédique, 1959) 127–175.

[8]John Crook, *Law and Life of Rome* (Ithaca: Cornell University, 1967) 114–115; H. F. Jolowicz, *Historical Introduction to the Study of Roman Law* (Cambridge: Cambridge University, 1967) 249–250.

[9]Jerome Carcopino, *Daily Life in Ancient Rome. The People and the City at the Height of the Empire* (New Haven: Yale University, 1940) 76, 78 stresses this emancipation. See Jolowicz, *Historical Introduction* 118–120.

[10]J. P. V. D. Balsdon, *Life and Leisure in Ancient Rome* (New York: McGraw-Hill, 1969) 83.

[11]Balsdon, *Roman Women* 179–180.

[12]Pomeroy, *Goddesses* 152.

[13]Alan Watson, *The Law of Persons in the Later Roman Republic* (Oxford: Clarendon, 1967) 19–29; Friedländer, *Roman Life* 236–238; Carcopino, *Daily Life* 80–81. But see Crook, *Law and Life* 103–104, who is more cautious.

[14]Carcopino, *Daily Life* 95–100 on the ease of divorce; Jolowicz, *Historical Introduction* 245–246; Watson, *The Law of Persons* 48–57.

[15]Crook, *Law and Life* 119–132; Jolowicz, *Historical Introduction* 260–262.

[16]See also Susan Treggiari, "Jobs for Women," *American Journal of Ancient History* 1 (1976) 76–104; Beryl Rawson, "Family Life among the Lower Classes in Rome in the First Two Centuries of the Empire," *Classical Philology* 61 (1966) 71–83.

[17]G. E. M. de Ste. Croix, "Why Were the Early Christians Persecuted?" in M. I. Finley (ed.), *Studies in Ancient Society* (Past and Present Series; London: Routledge and Kegan Paul, 1974) 217–219.

[18]Ibid., 226. Cp. 1 Pet 2:14.

[19]H. Last, "Christenverfolgung II (juristisch)," *RAC* 2 (1954) 1208–1228, at 1220.

[20]Cited ibid., 1221.

Appendix V

Roman Stoics and Plutarch on Equality between Husband and Wife

Several scholars contrast the Stoic principle of equality with the domestic code which stresses the subordination of wives. Crouch considers it difficult to imagine a Stoic or a wandering popular philosopher asserting that a woman should be submissive to her husband.[1] Crouch appeals to Vogt's conclusion: "Here [in the Stoic Musonius], the ethical equality of the sexes with all its consequences is recognized."[2] Musonius was a "women's liberationist" of the first century A.D., but Vogt's generalization goes too far. Musonius argued *That Women Too Should Study Philosophy* (*Or.* III). Musonius states the egalitarian *theory* that women have the same senses as men, the same parts of the body (?), and a natural inclination toward virtue (38,26–40,2 Lutz). But he is aware of the objection that the *practical* results of his theory will be that women will abandon their households when they ought to be at home spinning (42,11–15 Lutz). Musonius responds to the objection by discussing the four cardinal virtues which a woman who studies philosophy would be taught, and all four are explained in a practical mold. "In the first place a woman must be a good housekeeper"; Musonius typically places this assertion in the context of the feminine virtue of chastity and self-control (40,10–12 and 17 Lutz; cp. Dionysius Hal., *Rom. Ant.* II.24–25).[3] Similarly in *Or.* IV, *Should Daughters Receive the Same Education as Sons*, Musonius refers to virtue which is "equally appropriate to the *nature* of both" sexes (46,32 Lutz). He expands on the four cardinal virtues in a practical way in light of an objection: his theory means that men should learn spinning and women should exercise in the gymnasium (46,13–15 Lutz). No, he says, indoor work is more suitable for women, outdoor work for men, but occasionally, when it is fitting, this might be varied (46,16–31 Lutz). So the old distinction—men outside the house and women inside—is rejected in theory but largely retained in practice. In this way, Musonius counters the popular (male) impression that Stoic ethics are impractical. Discussing *Sexual Indulgence* (*Or.* XII), Musonius argues that the husband as well as the wife

should limit sexual activity to one's married partner, a limit which excludes
the husband's relations with slave girls, but he argues as follows:

> And yet surely one will not expect men to be less moral ($\chi\epsilon\ell\rho ovas$) than women, nor
> less capable of disciplining their desires, thereby revealing the stronger in judgment
> inferior to the weaker ($\tau o\dot{v}s$ $\dot{\iota}\sigma\chi v\rho o\tau\epsilon\rho ovs$ $\tau\dot{\eta}v$ $\gamma v\dot{\omega}\mu\eta v$ $\tau\hat{\omega}v$ $\dot{\alpha}\sigma\theta\epsilon v\epsilon\sigma\tau\epsilon\rho\omega v$), the rulers
> to the ruled ($\tau o\dot{v}s$ $\ddot{\alpha}\rho\chi ov\tau as$ $\tau\hat{\omega}v$ $\dot{\alpha}\rho\chi o\mu\epsilon v\omega v$). In fact, it behooves men to be much
> better ($\pi o\lambda\dot{v} . . . \kappa\rho\epsilon\ell\tau\tau ovas$) if they expect to be superior ($\pi\rho o\epsilon\sigma\tau\dot{\alpha}va\iota$) to women, for
> surely if they appear to be less self-controlled they will also be baser characters
> ($\kappa\alpha\kappa\ell ov\epsilon s$). (86,38–88,4 Lutz).

In practice, even Musonius is still willing to employ the typical Greek
distinctions between man and woman: stronger-weaker, ruler-ruled, better-
worse.

Musonius' pupil Hierocles was discussed in chap. 1. He too assumed
without argument that the husband would rule the wife (Stob. IV.22.23;
IV.503,12–16 Hense, quoted above p. 4). This was a secure assumption in the
early second century A.D.; Hierocles could use it as the basis for another
argument: the house is incomplete without a wife.

These references to Musonius and Hierocles are convincing evidence that
Thraede's interpretation of Columella, who wrote in the time of Nero, is
exaggerated. Thraede presents Columella as proof that the Neopythagorean
household ethic was not actually practiced any more.[4] Columella (*On
Agriculture* XII Preface 5) insists that God assigned domestic affairs to
women, open air activities to men, a principle, he notes, expressed by both
Xenophon and Cicero (XII Preface 7; XII.2.6). Both Greek and Roman
fathers can remember when domestic labor was the sphere of the married
woman, but nowadays, he says, most women abandon themselves to luxury
and idleness so that the house must be managed by a bailiff's wife (XII Preface
7–10). Columella does provide evidence that wives of wealthy husbands did
not perform the traditional duties. However, it is squeezing too much out of
this isolated text to take it as evidence that the old social roles were dead or
that the wife had become the social, political equal of her husband. Hierocles
is more liberal than Columella, arguing that the wife should do work outside
the house, but he retains the assumption that she should be subordinate.

Thraede[5] speaks of the Stoic principle of equality as the polar opposite of
Academic and Peripatetic thought, which maintained the natural inequality
of people. He appeals to Antisthenes, later followed by the Stoics, who said,
"Virtue is the same for women as for men" (Diog. Laert. VI.12).[6] He notes von
Arnim's reference to Chrysippus:

> And we admit that the same nature exists in every race, and the same virtue. As far as
> respects human nature the woman does not possess one nature, and the man exhibit
> another, but the same: so also with virtue. (in Clement, *Stromata* IV.8)[7]

> But if the nature of man is capable of wisdom, it was befitting that both workmen, and
> country people, and women, and all, in short, who bear the human form, should be

taught to be wise; and that people should be brought together from every language, and condition, and sex, and age. . . . The Stoics moreover, perceived this, who said that philosophy was to be studied both by slaves and women. (in Lactantus, *Divine Institutes* III.25)[8]

Following Cancik-Lindemaier, Thraede refers to the Stoic Antipater.[9] Cancik-Lindemaier speaks of Antipater's making possible the equality of men and women.[10] Thraede thinks Antipater an example of the "advanced conception of marriage"[11] which, as Xenophon and Isocrates show, was not only esoteric school doctrine but a popular point of view. In Plutarch, *Bravery of Women*, the traditional division between the wife's domestic activity and the husband's public activity is nullified, and the obedience of the wife hardly plays a role any more.[12] The male head of the house remains dominant, but this is a concession to social reality and should not be overstressed. These texts demonstrate that in the time of Augustus there was a "liberalizing process under the influence of Hellenistic thought," a reaction which led to a "genuine equality of the sexes."[13]

Thraede's enthusiastic interpretation of these texts needs qualification. Antipater, *Concerning Marriage*[14] is addressed to men who think that marriage is a burden which reduces personal freedom (256,1–2, 26–27).[15] These young men are given to intemperance and easy pleasures, a kind of life they consider god-like (255,35–36). Antipater wrote in light of specific problems in some cities where there was weakness, anarchy, and a tendency toward frivolous lechery which led to marriage being thought irksome (255,32–34). Antipater responds:

> Life with a wife seems to appear troublesome to some men because of their inability to rule (διὰ τὸ μὴ δύνασθαι ἄρχειν), since they are slaves of pleasure, some of them captured by beauty, others by a dowry. Certain things they willingly and corruptly surrender to a wife, and do not teach her anything concerning household management (περὶ οἰκονομίας), nor the growth of a household [i.e., having many children; cp. 254,28–255,10], nor for what reason they engage in sexual intercourse, nor do they produce in her honorable opinions concerning the gods, piety, and religious feeling, nor set before her the deadliness of luxury (wantonness), nor pleasure's lack of benefits. . . . (256,2–9. My trans.)

He concludes that if one considers and recommends these things, a wife is the pleasantest and lightest burden (256,14–17). Over against those who think that the introduction of a wife burdens life (256,26), he argues that if someone takes in addition "another like himself" (οἷον ἑαυτὸν ἕτερον) (it makes no difference whether this one is female or male), all the work might be done much more easily (256,30–33). Cancik-Lindemaier interprets this sentence as a proclamation of the equality of the sexes.[16] Epictetus, *Dis.* 3.22.68, uses parallel language, which means that Cancik-Lindemaier's interpretation of this sentence may be correct. But the theory of domestic equality in Epictetus and in Antipater results in different practical consequences! In Epictetus the

Cynic should be "free from distraction, wholly devoted to the service of God" (3.22.69), so he should not marry (3.22.76 and 81). But in Antipater,if a *male* wishes to lead a life of leisure devoted to reason or to political deeds or both, he should marry one to manage the house for him and make himself free from distractions (ἑαυτὸν ἀπερίσπαστον) concerning the necessities of life (256,33–257,10).[17]

In practice, the Roman Stoic Antipater did not advocate equality of the sexes. He was concerned that cities and households, like a flock of sheep or a herd of cattle (254,28–30), could not be preserved without offspring, without marriage. Like Musonius, he *assumes* in practice that the husband should rule and that the wife should manage the house. The wife should be taught "concerning household management." Thraede's repeated *contrast* between the Stoic principle of equality and the Peripatetic doctrine of inequality[18] is overdrawn at a key point: the Roman Stoics Antipater, Musonius, and Hierocles *assumed* in practice what Aristotle had argued in theory: husbands should rule their wives.[19] Actually, Antipater's list of what husbands have failed to teach their wives (256,2–9, translated above) has a number of parallels to duties of wives as listed by the Neopythagoreans Callicratidas and Perictione (above pp. 56–58, 97, 101). Antipater does say that the wife is to make pleasing her husband the aim and end of life, her parents willingly retiring to allow the primary good will (εὐνοία) to be assigned to the husband, and the same is true of the husband's attitude toward the wife (255,20–25). Cancik-Lindemaier stresses this beautiful idea but incorrectly interprets it as exemplifying domestic equality between husband and wife.[20] I conclude that, despite their egalitarian theory, these Roman Stoics were willing to accept Aristotelian ideas in practice.[21]

Thraede appeals primarily to Plutarch, *Bravery of Women*, who states that "man's virtues and woman's virtues are one and the same" (242F). Thraede asserts that here "the traditional division house/public life has been neutralized."[22] Wicker[23] is more accurate in distinguishing Plutarch's theoretical approach in the *Bravery of Women* from his practical, paraenetic purpose in *Advice to Bride and Groom*. In the former text he does laud the public as well as the private virtue of women, although he also praises these heroines for characteristically feminine qualities.[24] This theoretical work does conclude with the description of a Persian woman who is able to administer the government excellently when told to do so by her husband (263C). Typical of Greek women, however, are Megisto and Aretaphila. Megisto replies to Aristotimus the tyrant: "If you were a sensible man, you would not be talking to women about husbands, but you would send to them, as to those having authority over us" (252B). And Aretaphila, when Nicocrates the despot killed her husband and forced her to become his wife, plotted to poison him. When she successfully disposed of him, the men of Cyrene asked her to

share with the best citizens in the control and management of the government. But she, as one who had played through a drama of varying sort and of many roles up to the winning of the prize, when she saw the city free, withdrew at once to her own quarters among the women, and, rejecting any sort of meddling in affairs (πολυπραγμονεῖν), spent the rest of her life quietly at the loom in the company of her friends and family. (257DE. Trans. Babbitt)[25]

Plutarch's *Dialogue on Love*[26] is a dispute about whether homosexual or heterosexual relations are to be called "love." The setting is the attraction of Ismenodora, a beautiful, wealthy widow, for Baccon, a boy.[27] In discussing this situation, Protogenes objects: legislators support marriage because it produces children, but marriage has nothing to do with love (750C). Pisias, the homosexual lover of Baccon, criticizes Ismenodora: "We can see her determination to command and to dominate. . . . For such wealth makes women frivolous" (752EF).[28] But the key speech on the question of authority is by Plutarch himself (753B–754E).[29] Other men have married wealthy women and held their own without servility; the wife was controlled and guided with profit and justice (754B). Plutarch does not support democratic equality in marriage:

No one is his own master, no one is unrestricted. Since this is so, what is there dreadful about a sensible older woman piloting the life of a young man? She will be useful because of her superior intelligence. (754D. Trans. Helmbold)[30]

Pisias gives an Aristotelian objection to an older wife ruling her husband: when women are free, the city is on the way to anarchy, and women take over the state (755BC)! Even Plutarch retains a hierarchical conception of marriage while arguing that age and intelligence are more important than sex in determining who is to rule.

These texts do not support Thraede's conclusion that the obedience of the wife hardly plays a role in Plutarch.[31] Plutarch does argue that there are exceptional circumstances, usually when the community is being threatened by tyranny,[32] which allow a woman to be politically active, and he argues theoretically that an older wife may rule a teenage husband. But despite Thraede's criticism of Schrage,[33] the Roman Stoics Antipater, Musonius, and Hierocles as well as the Middle Platonist Plutarch demonstrate that the subordination of wives was general, contemporary Hellenistic practice. Some writers held the Stoic theory of the natural equality of the sexes while encouraging the Aristotelian practice of the subordination of wives to husbands. Schrage correctly cites Plutarch, *Advice to Bride and Groom* 142DE, as an example of Plutarch's view that, in practice, a wife should be subordinate to her husband.[34] Those Hellenistic philosophers discussed above, whom modern authors have interpreted as egalitarians, in practice urged the subordination of wives, and their practical philosophical views[35] are properly compared, not contrasted, with the practical, paraenetic domestic codes in the New Testament.

NOTES TO APPENDIX V

[1]James Crouch, *Colossian Haustafel* 107. Contrast C. E. Manning, "Seneca and the Stoics on the Equality of the Sexes," *Mnemosyne* 26 (1973) 172: "The relegation of women to a secondary place in society was quite consistent with the doctrines of the middle and late Stoa. . . . The development of the doctrine of the καθήκοντα or *officia* undoubtedly led the Stoics of a late period to support more conventional morality." He concludes that to speak of a Stoic concept of the equality of the sexes requires so many reservations that the term equality should be dispensed with (p. 176).

[2]Crouch, *Colossian Haustafel* 107 citing Josef Vogt, *Von der Gleichwertigkeit der Geschlechter in der bürgerlichen Gesellschaft der Griechen* (Akademie der Wissenschaften und der Literatur, Abhandlungen der geistes- und sozialwissenschaftliche Klasse; Mainz: Franz Steiner, 1960) 42. A similar exaggeration of Musonius' views is given by M. Barth, *Ephesians. Translation and Commentary on Chapters 4–6* (AB; Garden City: Doubleday, 1974) 658. More accurately, P. A. Stadter, *Plutarch's Historical Methods. An Analysis of the Mulierum Virtutes* (Cambridge: Harvard University, 1965) 4–5, describes Musonius as "liberal yet practical."

[3]See my article "Two Apologetic Encomia: Dionysius on Rome and Josephus on the Jews," *JSJ* (forthcoming 1981).

[4]K. Thraede, "Ärger mit der Freiheit. Die Bedeutung von Frauen in Theorie und Praxis der alten Kirche," in G. Scharffenorth, ed., *"Freunde in Christus werden . . ." Die Beziehung von Mann und Frau als Frage an Theologie und Kirche* (Berlin: Burckhardthaus, 1977) 68–69, 86. Cp. Thraede, "Frau," *RAC* 8 (1972) 203, 206, 210, 217, 239.

[5]Thraede, "Ärger" 55, citing H. von Arnim, ed., *Stoicorum Veterum Fragmenta* (Leipzig: B. G. Teubner, 1921) 3:58–59 (Chrysippus, fragments 245–254) and Epictetus, *Dis.* 3.7.20. The Epictetus reference is irrelevant to the discussion of equality.

[6]Thraede, "Ärger" 51, 63.

[7]Trans. Roberts and Donaldson, ANF 2:419. Clement, in the same chapter, thinks this compatible with the assertion that women are destined for "child-bearing and housekeeping." Cp. Thraede, "Frau" 239. Musonius argued the same point. For Roman Stoics the theoretical principle that men and women have the same virtue (courage, etc.) does not necessarily mean that in practice they should have the same domestic, social, and political functions.

[8]Trans. Roberts and Donaldson, ANF 7:95.

[9]Hildegard Cancik-Lindemaier, "Ehe und Liebe. Entwürfe griechischer Philosophen und römischer Dichter," in Hubert Cancik et al., *Zum Thema Frau in Kirche und Gesellschaft. Zur Unmündigkeit verurteilt?* (Stuttgart: Katholisches Bibelwerk, 1972) 56–62. Thraede, "Ärger" 58–59.

[10]Cancik-Lindemaier, "Ehe und Liebe" 62.

[11]Thraede, "Ärger" 59. One wonders about this "advanced conception of marriage" when Xenophon is used as an example! See his work *Concerning Household Management* chaps. 7–10.

[12]Thraede, "Ärger" 60, 85. Cp. Thraede, "Frau" 215.

[13]Thraede, "Ärger" 44, 81.

[14]The text is in von Arnim, *Stoicorum Veterum Fragmenta* III.254,23–257,10. It is translated by K. Gaiser, *Für und wider die Ehe. Antike Stimmen zu einer offenen Frage* (Dialog mit der Antike 1; Munich: Heimeran, 1974) 36–39. For a discussion of whether it is Antipater of Tarsus (head of the Stoic school c. 130–120 B.C.) or Antipater of Tyre (1st century B.C.), see Hermann Cohn, *Antipater von Tarsos. Ein Beitrag zur Geschichte der Stoa* (Berlin: Carl Fromholz, 1905) 15–18, 80–82.

[15]See K. Praechter, *Hierokles der Stoiker* (Leipzig: T. Weicher, 1901) 141.

[16]Cancik-Lindemaier, "Ehe und Liebe" 60, 61, 62. Gaiser, *Für und wider die Ehe* 71 observes that Aristotle (EE VII 1245a 30; NE IX 1170b 6) calls a true friend a "second self."

[17]Compare and contrast 1 Cor 7:32–35. Praechter, *Hierokles* 144.

[18]Thraede, "Ärger" 40, 53, 60, 63, 67–68.

[19]Hierocles in Stob. IV.22.23; IV.503,12–16 Hense (quoted above p. 4). Musonius, *Or.* XII, *On Sexual Indulgence* 86,38–88,4 Lutz (quoted above p. 144). Antipater, *On Marriage* III.256,3 von Arnim (quoted above).

[20]Cancik-Lindemaier, "Ehe und Liebe" 60–61. This idea in Antipater has parallels in Plutarch, *Dialogue on Love* 769DF. See G. Delling, "Eheleben," *RAC* 4 (1959) 694–696. Thraede, "Frau" 206, 209 incorrectly asserts that equality between the husband and wife is a condition of marital harmony according to the Stoics. Contrast G. Vlastos, "The Individual as an Object of Love in Plato," *Platonic Studies* (Princeton: Princeton University, 1973) 13: "[In Plato's *Republic*,] subjection to another's will is justified on the assumption that it may not only coexist with, but also promote, φιλία." Similarly, the Stoic Antipater spoke both of the husband's ruling and teaching his wife to manage the house and of marital good will.

[21]Praechter, *Hierokles* 149–150. Cancik-Lindemaier, "Ehe und Liebe" 53.

[22]Thraede, "Ärger" 59–60.

[23]Kathleen O'Brien Wicker, "Mulierum virtutes (Moralia 242E–263C)," in Hans Dieter Betz, ed., *Plutarch's Ethical Writings and Early Christian Literature* (Studia ad Corpus Hellenisticum Novi Testamenti 4; Leiden: E. J. Brill, 1978) 120 and Wicker, "First Century Marriage Ethics: A Comparative Study of the Household Codes and Plutarch's Conjugal Precepts," in J. W. Flanagan and A. W. Robinson, eds., *No Famine in the Land. Studies in Honor of John L. McKenzie* (Missoula: Scholars Press, 1975) 148.

[24]Wicker, "Mulierum virtutes" 114–115.

[25]Ibid., 120, n. 50.

[26]Plutarch may have used Musonius as a source for this work. See K. Ziegler, "Plutarchos," *PW* 21 (1951) 797.

[27]Typically, of course, the *bride* was a girl of 15 or 16. Thraede, "Frau" 210, 222.

[28]Antipater, *On Marriage* 256,3–5 objects to the enslavement of husbands by beautiful, wealthy wives.

[29]Hubert Martin, Jr., "Amatorius (Moralia 748E–771E)," in H. D. Betz, ed., *Plutarch's Ethical Writings and Early Christian Literature* (Studia ad Corpus Hellenisticum Novi Testamenti 4; Leiden: E. J. Brill, 1978) 476.

[30]Martin, "Amatorius" 479 gives parallels precisely to NT household codes.

[31]Cited n. 12 above.

[32]Wicker, "Mulierum virtutes" 120.

[33]Thraede, "Ärger" 61, 122 mistakenly criticizes W. Schrage, "Zur Ethik der neutestamentlichen Haustafeln," *NTS* 21 (1975) 13 on this point.

[34]Thraede, "Ärger" 36, 61 accuses Schrage of the methodological error of isolating this citation. But cp. Plutarch, *Lycurgus* 14.1 (see above p. 36), *Antony* 10 (above p. 71), *Advice to Bride and Groom* 140D (above p. 85), 142E (above p. 98), 142D (above p. 99). Cp. Wicker, "First Century Marriage Ethics" 142, 146, 148. She then refers to "the Jewish emphasis on the subordination of the wife" (149). However, those Jewish writers who stress wives' subordination are the Hellenistic Jews Philo and Josephus, and their sources for the idea are Platonic and Aristotelian. Cp. p. 58, n. 8.

[35]For "philosophy" used in this sense see Plutarch, *Advice to Bride and Groom* 138BC; *On Brotherly Love* 479F; ps.-Plutarch, *The Education of Children* 7DE, 8A; Musonius, *Or.* III, *That Women Too Should Study Philosophy*.

BIBLIOGRAPHY

TEXTS AND TRANSLATIONS

Aboth de Rabbi Nathan. Ed. S. Schechter. Reprinted New York: Philipp Feldheim, 1945. Originally published Vienna, 1887.

Aboth Rabbi Nathan. Trans. J. Goldin. Yale Judaica Series 10. New Haven: Yale University, 1955.

Achilles Tatius. *Clitophon and Leucippe.* 2nd ed. Trans. S. Gaselee. LCL. Cambridge: Harvard University, 1961.

Albinus. *Epitome.* Ed. and trans. P. Louis. Paris: Société d'édition "Les Belles Lettres," 1945.

_____. *Introduction to the Doctrines of Plato.* Trans. H. Cary and G. Burgess. In *The Works of Plato*, vol. 6, The Bohn Classical Library, 241–314. London: George Bell and Sons, 1891.

Antipater, *On Marriage.* Trans. K. Gaiser. In *Für und wider die Ehe. Antike Stimmen zu einer offenen Frage*, Dialog mit der Antike 1, 36–39. Munich: Heimeran, 1974.

Aphthonius. "The Progymnasmata of Aphthonius in Translation," trans. R. Nadeau. *Speech Monographs* 19 (1952) 264–285.

Apocrypha and Pseudepigrapha of the Old Testament. 2 vols. Ed. R. H. Charles. Oxford: Clarendon, 1913.

The Apostolic Fathers. 2 vols. Trans. K. Lake. LCL. Cambridge: Harvard University, 1952.

The Apostolic Fathers. 5 vols. Ed. J. B. Lightfoot. New York: Macmillan, 1885–1890.

Apuleius. *De Platone.* Ed. P. Thomas. Stuttgart: B. G. Teubner, 1908, 1970.

_____. *On the Doctrines of Plato.* Trans. H. Cary and G. Burgess. In *The Works of Plato*, vol. 6, The Bohn Classical Library, 323–403. London: George Bell and Sons, 1891.

_____. *The Golden Ass (Metamorphoses).* 2nd ed. Trans. S. Gaselee. LCL. Cambridge: Harvard University, 1971.

Aristides. *Panathenaic.* Vol. 1 of 4 vols. Trans. C. A. Behr. LCL. Cambridge: Harvard University, 1973.

_____. "The Civilizing Power: A Study of the Panathenaic Discourse of Aelius Aristides against the Background of Literature and Cultural Conflict with Text, Translation and Commentary." Ed. and trans. J. H. Oliver. In *Transactions of the American Philosophical Society* n.s. 58, Part 1 (1968) 1–223.

_____. "The Ruling Power: A Study of the Roman Empire in the Second Century after Christ through the Roman Oration of Aelius Aristides." Ed. and trans. J. H. Oliver. In *Transactions of the American Philosophical Society* n.s. 43, Part 4 (1953) 871–1003.

Aristides ex recensione. Vol. 1. Ed. G. Dindorfii. Leipzig: Libraria Weidmannia, 1829.

Aristotle. *Nicomachean Ethics.* Trans. H. Rackham. LCL. Cambridge: Harvard University, 1926.

_____. *Politics.* Trans. H. Rackham. LCL. Cambridge: Harvard University, 1932.

Aristoteles Politik. Eingeleitet, kritisch herausgegeben und mit Indices versehen. Ed. A. Dreizehnter. Studia et testimonia antiqua 7. Munich: Wilhelm Fink, 1970.

_____. *The "Art" of Rhetoric.* Trans. J. H. Freese. LCL. Cambridge: Harvard University, 1926.

Aristotelis qui ferebantur librorum fragmenta. Ed. V. Rose. 2nd ed. Leipzig: B. G. Teubner, 1967. Originally published 1885.

Pseudo-Aristotle. *Oeconomica and Magna Moralia.* Trans. G. C. Armstrong. LCL. Cambridge: Harvard University, 1935.

Pseudo-Aristotle. *Rhetorica ad Alexandrum.* 2nd ed. Trans. H. Rackham. LCL. Cambridge: Harvard University, 1957.

Athenaeus. *Deipnosophists.* 7 vols. Trans. C. B. Gulick. LCL. Cambridge: Harvard University, 1927-1941.

Augustine. *De Civitate Dei.* Corpus christianorum, Series Latina, vols. 47-48. Turnhout, Belgium: Typografhi Brepols, 1955.

Bryson. *Der Oikonomikos des Neupythagoreers 'Bryson' und sein Einfluss auf die islamische Wissenschaft. Edition und Übersetzung der erhaltenen Versionen.* Ed. and trans. M. Plessner. Orient und Antike 5. Heidelberg: C. Winter, 1928.

Pseudo-Callisthenes. *Der griechische Alexanderroman.* Ed. Ursula von Lauenstein. Beiträge zur klassischen Philologie 4. Meisenheim am Glan: Anton Hain, 1962.

Cicero. *De Finibus.* 2nd ed. Trans. H. Rackham. LCL. Cambridge: Harvard University, 1931.

_____. *De Legibus.* Trans. C. W. Keyes. LCL. Cambridge: Harvard University, 1928.

_____. *Letters to Atticus.* 3 vols. Trans. E. O. Winstedt. LCL. Cambridge: Harvard University, 1912-1918.

_____. *De Natura Deorum.* Trans. H. Rackham. LCL. Cambridge: Harvard University, 1933.

_____. *De Re Publica.* Trans. C. W. Keyes. LCL. Cambridge: Harvard University, 1928.

_____. *De Senectute, De Amicitia, De Divinatione.* Trans. W. A. Falconer. LCL. Cambridge: Harvard University, 1923.

_____. *Tusculan Disputations.* 2nd ed. Trans. J. E. King. LCL. Cambridge: Harvard University, 1945.

Clemens Alexandrinus. *Stromata I-IV.* Ed. O. Stählin. GCS. Leipzig: J. C. Heinrichs, 1906.

Pseudo-Clemens Romanus. *Die Pseudoklementinen.* Ed. B. Rehm. GCS. Berlin: Akademie, 1965.

Columella. *On Agriculture.* 3 vols. Trans. H. B. Ash. LCL. Cambridge: Harvard University, 1941.

Didascalia Apostolorum. The Syriac Version Translated and Accompanied by the Verona Latin Fragments with an Introduction and Notes by R. Hugh Connolly. Oxford: Clarendon, 1929.

Dio Cassius. *Roman History.* 9 vols. Trans. E. Cary. LCL. Cambridge: Harvard University, 1905-1906.

Dio Chrysostom. *Orations.* 5 vols. Trans. J. W. Cohoon and H. L. Crosby. LCL. Cambridge: Harvard University, 1932-1951.

Diodorus Siculus. *Library of History.* 12 vols. Trans. C. H. Oldfather et al. LCL. Cambridge: Harvard University, 1933-1957.

Diogenes Laertius. *Lives and Opinions of Eminent Philosophers.* 2 vols. Trans. R. D. Hicks. LCL. Cambridge: Harvard University, 1925. Vol. 2 revised 1938.

Dionysius of Halicarnassus. *Roman Antiquities.* 7 vols. Trans. E. Cary. LCL. Cambridge: Harvard University, 1937-1950.

_____. *The Three Literary Letters.* Ed. and trans. W. R. Roberts. Cambridge: Cambridge University, 1901.

Pseudo-Dionysius of Halicarnassus. *Ars Rhetorica.* Vol. 6. Ed. H. Usener and L. Radermacher. Leipzig: B. G. Teubner, 1919.

Epictetus. *Discourses and Encheiridion.* 2 vols. Trans. W. A. Oldfather. LCL. Cambridge: Harvard University, 1927.

Epicurus: The Extant Remains. Ed. Cyril Bailey. Oxford: Clarendon, 1926.

Euripides. *Bacchanals.* Trans. A. S. Way. LCL. Cambridge: Harvard University, 1912.

_____. *Suppliants.* Trans. A. S. Way. LCL. Cambridge: Harvard University, 1912.

Eusebius. *Die Kirchengeschichte.* Ed. E. Schwartz. GCS. Leipzig: J. C. Heinrichs, 1908.
_____. *Evangelicae Praeparationis.* 5 vols. Ed. and trans. E. H. Gifford. London: H. Frowde, 1903.
_____. *Die Theophanie.* Ed. E. Klostermann. GCS 3/2. Leipzig: J. C. Heinrichs, 1904.
Favorin von Arelate. *Der erste Teil der Fragmenta.* Ed. Echart Mensching. Berlin: Walter de Gruyter, 1963.
Heraclides Lembus. *Excerpta Politarum.* Ed. and trans. M. R. Dilts. Greek, Roman and Byzantine Monograph 5. London: William Clowes and Sons, 1971.
Hermogenes. *Progymnasmata.* Ed. H. Rabe. Leipzig: B. G. Teubner, 1913.
Herodotus. 4 vols. Trans. A. D. Godley. LCL. Cambridge: Harvard University, 1920–1938.
Hippolytus. *Didascalia et constitutiones apostolorum.* Ed. F. X. Funk. Paderbornae: Libraria Ferdinandi Schoeningh, 1905.
Horace. *Odes and Epodes.* 3rd ed. Trans. C. E. Bennett. LCL. Cambridge: Harvard University, 1968.
_____. *Satires, Epistles, Ars Poetica.* 2nd ed. Trans. H. R. Fairclough. LCL. Cambridge: Harvard University, 1929.
Iamblichos. Pythagoras; Legende, Lehre, Lebensgestaltung. Griechisch und Deutsch. Ed. and trans. M. von Albrecht. Zürich: Artemis, 1963.
Pseudo-Ignatius. *Tarsians, Antiochians,* and *Hero.* Trans. A. Roberts and J. Donaldson. In *Ante-Nicene Fathers* 1:107–115. Grand Rapids: Eerdmans, 1950.
Isocrates. *Panegyricus.* Trans. G. Norlin and L. Van Hook. LCL. Cambridge: Harvard University, 1928.
Joseph and Asenath. Trans. E. W. Brooks. London: Society for Promoting Christian Knowledge, 1918.
Joseph et Aséneth. Ed. and trans. M. Philonenko. SPB. Leiden: E. J. Brill, 1968.
Josephus. 9 vols. Trans. H. St. J. Thackeray and R. Marcus et al. LCL. Cambridge: Harvard University, 1927–1965.
Des Flavius Josephus Schrift gegen den Apion, Text und Erklärung (with concordance). Ed. J. G. Muller. Basel: Bahnmaier (C. Detloff), 1877.
Julian. *The Works of the Emperor Julian.* 3 vols. Trans. W. C. Wright. LCL. Cambridge: Harvard University, 1913–1923.
Justin. *Die älteste Apologeten; Texte mit kurzen Einleitungen.* Ed. E. J. Goodspeed. Göttingen: Vandenhoeck and Ruprecht, 1914.
Justinus. *Historiai Philippicae.* Ed. F. Ruhl. Leipzig: B. G. Teubner, 1886.
Juvenal and Persius. Trans. G. G. Ramsey. LCL. Cambridge: Harvard University, 1918.
Libanii Opera. Vol. 1. Ed. R. Foerster. Leipzig: B. G. Teubner, 1903.
"Libanius' Oration in Praise of Antioch (Oration XI), Translated with Introduction and Commentary," by G. Downey. *Proceedings of the American Philosophical Society* 103 (1959) 652–686.
Livy. *History.* 14 vols. Trans. E. T. Sage. LCL. Cambridge: Harvard University, 1936.
Lucian. *On Slander.* Vol. 1 of 8 vols. Trans. A. M. Harmon. LCL. Cambridge: Harvard University, 1913.
Marcus Aurelius Antonius. *Meditations.* 2nd ed. Trans. C. R. Haines. LCL. Cambridge: Harvard University, 1930.
Martial. *Epigrams.* 2 vols. Trans. W. C. A. Ker. Rev. ed. LCL. Cambridge: Harvard University, 1968.
Menander. περὶ ἐπιδεικτικῶν. Ed. L. Spengel. In *Rhetores Graeci* 3:331–367. Leipzig: B. G. Teubner, 1856.
Midrash Rabbah. 9 vols. Ed. M. A. Mirkin. Tel Aviv: Yavneh, 1956–1964.
Midrash Rabbah. 10 vols. Trans. H. Freedman and M. Simon. London: Soncino, 1939.
Midrash Suta. Ed. S. Buber. Vilna: Romm, 1925.
Der tannaitische Midrasch Sifre zu Numeri. Trans. K. G. Kuhn. Rabbinische Texte. Stuttgart: W. Kohlhammer, 1959.

C. Musonii Rufi Relequiae. Ed. O. Hense. Leipzig: B. G. Teubner, 1905.

Musonius Rufus. The Roman Socrates. Ed. and trans. C. Lutz. Yale Classical Studies 10. New Haven: Yale University, 1947.

Novum Testamentum Graeci. 25th ed. revised E. Nestle and K. Aland. Stuttgart: Württembergische Bibelanstalt, 1963.

'Ocellus Lucanus,' Text und Kommentar. Ed. R. Harder. Berlin: Weidmann, 1926.

Ocellus Lucanus, On the Nature of the Universe. Trans. T. Taylor. London: Printed for the Translator, 1891.

Die Oracula Sibyllina. Ed. J. Geffcken. GCS. Leipzig: J. C. Heinrichs, 1902.

Origen. *Gegen Celsus.* 2nd ed. Ed. P. Koetschau. GCS. Berlin: Akademie, 1959.

_____. *Contra Celsum.* Trans. H. Chadwick. Cambridge: Cambridge University, 1953.

Ovid. *The Art of Love and Other Poems.* 2nd ed. Vol. 2 of 6 vols. Trans. J. H. Mozley. LCL. Cambridge: Harvard University, 1939.

_____. *Heroides, Amores.* Vol. 1 of 6 vols. Trans. G. Showerman. LCL. Cambridge: Harvard University, 1914.

_____. *Metamorphoses.* Vols. 3–4 of 6 vols. Trans. R. J. Miller. LCL. Cambridge: Harvard University, 1916. Vol. 3 revised 1921.

_____. *Tristia, Ex Ponto.* Vol. 6 of 6 vols. Trans. A. L. Wheeler. LCL. Cambridge: Harvard University, 1924.

The Oxyrhynchus Papyri, Part XI. Eds. B. P. Grenfell and A. S. Hunt. Oxford: Oxford University, 1915.

Philo. 10 vols. Trans. F. H. Colson. LCL. Cambridge: Harvard University, 1929–1962.

Philodemi περὶ οἰκονομίας qui dicitur Libellus. Ed. C. Jensen. Leipzig: B. G. Teubner, 1906.

Philodems Abhandlungen über die Haushaltung und über den Hochmut und Theophrasts Haushaltung und Charakterbilder, Griechisch und Deutsch mit kritischen und erklärenden Anmerkungen. Trans. Johann Adam Hartung. Leipzig: Wilhelm Engelmann, 1857.

Philodemi Volumina Rhetorica. Vol. 2. Ed. S. Sudhaus. Leipzig: B. G. Teubner, 1896.

"The Rhetorica of Philodemus." Trans. H. M. Hubbell. *Transactions of the Connecticut Academy of Arts and Sciences* 23 (1920) 243–282.

"Pseudo-Phocylides." Trans. B. S. Easton. *ATR* 14 (1932) 222–228.

Pseudo-Phocylides. "Über das Phokylideische Gedicht." In *Gesammelte Abhandlungen*, by Jacob Bernays, ed. H. K. Usener, 1:192–261. Berlin: Wilhelm Hertz, 1885.

Plato. 12 vols. Trans. H. N. Fowler et al. LCL. Cambridge: Harvard University, 1914–1927.

The Works of Plato. Vol. 6. Trans. G. Burgess. The Bohn Classical Library. London: George Bell and Sons, 1891.

Pliny the Elder. *Natural History.* Vol. 1 of 2 vols. Trans. H. Rackham. LCL. Cambridge: Harvard University, 1949.

Plutarch. *Moralia.* 16 vols. Trans. F. C. Babbitt et al. LCL. Cambridge: Harvard University, 1927–1969.

_____. *The Parallel Lives.* 11 vols. Trans. B. Perrin. LCL. Cambridge: Harvard University, 1914–1926.

Porphyrii philosophi Platonici opuscula tria. Ed. A. Nauck. Leipzig: B. G. Teubner, 1860.

Porphyry. *To Marcella.* Ed. and trans. W. Potscher. Philosophia Antiqua 15. Leiden: E. J. Brill, 1969.

Quintilian. *Institutio oratoria.* Vol. 1 of 4 vols. Trans. H. E. Butler. LCL. Cambridge: Harvard University, 1922.

Seneca. *Epistulae Morales.* 3 vols. Trans. R. M. Gummere. LCL. Cambridge: Harvard University, 1917–1943.

_____. *Moral Essays.* 3 vols. Trans. J. W. Basore. LCL. Cambridge: Harvard University, 1928–1935.

_____. *Diatribe in Seneca philosophi fragmenta I: Fragmenta De matrimonio.* Ed. E. Bickel. Leipzig: B. G. Teubner, 1915.

Septuaginta. Id est Vetus Testamentum graece iuxta LXX interpretes. 6th ed. 2 vols. Ed. A. Rahlfs. Stuttgart: Württembergische Bibelanstalt, 1959.

Sextus Empiricus. 4 vols. Trans. R. G. Bury. LCL. Cambridge: Harvard University, 1933-1949.

Sifre: ספרי דבי רב עם תוספות מיר עין . Ed. M. Friedmann. Vienna: 1864. Reprinted New York: Om, 1948.

Sophocles. 2 vols. Trans. F. Storr. LCL. Cambridge: Harvard University, 1912.

Stobaeus. *Anthologium.* 5 vols. Eds. C. Wachsmuth and O. Hense. Berlin: Weidmann, 1958.

Strabo. *Geography.* 8 vols. Trans. H. L. Jones. LCL. Cambridge: Harvard University, 1929.

Suetonius. *The Lives of the Caesars.* 2 vols. Trans. J. C. Rolfe. LCL. Cambridge: Harvard University, 1913-1914. Vol. 1 revised 1951.

Tacitus. 5 vols. Trans. C. H. Moore. LCL. Cambridge: Harvard University, 1914-1937.

Talmud Babli: תלמוד בבלי עם כל המפרשים כאשר נדפס מקדם ועם. הספות חדשות. 20 vols. New York: S. Goldman-Otzar Hasefarim, 1958.

Tertullian. *Apology.* Trans. T. R. Glover. LCL. Cambridge: Harvard University, 1931.

Testaments of the Twelve Patriarchs. Ed. R. H. Charles. Oxford: Clarendon, 1908.

"Theophrastus περὶ νόμων." Ed. H. Hager. *Journal of Philology* 6 (1876) 1–27.

Valerius Maximus. *Factorum et Dictorum Memorabilium Libri.* Ed. C. Kempf. Stuttgart: B. G. Teubner, 1966.

Xenophon. 7 vols. Trans. C. L. Brownson et al. LCL. Cambridge: Harvard University, 1918–1967.

Xenophon of Ephesus. *Le roman d'Habrocomes et d'Anthia.* Ed. G. Dalmeyda. Collection des universités de France, pub. sous le patronage de l'Association Guillaume Budé. Paris: Société d'édition "Les Belles Lettres," 1962.

COLLECTED TEXTS AND TRANSLATIONS

von Arnim, H., ed. *Stoicorum Veterum Fragmenta.* 4 vols. Leipzig: B. G. Teubner, 1921.

Crönert, C., ed. *Kolotes und Menedemos. Texte und Untersuchungen zur Philosophen- und Literaturgeschichte.* Studien zur Palaeographie und Papyruskunde. Leipzig: Eduard Avenauius, 1906.

Diels, H., ed. and trans. *Die Fragmenta der Vorsokratiker.* 7th ed. 3 vols. Berlin: Weidmann, 1954.

Guthrie, Kenneth Sylvan, trans. *The Life of Pythagoras* and *Pythagorean Library.* 2 vols. in 1. Alpine: Platonist, 1919.

Hercher, R., ed. *Epistolographi Graeci.* Paris: Didot, 1873.

Pritchard, J. B. *Ancient Near Eastern Texts Relating to the Old Testament.* Princeton: Princeton University, 1950.

Reinach, T., ed. *Textes d'auteurs grecs et romains relatifs au Judaisme.* Heldesheim: Georg Olms, 1963. Originally published 1895.

Spengel, L., ed. *Rhetores Graeci.* 3 vols. Leipzig: B. G. Teubner, 1854.

Taylor, Thomas, trans. *Iamblichus' Life of Pythagoras, or Pythagoric Life. Accompanied by Fragments of the Ethical Writings of Certain Pythagoreans in the Doric Dialect; and a Collection of Pythagoric Sentences.* London: A. J. Valpy, 1818.

_____. *Political Fragments of Archytas, Charondas, Zaleucus and Other Ancient Pythagoreans Preserved by Stobaeus and also Ethical Fragments of Hierocles.* London: C. Whittingham, 1822.

Thesleff, H., ed. *The Pythagorean Texts of the Hellenistic Period.* Acta Academiae Aboensis Ser. A, Humaniora 30. Abo: Abo Akademi, 1965.

Walz, C., ed. *Rhetores Graeci.* 9 vols. Tübingen: J. G. Cotta, 1832.

Wehrli, F., ed. *Die Schule des Aristoteles: Texte und Kommentar.* 10 vols. Basel: B. Schwabe, 1944-1959.

GENERAL WORKS

Aalders, Gerhard Jean Daniel. *Die Theorie der gemischten Verfassung im Altertum*. Amsterdam: A. M. Hakkert, 1968.

Adcock, Sir Frank Ezra. "Early Greek Codemakers." *The Cambridge Historical Journal* 2 (1927) 95–105.

Alfoeldi, Andras. "Isiskult und Umsturzbewegung im letzen Jahrhundert der römischen Republik." *Schweizer Münzblätter* 5 (1954) 25–31.

Allen, D. J. "Magna Moralia and Nicomachean Ethics." *JHS* 77 (1957) 7–11.

_____. Review of Franz Dirlmeier, *Aristoteles: Eudemische Ethik* (1962), in *Gnomen* 38 (1966) 138–149.

Andresen, Carl. *Logos und Nomos. Die Polemik des Kelsos wider das Christentum*. Arbeiten zur Kirchengeschichte 30. Berlin: Walter de Gruyter, 1955.

Aptowitzer, Viktor. "Asenath, the Wife of Joseph." *HUCA* (1924) 239–306.

von Arnim, Hans. "Ariston (56)." PW 2 (1895) 957–959.

_____. "Kritolaos." PW 11 (1922) 1930–1932.

_____. *Arius Didymus' Abriss der peripatetischen Ethik*. Akademie der Wissenschaften in Wien, philosophisch-historische Klasse, Sitzungsberichte 204/3. Vienna: Hölder-Pichler-Tempsky, 1926.

_____. *Leben und Werke des Dio von Prusa mit einer Einleitung: Sophistik, Rhetorik, Philosophie in ihrem Kampf um die Jugendbildung*. Berlin: Weidmann, 1898.

_____. *Der neueste Versuch die Magna Moralia als unecht zu erweisen*. Akademie der Wissenschaften in Wien, philosophisch-historische Klasse, Sitzungsberichte 211/2. Vienna: Hölder-Pichler-Tempsky, 1929.

Bacher, Wilhelm. *Die Agada der Tannaiten*. 2nd ed. Strassburg: K. J. Teubner, 1965.

Bailey, Cyril. *The Greek Atomists and Epicurus*. Oxford: Clarendon, 1928.

Balch, David L. "Backgrounds of I Cor. 7: Sayings of the Lord in Q; Moses as an Ascetic ΘΕΙΟΣ ANHP in II Cor. 3." *NTS* 18 (1972) 351–364.

_____. "Two Apologetic Encomia: Dionysius on Rome and Josephus on the Jews." *JSJ* (forthcoming).

_____. "The Neopythagorean Moralists and the New Testament." In *Aufstieg und Niedergang der römischen Welt*, Teil II, Band 26, ed. H. Temporini and W. Haase. Berlin-New York: Walter de Gruyter, forthcoming.

Baldwin, Charles Sears. *Medieval Rhetoric and Poetic (to 1400) Interpreted from Representative Works*. New York: Macmillan, 1928.

Balkin, S. "The Alexandrian Source for Contra Apionem II." *JQR* n.s. 27 (1936) 1–32.

Balsdon, J. P. V. D. *Roman Women. Their History and Habits*. Westport: Greenwood, 1962.

_____. *Life and Leisure in Ancient Rome*. New York: McGraw-Hill, 1969.

Bamberger, Bernard Jacob. *Proselytism in the Talmudic Period*. Cincinnati: Hebrew Union College, 1939.

Bartchy, S. Scott. ΜΑΛΛΟΝ ΧΡΗΣΑΙ. *First-Century Slavery and I Corinthians 7:21*. SBLDS 11. Missoula: Scholars Press, 1973.

Barth, Markus. *Ephesians. Translation and Commentary on Chapters 4–6*. AB. Garden City: Doubleday, 1974.

Beare, Francis Wright. *The First Epistle of Peter*. 2nd ed. Oxford: B. Blackwell, 1958.

Becher, Ilse. *Das Bild der Kleopatra in der griechischen und lateinischen Literatur*. Berlin: Akademie, 1966.

_____. "Der Isiskult in Rom—ein Kult der Halbwelt?" *Zeitschrift für ägyptische Sprache und Altertumskunde* 96 (1970) 81–90.

_____. "Oktavians Kampf gegen Antonius und seine Stellung zu den ägyptischen Göttern." *Das Altertum* 11 (1965) 40–47.

Bernays, Jacob. *Gesammelte Abhandlungen*. 2 vols. Ed. H. Usener. Berlin: Wilhelm Hertz, 1885.

Best, Ernest. "I Peter and the Gospel Tradition." *NTS* 16 (1969–1970) 95–113.

Best, Ernest. *I Peter*. New Century Bible. London: Oliphants, 1971.
_____. "Spiritual Sacrifice. General Priesthood in the New Testament." *Int* 14 (1960) 273-299.
_____. "I Peter II 4–10—A Reconsideration." *NovT* 11 (1960) 270-293.
Beyer, Hermann W. "ἐπισκοπή." *TDNT* 2:606-607. Grand Rapids: Eerdmans, 1964.
Bishoff, A. "Exegetische Randbemerkungen." *ZNW* 9 (1908) 166-172.
Bishop, Eric F. F. "Oligoi in I Peter 3:20." *CBQ* 13 (1951) 44-45.
Blauw, Johannes. *The Missionary Nature of the Church in the New Testament. A Survey of the Biblical Theology of Mission.* New York: McGraw-Hill, 1962.
Blinzler, Joseph. "ΙΕΡΑΤΕΥΜΑ. Zur Exegese von I Petr. 2,5 u. 9." In *Episcopus. Festschrift für Michael Kardinal von Faulhaber*, 49-65. Regensburg: Gregorius, 1949.
Börner, Franz. *Untersuchungen über die Religion der Sklaven in Griechenland und Rom.* 4 parts. Akademie der Wissenschaften und der Literatur, Abhandlungen der geistes- und sozialwissenschaftlichen Klasse. Mainz: Franz Steiner, 1947, 1960, 1961, 1963.
Boismard, M.-E. *Quatre hymnes baptismales dans la première Épître de Pierre.* Paris: Éditions du Cerf, 1961.
_____. "Une liturgie baptismale dans la Prima Petri." *RB* 63 (1956) 182-208 and 64 (1957) 161-183.
Bolkestein, Hendrik. *Wohltätigkeit und Armenpflege im vorchristlichen Altertum: Ein Beitrag zum Problem 'Moral und Gesellschaft'.* Utrecht: A. Oosthoek, 1939.
Bornemann, Wilhelm. "Der erste Petrusbrief—eine Taufrede des Silvanus?" *ZNW* 19 (1919-1920) 143-165.
Boulanger, André. *Aelius Aristide et la sophistique dans la province d'Asie au IIᵉ siècle de notre ère.* Paris: Anciennes Maisons Thorin et Fontenmoing, 1923.
Bowersock, G. W. *Augustus and the Greek World.* Oxford: Clarendon, 1965.
Boyance, Pierre. "Sur la vie pythagoricienne." *Revue des études grecques* 52 (1939) 36-50.
_____. Review of Michelangelo Giusta, *I dossografi di etica* 1 in *Latomus* 26 (1967) 246-249.
Bradley, D. G. "The Topos as a Form in Pauline Paraenesis." *JBL* 72 (1953) 238-246.
Brandt, W. "Wandel als Zeugnis nach dem I.Petrusbrief." In *Verbum Dei Manet in Aeternum*, Festschrift für Otto Schmitz, ed. W. Foerster, 10-25. Wittenberg: Luther, 1955.
Braun, Egon. *Die Kritik der lakedaimonischen Verfassungen in den Politika des Aristoteles.* Kärntner Museumschriften 12. Klagenfurt: Landesmuseum für Kärntner, 1956.
Braunert, Horst. "Staatstheorie und Staatsrecht in Hellenismus." *Saeculum* 19 (1968) 47-66.
Brink, C. O. "Οἰκείωσις and Οἰκειότης. Theophrastus and Zeno on Nature in Moral Theory." *Phronesis* 1 (1955-1956) 123-145.
Brink, K. L. "Peripatos." PWSup 7 (1940) 899-947.
Brunner, Otto. "'Das ganze Haus' und die alteuropaische 'Oekonomik'." *Neue Wege der Sozialgeschichte* (1956) 33-61.
Burgess, Theodore C. "Epideictic Literature." *The University of Chicago Studies in Classical Philology* 3 (1902) 89-248.
Burkert, Walter. "Hellenistische Pseudopythagorica." *Philologus* 105 (1961) 16-43 and 226-246.
_____. "Zur geistesgeschichtlichen Einordnung einiger Pseudopythagorica." In *Pseudepigrapha*, ed. K. von Fritz, 23-55. Entretiens sur l'antiquité classique 18. Geneva: Fondation Hardt, 1972.
_____. Review of H. Thesleff, *An Introduction to the Pythagorean Writings of the Hellenistic Period* in *Gnomon* 34 (1965) 763-768.
_____. Review of H. Thesleff, *The Pythagorean Texts of the Hellenistic Period* in *Gnomon* 39 (1967) 548-556.
Burnet, John. *Early Greek Philosophy.* 4th ed. London: A. and C. Black, 1930.
Cancik-Lindemaier, Hildegard. "Ehe und Liebe. Entwürfe griechischer Philosophen und römischer Dichter." In *Zum Thema Frau in Kirche und Gesellschaft. Zur Unmündigkeit verurteilt?*, by Hubert Cancik et al., 47-80. Stuttgart: Katholisches Bibelwerk, 1972.
Cappelle, Wilhelm. "Griechische Ethik und römischer Imperialismus." *Klio* 25 (1932) 86-113.

Carcopino, Jerome. *La basilique pythagoricienne de la Porta Majeure*. Paris: L'Artisan du Livre, 1926.

_____. *Daily Life in Ancient Rome. The People and the City at the Height of the Empire*. New Haven: Yale University, 1940.

Carrington, Phillip. *The Primitive Christian Catechism. A Study in the Epistles*. Cambridge: Cambridge University, 1940.

Chadwick, Henry. "Florilegium." *RAC* 8 (1969) 1131-1160.

Chevallier, Max-Alain. "I Pierre 1/1 à 2/10. Structure littéraire et conséquences exégétiques." *RHPR* 51 (1971) 129-142.

von Christ, Wilhelm; Schmid, Wilhelm; and Stählin, Otto. *Geschichte der griechischen Literatur*. Vol. 2. Munich: C. H. Beck, 1934.

Chroust, Anton-Hermann. "Aristotle's *On Justice*." In *Aristotle. New Light on His Life and on Some of His Lost Works* 2:71-85. Notre Dame: University of Notre Dame, 1973.

Clark, Donald Lemen. *Rhetoric in Graeco-Roman Education*. New York: Columbia University, 1957.

Cohn, Hermann. *Antipater von Tarsos. Ein Beitrag zur Geschichte der Stoa*. Berlin: Carl Fromholz, 1905.

Cohn, Leopold. "Apion (3)." *PW* 1 (1894) 2803-2806.

Crook, John. *Law and Life of Rome*. Ithaca: Cornell University, 1967.

Cross, Frank Leslie. *I Peter. A Paschal Liturgy*. London: A. R. Mowbray, 1954.

Crouch, James E. *The Origin and Intention of the Colossian Haustafel*. FRLANT 109. Göttingen: Vandenhoeck and Ruprecht, 1972.

Cumont, Franz. *The Oriental Religions in Roman Paganism*. Chicago: Open Court, 1911.

Dalton, William Joseph. *Christ's Proclamation to the Spirits. A Study of I Peter 3:18-4:6*. An Bib 23. Rome: Pontifical Biblical Institute, 1965.

Danielou, Jean. *Gospel Message and Hellenistic Culture*. Philadelphia: Westminster, 1973.

Danker, Frederick W. "I Peter 1,24-2,17—A Consolatory Pericope." *ZNW* 58 (1967) 93-102.

_____. Review of J. H. Elliott, *The Elect and the Holy* (1966) in *CTM* 38 (1967) 329-332.

Daube, David. "κερδαίνω as a Missionary Term." *HTR* 40 (1947) 109-120.

Delatte, Armand. *Essai sur la politique pythagoricienne*. Paris: E. Champion, 1922.

Delling, Gerhard. "Zur Taufe von 'Häusern' im Urchristentum." *NovT* 7 (1965) 285-311.

_____. "Eheleben," "Ehescheidung." *RAC* 4 (1959) 691-719.

Dibelius, Martin. *Der Brief des Jakobus*. MeyerK. Göttingen: Vandenhoeck and Ruprecht, 1957.

_____. *From Tradition to Gospel*. Trans. B. L. Wolff. New York: Charles Scribner's Sons, 1935.

_____. *Geschichte der urchristlichen Literatur*. 2 vols. Berlin and Leipzig: Walter de Gruyter, 1926.

_____. *An die Kolosser, an die Epheser, an Philemon*. HNT. Tübingen: Mohr, 1913.

Dibelius, Martin, and Conzelmann, Hans. *The Pastoral Epistles*. Hermeneia. Philadelphia: Fortress, 1972.

Dickason, Anne. "Anatomy and Destiny: The Role of Biology in Plato's Views of Women." In *Women and Philosophy. Toward a Theory of Liberation*, ed. Carol C. Gould and Marx W. Wartofsky, 45-53. New York: G. P. Putnam's Sons, 1976.

Dickey, Samuel. "Some Economic and Social Conditions of Asia Minor Affecting the Expansion of Christianity." In *Studies in Early Christianity*, ed. S. J. Case, 393-416. New York: Century, 1928.

Diels, Hermann. *Doxographi graeci*. Berlin and Leipzig: Walter de Gruyter, 1929.

Dietrich, Dieter. "Die Ausbreitung der alexandrinischen Mysteriengötter Isis, Osiris, Serapis und Horus in griechisch-römischer Zeit." *Das Altertum* 14 (1968) 201-211.

Dirlmeier, Franz. "Die Zeit der 'Grossen Ethik'." *RhM* N.F. 88 (1939) 214-243.

Doerrie, Heinrich. "Der nachklassische Pythagoreismus." *PW* 24 (1963) 268-277.

_____. "Der Platoniker Eudorus von Alexandria." *Hermes* 79 (1944) 25-39.

Drews, Robert. *The Greek Accounts of Eastern History*. Washington, D. C.: Center for Hellenic Studies, 1973.

Duering, Ingemar. "Aristoteles." *PWSup* 11 (1968) 159-336.

Dupar, Kenneth W. *A Study in New Testament Haustafeln*. Dissertation Edinburgh, 1971.

Dvornik, Francis. "Hellenistic Political Philosophy." In *Early Christian and Byzantine Political Philosophy* 1:205–277. Dumbarton Oaks Studies 9. Locust Valley: J. J. Augustin, 1966.

Dyroff, Adolf. *Die Ethik der alten Stoa*. Berliner Studien für classische Philologie und Archaeologie, N.F. 2. New York: Arno, 1979. Originally published 1897.

Ehrenberg, Victor. "Polypragmosyne: A Study in Greek Politics." *JHS* 67 (1947) 46–67.

Elliott, John Hall. *The Elect and the Holy. An Exegetical Examination of I Peter 2:4–10 and the Phrase βασίλειον ἱεράτευμα*. NovTSup 12. Leiden: E. J. Brill, 1966.

_____. "Ministry and Church Order in the NT: A Traditio-Historical Analysis (I Pt. 5,1–5 + plls.)." *CBQ* 32 (1970) 367–391.

_____. "The Rehabilitation of an Exegetical Step-Child: I Peter in Recent Research." *JBL* 95 (1976) 243–254.

Farrington, Benjamin. *The Faith of Epicurus*. New York: Basic Books, 1967.

Finley, M. I. *Democracy Ancient and Modern*. New Brunswick: Rutgers University, 1973.

Förtsch, Barbara. *Die politische Rolle der Frau in der römischen Republik*. Würzburger Studien zur Altertumswissenschaft 5. Stuttgart: W. Kohlhammer, 1935.

Fraser, Peter Marshal. *Ptolemaic Alexandria*. 2 vols. Oxford: Clarendon, 1972.

_____. "Two Studies on the Cult of Serapis in the Hellenistic World." In *Opuscula Atheniensia* 3:1–54. Skifter Utgivna av Svenska Institutet I Athen, 4°, 7. Lund: C. W. K. Gleerup, 1960.

Freeman, Kathleen. *The Pre-Socratic Philosophers. A Companion to Diels' Fragmenta der Vorsokratiker*. 2nd ed. Cambridge: Harvard University, 1959.

Freymuth, Günther. "Zum Hieros Gamos in den antiken Mysterien." *Museum Helveticum* 21 (1964) 86–95.

Friedländer, Ludwig. *Roman Life and Manners under the Early Empire*. Vol 1. Trans. L. A. Magnus. New York: E. P. Dutton, 1913.

von Fritz, Kurt. *Pythagorean Politics in Southern Italy. An Analysis of the Sources*. New York: Columbia University, 1940.

_____. *The Theory of the Mixed Constitution in Antiquity. A Critical Analysis of Polybius' Political Ideas*. New York: Columbia University, 1954.

Gager, John G. *Moses in Graeco-Roman Paganism*. SBLMS 16. New York: Abingdon, 1972.

Gaiser, Konrad. *Für und wider die Ehe. Antike Stimmen zu einer offenen Frage*. Dialog mit der Antike 1. Munich: Heimeran, 1974.

Geffcken, Johannes. *Zwei griechische Apologeten*. Leipzig: B. G. Teubner, 1904.

Geiger, Franz. *Philon von Alexandria als sozialer Denker*. Tübinger Beiträge zur Altertumswissenschaft 14. Stuttgart: W. Kohlhammer, 1932.

Gigon, Olof. "Die Sklaverei bei Aristoteles." In *Entretiens sur l'antiquité classique* 11:245–276. Geneva: Fondation Hardt, 1965.

Ginzberg, Louis. *The Legends of the Jews*. 6 vols. Trans. H. Szold. Philadelphia: Jewish Publication Society of America, 1913.

Giusta, Michelangelo. *I dossografi di etica*. 2 vols. Università di Torino, Pubblicazioni della Facoltà di lettere e filosofia 15/3 and 15/4. Torino: G. Giappichelli, 1964 and 1967.

Goldstein, Horst. "Die politischen Paränesen in I Petr 2 und Röm 13." *Bib Leb* 15 (1974) 88–104.

Goodenough, Erwin R. *The Jurisprudence of the Jewish Courts in Egypt*. New Haven: Yale University, 1929.

Goppelt, Leonhard. "Prinzipien neutestamentlicher Sozialethik nach dem 1.Petrusbrief." In *Neues Testament und Geschichte. Historisches Geschehen und Deutung im Neuen Testament. Oscar Cullmann zum 70. Geburtstag*, ed. H. Baltensweiler and B. Reicke, 285–296. Tübingen: Mohr, 1972.

_____. *Der Erste Petrusbrief*. Ed. F. Hahn. MeyerK. Göttingen: Vandenhoeck and Ruprecht, 1978.

Grayeff, Felix. *Aristotle and His School*. New York: Barnes and Noble, 1974.

Grossmann, Gustav. *Politische Schlagwörter aus der Zeit des Peloponnesischen Krieges*. Zürich: Dissertationsdruckerei Leemann, 1950.

Gülzow, Henneke. *Christentum und Sklaverei in den ersten drei Jahrhunderten.* Bonn: R. Habelt, 1969.

Guthrie, W. K. C. *A History of Greek Philosophy.* Vol. 3. Cambridge: Cambridge University, 1969.

von Gutschmid, Alfred. "Vorlesungen über Josephos' Bücher gegen Apion." In *Kleine Schriften von Alfred von Gutschmid,* ed. Franz Ruhl, 4:336–589. Leipzig: B. G. Teubner, 1893.

Haddad, George. *Aspects of Social Life in Antioch in the Hellenistic-Roman Period.* Chicago: University of Chicago, 1949.

von Harnack, Adolf. *Geschichte der altchristlichen Literatur bis Eusebius:* Vol. 2. *Die Chronologie der altchristlichen Literatur bis Eusebius.* Leipzig: J. C. Heinrichs, 1897.

_____. *The Mission and Expansion of Early Christianity in the First Three Centuries.* 2nd ed. 2 vols. Trans. J. Moffatt. New York: G. P. Putnam's Sons, 1908. Vol. 1 republished by Harper, 1961.

Henkel, Hermann. *Studien zur Geschichte der griechischen Lehre vom Staat.* Leipzig: B. G. Teubner, 1872.

_____. "Zur Politik des Aristoteles II. Der Abriss der peripatetischen Oekonomik und Politik bei Stobaios und die Politik des Aristoteles." In *Gymnasium zu Seehausen in der Altmark,* 10–17. Stendal: Franzen und Grosse, 1875.

Henrichs, Albert. "Pagan Ritual and the Alleged Crimes of the Early Christians." In *Kyriakon, Festschrift Johannes Quasten,* ed. P. Granfield and J. A. Jungmann, 1:18–35. Münster: Aschendorff, 1970.

Hense, Otto. "Ariston bei Plutarch." *RhM* 46 (1890) 541–554.

_____. "Ioannes Stobaios." PW 9 (1916) 918–920.

Herrmann, Claudine. *Le rôle judiciare et politique des femmes sous la République romaine.* Collection Latomus 67. Brussels: Latomus, 1964.

Hill, David. "On Suffering and Baptism in I Peter." *NovT* 18 (1976) 181–189.

Hirzel, Rudolf. *Agraphos Nomos.* Abhandlungen der philologisch-historische Classe der königlich sächsischen Gesellschaft der Wissenschaften 20, Nr. 1. Leipzig: B. G. Teubner, 1903.

Hope, Richard. *The Book of Diogenes Laertius.* New York: Columbia University, 1930.

van der Horst, P. W. "Pseudo-Phocylides and the New Testament." *ZNW* 69 (1978) 187–202.

Immisch, Otto. Review of A. Delatte, *Essai sur la politique pythagoricienne* and G. Meantes, *Recherches sur le Pythagorisme* in *Philologische Wochenschrift* 43 (1923) 25–34.

_____. "Zum antiken Herrscherkult." In *Aus Roms Zeitwende. Von Wesen und Wirken des Augusteischen Geistes,* 3–36. Leipzig: Dietrich, 1931.

Jaeger, Werner. *Paideia: The Ideals of Greek Culture.* 3 vols. Trans. G. Highet. Oxford: B. Blackwell, 1939–1944.

_____. "Über Ursprung und Kreislauf des philosophischen Lebensideals." In *Sitzungsberichte der preussischen Akademie der Wissensehaften, philosophisch-historische Klasse,* 25:390–421. Berlin: Akademie der Wissenschaften, 1928. E.T. "On the Origin and Cycle of the Philosophic Ideal of Life." In *Aristotle,* Appendix II. 2nd ed. London: Oxford University, 1948.

Joël, Karl. *Der echte und der Xenophontische Sokrates.* 2 vols. Berlin: R. Gartners Verlagsbuchhandlung, 1901.

Johnson, Sherman E. "Asia Minor and Early Christianity." In *Christianity, Judaism and Other Greco-Roman Cults, Studies for Morton Smith at Sixty,* ed. Jacob Neusner, 2:77–145. Leiden: E. J. Brill, 1975.

Jolowicz. J. F. *Historical Introduction to the Study of Roman Law.* Cambridge: Cambridge University, 1967.

Joly, Robert. Review of M. Giusta, *I dossografi di etica* in *L'antiquité classique* 35 (1966) 289–290 and 38 (1969) 308–309.

Jones, C. P. *The Roman World of Dio Chrysostom.* Loeb Classical Monographs. Cambridge: Harvard University, 1978.

Judge, Edwin Arthur. *The Social Pattern of the Christian Groups in the First Century. Some Prolegomena to the Study of the New Testament Ideas of Social Organization.* London: Tyndale, 1960.

Juster, Jean. *Les juifs dans l'empire romain. Leur condition juridique, économique et sociale.* 2 vols. Paris: Librairie Paul Guethner, 1914.

Kamlah, Ehrhard. "ὑποτάσσεσθαι in den neutestamentlichen Haustafeln." In *Verborum Veritas. Festschrift für Gustav Stählin zum 70. Geburtstag,* ed. O. Böcher and K. Haacker, 237–243. Wuppertal: Theologischer Verlag Brockhaus, 1970.

Karris, R. J. *The Function and Sitz im Leben of the Paraenetic Elements in the Pastoral Epistles.* Th.D. dissertation, Harvard University, 1971.

Kaser, Max. *Roman Private Law.* Trans. R. Dannerbring. Durban: Butterworths, 1968.

Kelly, John Norman Davidson. *A Commentary on the Epistles of Peter and of Jude.* HNTC. New York: Harper and Row, 1969.

Kennedy, George A. *The Art of Persuasion in Greece.* Princeton: Princeton University, 1963.
_____. *The Art of Rhetoric in the Roman World 300 B.C.–A.D. 300.* Princeton: Princeton University, 1972.

Kerferd, G. B. "Ethical Doxographers." *The Classical Review* 81 (1967) 156–158 and 85 (1971) 371–373.

Klein, Gottlieb. *Der älteste christliche Katechismus und die jüdische Propaganda-Literatur.* Berlin: B. Reimer, 1909.

Klijn, A. F. J. "Die Ethik des neuen Testaments. Eine Umschau." *Nederlands Theologisch Tijdschrift* 24 (1969-1970) 241-249.

Knopf, Rudolf. *Die Briefe Petri und Juda.* MeyerK. Göttingen: Vandenhoeck and Ruprecht, 1912.

Koch, Hal. *Pronoia und Paideusis. Studien über Origenes und sein Verhältnis zum Platonismus.* Berlin: Walter de Gruyter, 1932.

Krodel, Gerhard. "The First Letter of Peter." In *Hebrews, James, 1 and 2 Peter, Jude, Revelation,* by Reginald H. Fuller et al., 50-80. Proclamation Commentaries. Philadelphia: Fortress, 1977.

Kunkel, Wolfgang. *An Introduction to Roman Legal and Constitutional History.* Trans. J. M. Kelly. Oxford: Clarendon, 1973.

de Labriolle, Pierre. *La reaction painne: Étude sur la polémique antichrétienne du Ier au VIe siècle.* Paris: L'Artisan du Livre, 1934.

Last, H. "Christenverfolgung II (juristisch)." *RAC* 2 (1954) 1208-1228.

Latte, Kurt. *Römische Religionsgeschichte.* Handbuch der Altertumswissenschaft, 5. Abt. T. 4. Munich: C. H. Beck, 1960.

Leaney, A. R. C. "I Peter and the Passover: An Interpretation." *NTS* 10 (1963-1964) 238-251.

Lee, Clarence L. "Social Unrest and Primitive Christianity." In *The Catacombs and the Coliseum. The Roman Empire as the Setting of Primitive Christianity,* ed. S. Benko and J. J. O'Rourke, 121-138. Valley Forge: Judson: 1971.

Leipoldt, Johannes. *Dionysos.* Angelos Beiheft 3. Leipzig: Eduard Pfeiffer, 1931.

Leon, Harry Joshua. *The Jews of Ancient Rome.* Philadelphia: Jewish Publication Society of America, 1960.

Liebich, Werner. *Aufbau, Absicht und Form der Pragmateiai Philodems.* Dissertation Ost-Berlin: Photokopie von der Autor, 1956, 1960.

Lohmeyer, Ernst. *Die Briefe an die Philipper, an die Kolosser und an Philemon.* MeyerK. Göttingen: Vandenhoeck and Ruprecht, 1954.

Lohse, Eduard. *A Commentary on the Epistles to the Colossians and to Philemon.* Trans. W. R. Poehlmann and R. J. Karris. Hermeneia. Philadelphia: Fortress, 1971.
_____. "Paränese und Kerygma im 1.Petrusbrief." *ZNW* 45 (1954) 68-89.

Long, A. A. "Aristotle's Legacy to Stoic Ethics." *Institute of Classical Studies (University of London), Bulletin* Number 15 (1968) 72-85.

Lyonnet, Stanislas. "Note sur le plan de l'Épître aux Romains." *Recherches de science religieuse* 39 (1951-1952) 301-316.

McDonald, A. H. "Rome and the Italian Confederation (200-186 B.C.)." *JRS* 34 (1944) 11-33.

MacMullen, Ramsey. *Enemies of the Roman Order. Treason, Unrest and Alienation in the Empire.* Cambridge: Harvard University, 1966.

Malherbe, Abraham J. "Hellenistic Moralists and the New Testament." In *Aufstieg und Niedergang der römischen Welt*, Teil II, Band 26, ed. H. Temporini and W. Haase. Berlin: Walter de Gruyter, forthcoming.

_____. "The Apologetic Theology of the Preaching of Peter." *Restoration Quarterly* 13 (1970) 205-223.

_____. *Social Aspects of Early Christianity.* Baton Rouge: Louisiana State University, 1977.

_____. "The Structure of Athenagoras, 'Supplicatio pro Christianis'." *VC* 23 (1969) 1-20.

Manning, C. E. "Seneca and the Stoics on the Equality of the Sexes." *Mnemosyne* 26 (1973) 170-177.

Marrou, Henri-Irenee. *A History of Education in Antiquity.* Trans. G. Lamb. New York: Sheed and Ward, 1956.

Martin, Hubert, Jr. "Amatorius (Moralia 748E-771E)." In *Plutarch's Ethical Writings and Early Christian Literature*, ed. H. D. Betz, 442-537. Studia ad Corpus Hellenisticum Novi Testamenti 4. Leiden: E. J. Brill, 1978.

Martini, Heinrich Edgar. "Dikaiarchos." PW 5 (1903) 546-563.

Matz, Friedrich. ΔIONYΣIAKH TEΛETH. *Archäologische Untersuchungen zum Dionysoskult in hellenistischer und römischer Zeit.* Akademie der Wissenschaften und der Literatur, Abhandlungen der geistes- und sozialwissenschaftliche Klasse. Mainz: F. Steiner, 1964.

Meeks, Wayne A. "The Image of the Androgyne: Some Uses of a Symbol in Earliest Christianity." *HR* 13 (1974) 165-208.

Merkelbach, Reinhold. *Roman und Mysterium in der Antike.* Munich: C. H. Beck, 1962.

Meyer, Eduard. "Die Sklaverei im Altertum." In *Kleine Schriften zur Geschichtstheorie und zur wirtschaftlichen und politischen Geschichte des Altertums*, 169-212. Halle: M. Niemeyer, 1910.

Michaels, J. Ramsey. "Eschatology in I Peter iii.17." *NTS* 13 (1966-1967) 394-401.

Michel, A. "Quelques aspects de la rhétorique chez Pilon." In *Philon d'Alexandrie, Lyon 11-15 Septembre 1966*, 81-103. Paris: Éditions du centre national de la recherche scientifique, 1967.

Milobenski, Ernst. *Der Neid in der griechischen Philosophie.* Klassisch-philologische Studien 29. Wiesbaden: O. Harrassowitz, 1964.

Minar, Edwin LeRoy. *Early Pythagorean Politics in Practice and Theory.* Baltimore: Waverly, 1942.

Moehring, Horst R. "The Persecution of the Jews and the Adherents of the Isis Cult at Rome A.D. 19." *NovT* 3 (1959) 293-304.

Moore, George Foot. *Judaism.* 2nd ed. New York: Schocken, 1971. Vol. 1 originally published 1927.

Moraux, Paul. *La dialogue "Sur la justice:" à la recherche de l'Aristote perdu.* Louvain: Publications universitaires, 1957.

_____. "From the Protrepticus to the Dialogue On Justice." In *Aristotle and Plato in the Mid-Fourth Century*, ed. I. Düring and G. E. L. Owen, 113-132. Göteborg, 1960.

Morrison, J. S. "Pythagoras of Samos." *The Classical Quarterly* 50 (1956) 135-156.

Moule, C. F. D. "The Nature and Purpose of I Peter." *NTS* 3 (1956-1957) 1-11.

Muehl, Max. "Die Gesetze des Zaleukos und Charondas." *Klio* 22 (1929) 105-124 and 432-463.

Mutschmann, Hermann. Review of Willy Kraemer, *De Aristoteles, qui fertur, Oeconomicorum libro primo* in *Wochenschrift für klassische Philologie* 5 (1912) 118-123.

Nauck, Wolfgang. "Freude im Leiden." *ZNW* 46 (1955) 68-80.

Nilsson, Martin P. *The Dionysiac Mysteries of the Hellenistic and Roman Age.* Lund: C. W. K. Gleerup, 1957.

_____. *Geschichte der griechischen Religion.* 3rd ed. 2 vols. Munich: C. H. Beck, 1967.

Nock, Arthur Darby. *Conversion: The Old and the New in Religion from Alexander the Great to Augustine of Hippo.* New York: Oxford University, 1961. Originally published 1933.
_____. "Notes on Ruler-Cult, I–IV." *JHS* 48 (1928) 21–43.
_____. "Posidonius." *JRS* 49 (1959) 5–9.
_____. "The Praises of Antioch." *The Journal of Egyptian Archaeology* 40 (1954) 76–82.
_____. "Sarcophagi and Symbolism." *American Journal of Archaeology* 50 (1946) 140–170.
Norden, Eduard. "Beiträge zur Geschichte der griechischen Philosophie." *Jahrbücher für classische Philologie*, Supplementband 19 (1893) 373–385.
Oepke, A. "Ehe I." *RAC* 4 (1959) 650–666.
Oltramare, André. *Les origines de la diatribe romaine.* Lausanne: Librairie Payot, 1926.
Opelt, I. "Epitome." *RAC* 5 (1962) 944–973.
Orlinsky, Harry M. *The So-called "Servant of the Lord" and "Suffering Servant" in Second Isaiah.* VTSup 14. Leiden: E. J. Brill, 1967.
Otto, Walter F. *Dionysus. Myth and Cult.* Bloomington: Indiana University, 1965.
Paul, Shalom M. *Studies in the Book of the Covenant in Light of Cuneiform and Biblical Law.* VTSup 18. Leiden: E. J. Brill, 1970.
Pearce, T. E. V. "The Role of the Wife as CUSTOS in Ancient Rome." *Eranos, Acta Philologica Svecana* 72 (1974) 16–33.
Perdelwitz, R. *Die Mysterienreligionen und das Problem des I Petrusbriefes. Ein literarischer und religionsgeschichtlicher Versuch.* Religionsgeschichtliche Versuche und Vorarbeiten 11. Giessen: Alfred Töpelmann, 1911.
Pirenne, Jacques. *Histoire des institutions et du droit privé de l'ancienne Egypte.* Vol. 2. Brussels: Édition de la Fondation egyptologique reine Elizabeth, 1934.
_____. "Le statut de la femme dans l'ancienne Egypte." In *La femme. Recueils de la Société Jean Bodin* 11:63–77. Brussels: Librairie encyclopédique, 1959.
Pohlenz, Max. *Staatsgedanke und Staatslehre der Griechen.* Leipzig: Quelle and Meyer, 1923.
_____. *Die Stoa. Geschichte einer geistigen Bewegung.* 2nd ed. 2 vols. Göttingen: Vandenhoeck and Ruprecht, 1955.
_____. Review of Heinz Gomoll, *Der stoische Philosoph Hekaton* in *Göttingische gelehrte Anzeigen* 197 (1935) 104–111.
Pomeroy, Sarah B. "Selected Bibliography on Women in Antiquity." *Arethusa* 6 (1973) 125–157.
_____. *Goddesses, Whores, Wives and Slaves. Women in Classical Antiquity.* New York: Schocken, 1975.
Praechter, Karl. *Hierokles der Stoiker.* Leipzig: T. Weicher, 1901.
_____. "Metopos, Theages und Archytas bei Stobaeus." *Philologus* 50 (1891) 49–57.
Préaux, Claire. "Le statut de la femme à l'époque hellénistique principalement en Egypte." In *La femme. Recueils de la Société Jean Bodin* 11:127–175. Brussels: Librairie encyclopédique, 1959.
von Rad, Gerhard. *Old Testament Theology.* 2 vols. Trans. D. Stalker. New York: Harper and Row, 1962–1965.
Radermacher, L. "Menandros (16)." *PW* 15 (1931) 762–764.
Rawson, Beryl. "Family Life among the Lower Classes in Rome in the First Two Centuries of the Empire." *Classical Philology* 61 (1966) 71–83.
Rech, Hans. *Mos maiorum. Wesen und Wirkung der Tradition in Rom.* Marburg: Lengricher, 1936.
Redfors, Josef. *Echtheitskritische Untersuchung der apuleischen Schriften De Platone und De Mundo.* Trans. G. Burges. Lund: Akademisk avhandling, 1960.
Regenbogen, O. "Theophrastos." *PWSup* 7 (1940) 1354–1562.
Rengstorf, Karl Heinrich. *Mann und Frau im Urchristentum.* Arbeitsgemeinschaft für Forschung des Landes Nordrhein-Westfalen, Abhandlungen Geisteswissenschaften 12. Cologne: Westdeutscher, 1954.
_____. "Die neutestamentliche Mahnungen an die Frau sich dem Manne unterzuordnen." In *Verbum Dei Manet in Aeternum.* Festschrift für Otto Schmitz, ed. W. Foerster, 131–145. Wittenberg: Luther, 1955.

Ritter, J. "Politik und Ethik in der praktischen Philosophie des Aristoteles." *Philosophisches Jahrbuch* 74 (1967) 235–253.

Rivaud, A. "Platon et la politique pythagoricienne." In *Mélanges Gustave Glotz* 2:779–792. Paris: Presses universitaires de France, 1932.

Roberts, William. *The History of Letter-Writing from the Earliest Period to the Fifth Century.* London: W. Pickering, 1843.

Rohde, Erwin. "Die Quellen des Iamblichus in seiner Biographie des Pythagoras." In *Kleine Schriften* 2:102–172. Tübingen and Leipzig: Mohr, 1901.

Rossi, Alice S., ed. *Essays on Sex Equality by John Stuart Mill and Harriet Taylor Mill.* Chicago: University of Chicago, 1970.

Rostovtzeff, Mikhail Ivanovich. "Augustus." In *Mitteilungen des deutschen archaeologischen Instituts, Römische Abteilung* 38/39: 281–299. Munich: Münchener Verlag und graphische Kunstanstalten, 1923–1924.

_____. *Mystic Italy.* New York: H. Holt, 1927.

Rutland, Linda W. "Women as Makers of Kings in Tacitus' *Annals.*" *Classical World* 72 (1978) 15–29.

Ryffel, Heinrich. *Metabole Politeion. Der Wandel der Staatsverfassungen; Untersuchungen zu einem Problem der griechischen Staatstheorie.* Bern: P. Haupt, 1949.

de Ste. Croix, G. E. M. "Why Were the Early Christians Persecuted?" *Past and Present* 26 (1963) 6–38. Reprinted in *Studies in Ancient Society,* ed. M. I. Finley, 210–249. Past and Present Series. London: Routledge and Kegan Paul, 1974.

Sampley, J. Paul. *"And the two shall become one flesh." A Study of Traditions in Ephesians 5:21–33.* SNTSMS 16. Cambridge: Cambridge University, 1971.

Schlaifer, R. "Greek Theories of Slavery from Homer to Aristotle." In *Slavery in Classical Antiquity,* ed. M. I. Finley, 93–132. Cambridge: W. Heffer, 1960.

Schmid, Wilhelm. "Genethlios (2)." PW 7 (1912) 1134–1135.

Schneider, Carl. *Kulturgeschichte des Hellenismus.* 2 vols. Munich: C. H. Beck, 1969.

Schrage, Wolfgang. "Zur Ethik der neutestamentlichen Haustafeln." *NTS* 21 (1975) 1–22.

Schroeder, David. *Die Haustafeln des neuen Testaments (ihre Herkunft und theologischer Sinn).* Dissertation Hamburg: Mikrokopie, 1959.

Schürer, Emil. *Geschichte des jüdischen Volkes in Zeitalter Jesu Christi.* 4th ed. Vol. 3. Leipzig: J. D. Heinrichs, 1909.

_____. *A History of the Jewish People in the Time of Jesus Christ.* 4 vols. Trans. S. Taylor and P. Christie. New York: Charles Scribner's Sons, 1891.

Schulz, S. "Evangelium und Welt. Hauptprobleme einer Ethik des neuen Testaments." In *Neues Testament und christliche Existenz,* Festschrift H. Braun, ed. H. D. Betz and L. Schottroff, 483–501. Tübingen: Mohr, 1973.

Scott, Kenneth. "The Identification of Augustus with Romulus-Quirinus." *Transactions of the American Philological Association* 56 (1925) 82–105.

Seeberg, Alfred. *Die beiden Wege und das Aposteldekret.* Leipzig: A. Deichert, 1906.

_____. *Die Didache des Judentums und der Urchristenheit.* Leipzig: A. Deichert, 1908.

_____. *Das Evangelium Christi.* Leipzig: A. Deichert, 1905.

_____. *Der Katechismus der Urchristenheit.* Leipzig: A. Deichert, 1903.

Segal, Charles. "The Menace of Dionysus: Sex Roles and Reversals in Euripides' Bacchae." *Arethusa* 11 (1978) 185–202.

Selwyn, Edward Gordon. "Eschatology in I Peter." In *The Background of the New Testament and its Eschatology, In Honour of C. H. Dodd,* ed. W. D. Davies and D. Daube, 394–401. Cambridge: Cambridge University, 1956.

_____. *The First Epistle of St. Peter.* 2nd ed. London: Macmillan, 1958.

_____. "The Persecutions in I Peter." In *Bulletin of the Studiorum Novi Testamenti Societas* Nos. 1–3: 39–50. Cambridge: Cambridge University, 1963. Originally published 1950.

Shutt, R. J. H. *Studies in Josephus.* London: Society for the Preservation of Christian Knowledge, 1961.

Sinclair, Thomas Alan. *A History of Greek Political Thought*. London: Routledge and Kegan Paul, 1952.

Smallwood, E. Mary. "Some Notes on Jews under Tiberius." *Latomus* 15 (1956) 314–329.

_____. *The Jews under Roman Rule. From Pompey to Diocletian*. Studies in Judaism in Late Antiquity 20. Leiden: E. J. Brill, 1976.

Smith, Jonathan Z. "Adde Parvum Parvo Magnus Acervus Erit." *HR* 11 (1971–1972) 56–90.

_____. "Native Cults in the Hellenistic Period." *HR* 11 (1971–1972) 236–249.

Sperling, Arthur Gotthard. "Apion der Grammatiker und sein Verhältnis zum Judentum: Ein Beitrag zu einer Einleitung in die Schriften des Josephos." *Programm des Gymnasiums zum heiligen Kreuz in Dresden* Nr. 491, pp. iii–xxii. Dresden: Lehmann, 1886.

Stadter, Philip A. *Plutarch's Historical Methods. An Analysis of the Mulierum Virtutes*. Cambridge: Harvard University, 1965.

Staerman, Elene Michajlovna. *Die Krise der Sklavenhalterordnung im Westen des römischen Reiches*. Aus dem Russischen übersetzt von Wolfgang Seyfarth. Berlin: Akademie, 1964.

Steck, Odil Hannes. *Israel und das gewaltsame Geschick der Propheten*. Neukirchen-Vluyn: Neukirchener, 1967.

Stegemann, Willy. "Nikostratos (27)," *PW* 17 (1936) 551–553.

Steinmetz, Peter, ed. *Schriften zu den Politika des Aristoteles*. Hildesheim: Georg Olms, 1973.

Stern, M. "The Jews in Greek and Latin Literature." In *The Jewish People in the First Century*, ed. S. Safrai and M. Stern, 2:1101–1159. Compendia Rerum Judaicarum ad Novum Testamentum. Philadelphia: Fortress, 1976.

Strack, Hermann L., and Billerbeck, Paul. *Kommentar zum neuen Testament aus Talmud und Midrasch*. 5 vols. 5th ed. Munich: C. H. Beck, 1969. Originally published 1922–1928.

Strobel, August. "Zum Verständnis von Röm. 13." *ZNW* 47 (1956) 67–93.

Stuhlmacher, Peter. "Christliche Verantwortung bei Paulus und seinen Schülern." *EvT* 28 (1968) 165–186.

Sudhaus, S. "Aristoteles in der Beurteilung des Epikur und Philodem." *RhM* 48 (1893) 552–564.

Swidler, Leonard. *Women in Judaism. The Status of Women in Formative Judaism*. Metuchen: Scarecrow, 1976.

Theiler, Willy. "Die grosse Ethik und die Ethiken des Aristoteles." *Hermes* 69 (1934) 353–379.

_____. "Philo von Alexandria und der Beginn des kaiserzeitlichen Platonismus." In *Parusia, Studien zur Philosophie Platons und zur Problemgeschichte des Platonismus*, Festgabe für Johannes Hirschberger, ed. Kurt Flasch, 199–218. Frankfurt/Main: Minerva, 1965.

_____. Review of A. Delatte, *Essai sur la politique pythagoricienne* and other works in *Gnomon* 2 (1926) 147–156.

_____. Review of R. Harder, *Ocellus Lucanus* in *Gnomon* 2 (1926) 585–597.

_____. Review of A. Rostagni, *Il verbo di Pitagora* in *Gnomon* 1 (1925) 146–154.

_____. "Bau und Zeit der Aristotelischen Politik." *Museum Helveticum* 9 (1952) 65–78.

Thesleff, Holger. *An Introduction to the Pythagorean Writings of the Hellenistic Period*. Acta Academiae Aboensis, Humaniora 24.3. Abo: Abo Akademi, 1961.

_____. "On the Problem of the Doric Pseudo-Pythagorica. An Alternative Theory of Date and Purpose." In *Pseudepigrapha*, ed. K. von Fritz, 57–87. Entretiens sur l'antiquité classique 18. Geneva: Fondation Hardt, 1972.

_____. Review of Adriana Della Casa, *Nigidio Figulo* in *Gnomon* 37 (1965) 44.

Thornton, T. C. G. "I Peter, A Paschal Liturgy?" *JTS* 12 (1961) 14–26.

Thraede, K. "Frau." *RAC* 8 (1972) 197–269.

_____. "Ärger mit der Freiheit. Die Bedeutung von Frauen in Theorie und Praxis der alten Kirche." In *"Freunde in Christus werden . . ." Die Beziehung von Mann und Frau als Frage an Theologie und Kirche*, ed. G. Scharffenorth, 35–182. Gelnhausen/Berlin: Burckhardthaus, 1977.

_____. "Frauen im Leben frühchristlichen Gemeinden." *Una Sancta* 32 (1977) 286–299.

_____. "Zum historischen Hintergrund der 'Haustafeln' des NT." In *Pietas. Festschrift für Bernhard Kötting*, ed. Ernst Dassmann and K. Suso Frank, 359–368. JAC Ergänzungsband 8. Munich: Aschendorff, 1980.

Treggiari, Susan. "Roman Social History: Recent Interpretations." *Histoire sociale. Social History.* Université d'Ottowa & Carleton University. 8 (1975) 149–164.

Treggiari, Susan. "Jobs for Women." *American Journal of Ancient History* 1 (1976) 76–104.

Trüdinger, Karl. *Studien zur Geschichte der griechisch-römischen Ethnographie.* Basel: Emil Birkhäuser, 1918.

Tuilier, André. "La notion de φιλία dans ses rapports avec certains fondements sociaux de l'épicurisme." In *Actes du VIIIᵉ Congrès,* Association Guillaume Budé, 318–329. Paris: Les Belles Lettres, 1969.

van Unnik, Willem Cornelis. "Die Anklage gegen die Apostel in Philippi (Apostelgeschichte 16,20f.)." In *Mullus,* Festschrift Theodor Klausner, ed. A. Stuiber and A. Hermann, 366–372. JAC Ergänzungsband 1. Münster/Westfalen: Aschendorff, 1964.

_____. "Christianity according to I Peter." *Exp Tim* 68 (1956) 79–83.

_____. "The Critique of Paganism in I Peter 1:18." In *Neotestamentica et Semitica, Studies in Honour of Matthew Black,* ed. E. E. Ellis and M. Wilcox, 129–142. Edinburgh: T. and T. Clark, 1969.

_____. "First Century A.D. Literary Culture and Early Christian Literature." *Nederlands Theologisch Tijdschrift* 25 (1971) 28–43.

_____. "Die Rücksicht auf die Reaktion der Nicht-Christen." In *Judentum, Urchristentum, Kirche,* Festschrift für Joachim Jeremias, ed. W. Eltester, 221–234. BZNW 26. Berlin: Alfred Töpelmann, 1960.

_____. "The Teaching of Good Works in I Peter." *NTS* 1 (1954–1955) 92–110.

_____. *De verlossing I Petrus 1:18–19 en het probleem van den eersten Petrusbrief.* Mededulingen der Nederlandsche Akademie van Wetschappen. Afd. letterkunde. Nieuwe reeks, deel 5, n. 1. Amsterdam: Noord-hollandische uitg. mij., 1942.

Vaganay, Léon. "Le plan de l'Épître aux Hébreux." In *Memorial Lagrange,* 269–277. Paris: J. Gabalda, 1940.

Vatin, Claude. *Recherches sur le mariage et la condition de la femme marieé à l'époque héllenistique.* Paris: E. de Boccard, 1970.

Vidman, Ladislav. *Isis und Serapis bei den Griechen und Römern.* Religionsgeschichtliche Versuche und Vorarbeiten 29. Berlin: Walter de Gruyter, 1970.

Vlastos, Gregory. "The Individual as Object of Love in Plato." In *Platonic Studies,* 3–42. Princeton: Princeton University, 1973.

Voelke, André-Jean. *Les rapports avec autrui dans la philosophie grecque d'Aristote à Panétius.* Paris: J. Vrin, 1961.

de Vogel, Cornelia Johanna. *Pythagoras and Early Pythagoreans: An Interpretation of Neglected Evidence on the Philosopher Pythagoras.* Assen: Van Gorcum, 1966.

Vogt, Josef. *Struktur der antiken Sklavenkriege.* Akademie der Wissenschaften und der Literatur, Abhandlungen der geistes- und sozialwissenschaftliche Klasse. Mainz: Franz Steiner, 1957.

_____. *Von der Gleichwertigkeit der Geschlechter in der bürgerlichen Gesellschaft der Griechen.* Akademie der Wissenschaften und der Literatur, Abhandlungen der geistes- und sozialwissenschaftliche Klasse. Mainz: Franz Steiner, 1960.

Volkmann, R. *Die Rhetoric der Griechen und Römern.* 2nd ed. Leipzig: B. G. Teubner, 1885.

Walzer, Richard. *Magna Moralia und Aristotelische Ethik.* Neue philologische Untersuchungen 7. Berlin: Weidmann, 1929.

Wasser, Nathan. *Die Stellen der Juden gegenüber den Römern nach der rabbinischen Literatur von der Hasmonaeischen Zeit (ca. 165 v. Chr.) bis zum Hadrianische Kriege (132 n. Chr.).* Jersey City: Posy-Shoulson, 1933.

Watson, Alan. *The Law of Persons in the Later Roman Republic.* Oxford: Clarendon, 1967.

Weidinger, Karl. *Die Haustafeln, ein Stück urchristlicher Paraenese.* UNT 14. Leipzig: J. C. Heinrich, 1928.

Wendland, Heinz-Dietrich. "Zur sozialethischen Bedeutung der neutestamentlichen Haustafeln." In *Die Leibhaftigkeit des Wortes,* Festgabe für A. Koherle, ed. O. Michel and U. Mann, 34–46. Hamburg: Furche, 1958.

Wendland, P. "Die Therapeuten und die philonische Schrift vom beschaulichen Leben." *Jahrbücher für classische Philologie* 22 (1896) 693–770.

Wicker, Kathleen O'Brien. "First Century Marriage Ethics: A Comparative Study of the Household Codes and Plutarch's Conjugal Precepts." In *No Famine in the Land. Studies in Honor of John L. McKenzie*, ed. J. W. Flanagan and A. W. Robinson, 141–153. Missoula: Scholars Press, 1975.

_____. "Mulierum virtutes (Moralia 242E–263C)." In *Plutarch's Ethical Writings and Early Christian Literature*, ed. H. D. Betz, 106–134. Studia ad Corpus Hellenisticum Novi Testamenti 4. Leiden: E. J. Brill, 1978.

von Wilamowitz-Möllendorff, Ulrich. *Platon.* 2nd ed. 2 vols. Berlin: Weidmann, 1920.

Wilhelm, Friedrich. "Die Oeconomica der Neupythagoreer Bryson, Kallikratidas, Periktione, Phintys." *RhM* 70 (1915) 161–223.

Wilmes, Eugen. *Beiträge zur Alexandrinnerrede (Or. 32) des Dion Chrysostomos.* Bonn: Rheinische Friedrich-Wilhelms Universität, 1970.

Windisch, Hans. *Die katholischen Briefe.* 3rd ed. HNT. Tübingen: Mohr, 1951.

Witt, Reginald E. *Isis in the Graeco-Roman World.* Aspects of Greek and Roman Life. London: Thames and Hudson, 1971.

_____. "Isis-Hellas." In *Cambridge Philological Society Proceedings* 12:48–69. Cambridge: The Philological Society, 1966.

Zeller, Eduard. *Die Philosophie der Griechen in ihrer geschichtlichen Entwicklung.* 5th ed. Vol. 3. Leipzig: O. R. Reisland, 1923.

_____. "Über eine Berührung des jüngeren Cynismus mit dem Christentum." *Sitzungsberichte der königlichen preussischen Akademie der Wissenschaften zu Berlin* 23 (1893) 129–132.

Ziegler, K. "Plutarchos." PW 21/1 (1951) 636–962.

_____. "Polos (4)." PW 21/2 (1952) 1425.

Zipser, M. *Des Flavius Josephus Werk "Über das hohe Alter des jüdischen Volkes gegen Apion" nach hebraischen Originalquellen erläutert.* Vienna: Verlag der Beck'schen Universitäts-Buchhandlung, 1871.

BIBLICAL REFERENCES

OLD TESTAMENT

Gen

18:12	104
18:13	104
18:12–13	104
38:9	54

Exod

19:6	132, 133
20:12	7

Lev

9:9	104
17–19	12
18–19	6, 15
19:2	124
19:23–25	136

Num

5:23	104
6:26	104
6:26,42	104

Deut

5:16	7
21:18	17

Josh

7:19	111

1 Sam

18:27	134

1 Chr

29:21	134
29:23–24	98

2 Chr

8:12	134
23:18	134

Ps

8:7 [6]	98
9:14–15 [13–14]	133
33 [34]	11, 88, 129, 130
33 [34]:6	130
33:13–17 [34:12–16]	130
33 [34]:14–17	130
33 [34]:15b	104
61:2,6 [62:1,5]	98
106 [107]:14,10	133
106 [107]:22	133

Prov

3:34	128
24:21	96

Isa

8:12	95
18:7	134
42:6	132, 136
42:6, 8	133
42:6–9	132, 133, 135
42:8	135
43:20	135
43:21b	132, 133
53	19

Jer

6:15	87
10:15	87

Mal

1:6	17, 96
1:10	136
1:14	96
3:17,18,24 [4:4]	96

NEW TESTAMENT

Index of Ancient Authors

Index of Modern Authors

Subject Index*

*A list of selected terms and their occurrence.